PRAISE FOR *STANDOFF*

"Eye-opening and compelling . . . required reading for those who would call this land home."

—KIRKUS REVIEWS

"*Standoff* has the potential to launch a trend of orderly and pertinent analysis of the societal, cultural and structural issues that provide the context within which today's Indian Movement(s) operate and presents a challenge to Indian people whether we continue to play the game of accepting our 'place' in America or define who we are and what we want to be."

—SAM DELORIA, law professor emeritus, University of New Mexico

"Environmental activists, Indigenous rights activists, and allies should take note of the challenging, unjust, and at times beautiful accounts shared here, which illuminate the complexity of what it means to stand in solidarity in a colonial state."

—MARISA ELENA DUARTE, assistant professor, Arizona State University School of Social Transformation

"This is the kind of book we owe to young Indigenous kids. They deserve the truth, even if it hurts, and this brave, well-sourced journalism deserves to be named for what it will go down in history as: perhaps the most in-depth look at the #NoDAPL movement, coming from where it should: your nation and from within Indian country."

—DESIREE KANE, journalist

"Jacqueline Keeler weaves personal experience, cultural awareness, and journalistic acumen to tell a compelling story that compares and contrasts two r ncounters between federal land policy an **NAPA COUNTY LIBRARY** se lands. 'Whose land is it anyway?' Kee **580 COOMBS STREET** g the answer is a task that
NAPA, CA 94559

requires deep reflection from all of us who share these magnificent vistas."

—CHRIS LA TRAY, author of *Becoming Little Shell*

"Jacqueline Keeler, a master storyteller and reporter, crafts a knotty skein, twining together family traditions, Native and colonial histories, personal experiences, and crackerjack journalism. *Standoff* explores inequity and entitlement, seeking answers to what American land means to cultures with divergent values and uneven advantages."

—BETSY GAINES QUAMMEN, author of *American Zion*

STANDOFF

STANDOFF

Standing Rock, the Bundy Movement, and the American Story
of Sacred Lands

JACQUELINE KEELER

TORREY HOUSE PRESS

Salt Lake City • Torrey

First Torrey House Press Edition, March 2021
Copyright © 2021 by Jacqueline Keeler

Published by Torrey House Press
Salt Lake City, Utah
www.torreyhouse.org

MIX
Paper from
responsible sources
FSC
www.fsc.org   FSC® C011935

International Standard Book Number: 978-1-948814-27-0
E-book ISBN: 978-1-948814-50-8
Library of Congress Control Number: 2017947293

Cover photos by Stephanie Keith/REUTERS and Rob Kerr/AFP via Getty Images
Cover design by Kathleen Metcalf
Interior design by Rachel Buck-Cockayne
Distributed to the trade by Consortium Book Sales and Distribution

Torrey House Press offices in Salt Lake City sit on the homelands of Ute, Goshute, Shoshone, and Paiute nations. Offices in Torrey are in homelands of Paiute, Ute, and Navajo nations.

CONTENTS

INTRODUCTION

A young man holds a staff on a gray asphalt road surrounded by the prairie. It's October and the grass has turned gold and dry. The bent staff is decorated with eagle feathers. The youth, Danny Grassrope of the Kul Wicasa Oyate (Lower Brule Sioux Tribe), is wearing a red scarf over his head and beige pants and a T-shirt. The men wrestling with him and the staff are mostly in black uniforms, some in green jackets and beige polyester pants, most wearing riot gear helmets, a few wearing respirators, and all carrying guns in their holsters. His slight figure goes down, but still he hangs on to the staff. In the end, the law enforcement in riot gear take it and pin him down, pressing his face to the soft earth, and lashing his wrists behind his back with plastic handcuffs.

The Lakota youth that had begun the fight against the Dakota Access Pipeline (DAPL) had carried that staff across the country—from North Dakota to Washington, DC. They had run thousands of miles to request that the Army Corps of Engineers reconsider allowing the crude oil pipeline to be built just a mile north of the sole intake source of water for their reservation. The young man was not just fighting for an object, but for a symbol of that prayer—that prayer a new generation was carrying for the future.

The staff and other personal items like sacred pipes, *canunpa*, were later returned to the main Océti Saków in (Sioux) camp north of the Standing Rock Sioux Reservation. They came in plastic bags with numbers on them matching the numbers that were written on their owners' arms in jail. Elders I spoke to who held a ceremony to bless and cleanse them told me they smelled of urine and had evidently been peed on.

How did American citizens end up on either side of this standoff? The police in the armor and the young man armed only with a staff representing the prayers of his people?

The scenes of the raid of the 1851 Treaty Camp near the Dakota Access Pipeline construction corridor on October 28, 2016, did not resemble the post-racial America Obama's administration was supposed to usher in—an America where the lessons of the civil rights movement had been fully integrated into the power structure of the nation by the election of a Black man as leader of the free world.

Instead, Obama's administration oversaw the violent arrest of 142 water protectors that day. Images of the forcible removal of the camp are haunting. Tipis ripped open by white men in military uniforms. Native people being dragged out of a sweat lodge. A Native youth leader fighting to keep a medicine staff from the police. These scenes are reminiscent of the 1863 Whitestone Massacre that occurred not far from the 1851 Treaty Camp.

Just nine months earlier, along another state highway, LaVoy Finicum, an Arizona foster parent, is run off the road by a blockade set up by the Oregon State Police to capture the leaders of the armed takeover of Malheur National Wildlife Refuge. On the snowy roadside, surrounded by police cars, he gets out of a white SUV with his hands up. He speaks imperiously to the police, giving the impression he expects to be able to have a conversation as equals with them. In the month the armed occupiers, led by Ammon Bundy, son of scofflaw Nevada rancher Cliven Bundy, have held the wildlife refuge, they have enjoyed a respectful, if oppositional, relationship with the local county sheriff. They have been free to come and go from the refuge to get supplies or attend speaking engagements like the one they are heading to now: a meeting with the sheriff in the next county and a crowd of about a hundred locals. Finicum obviously felt he had the standing to have a talk with those who had guns pointed at him.

During an earlier media interview, when asked why he was sitting with a rifle draped across his lap at the refuge, he had said, "If you point a gun at me you know what to expect."

Now, with police guns pointed at him, he walks across the snow and reaches a few times toward a pocket in his denim jacket. Police later allege he had a gun tucked there. The third time he reaches, he is gunned down, becoming a martyr to the cause of public lands detractors.

What are we all fighting for? Are we so different from one another? What are the causes of this American standoff?

The lens we see the world and "our" America through, defines our personal understanding of history, often to the exclusion of other peoples that history has also touched. In this book, I illustrate and explore this exclusivity of viewpoint by comparing two "standoffs." I provide a frame to understand both how the Standing Rock Sioux Tribe perceives its history and asserts its rights as a nation, as an *oyate*, and how the Bundy family does so, and I contrast the two. The Bundys' armed supporters faced off against their own federal government even as they proclaimed their reverence for the US Constitution, which they keep in their shirt pockets.

The Bundy family and their supporters and the Standing Rock Sioux community represent relatively small populations—rural, anti-government white Americans and citizens of the nine tribes that comprise the Great Sioux Nation. However, these two groups lay claim, either through usage, US property law, or treaty negotiations, to the idea and sovereignty of America's remaining public lands, an area that encompasses some 640 million acres of federally owned land, 248 million of which is under the control of the Department of the Interior's Bureau of Land Management—nearly one-eighth the total landmass of the United States.

While each group articulates its respective struggle in opposition to the threat of an oppressive federal power bent on stripping it of its sovereignty as a People (tribal sovereignty) and as individuals (sovereign citizens) and even right to life, they differ in significant ways. For the tribe, the threat is corporate, and for the Bundys, it's the federal government; both are defined by roles assigned to them to play in the story America tells itself about itself. And so it is that "cowboys" and "Indians" meet, with starkly different degrees of success.

To call oneself an American is to claim the fruits and spoils of a revolution built from the philosophy and language of Locke, Jefferson, and Paine, something now understood to be the "American dream," which the Bundys and their followers call "liberty." In contrast, when I say I am Dakota, I am saying I am a child of an agreement my ancestors made with the land itself. In each of these identities, there is a story that defines kinship to the land, and the responsibilities that relationship entails.

In order to bolster its claims to the lands of Indigenous nations, including my own Dakota and Diné nations, the United States has sought to reframe that relationship with a story of its own. This story is called the Doctrine of Discovery, a legal fiction that self-servingly assigns legal title to the entirety of this hemisphere to "discovering Christian nations" as defined by a Medici pope in Rome in the fifteenth century.

This desire of these discovering Christian Nations to claim and consume whatever they can see reminds me of a Dakota ohunkaka story of the Iya. The Iya is a monster with an insatiable hunger that eats everything it encounters, including entire tribes. It is said that the campfires of the tribes could be seen glowing inside its body. People would live and die and spend their entire lives inside the creature. Of course, the story has a positive ending with a hero killing the Iya, freeing the nations, and marching out of the monster with them to repopulate a world left barren and bereft by the Iya's greed.

As people put their lives on the line, motivated by stories that define their relationships to the land and to each other, the standoffs of the Bundys and the Lakota/Dakota people demonstrate how these stories have power. This leaves us with questions: Whose stories will carry the day? Will it happen by the barrel of the gun or by ceremony? This is not an idle comparison. One standoff was armed, and one was not. Americans (mostly white Americans) own more guns than the Chinese army. And when Lakota and Dakota people gather, they reassemble themselves in the traditional encampments of tipis and pray with canunpas. These impulses point to the fundamentally different and distinct ideas of what makes one American and what makes one Adakȟóta.

In writing this book, I spent a great deal more time researching the rise of Mormonism in the United States than I had frankly expected to do. It is a subject I have successfully avoided most of my life, possibly because of the painful split it caused in my mother's Navajo family. Her family was, when she left it in the 1960s for college, a traditional Navajo family speaking the Diné language and practicing the culture to a degree unheard of for most Native people in America. When my mother and her sister, who had also left for college, returned for family reunions, they found their younger siblings and cousins entirely in the grip of Mormonism. While they were away, the younger children had been placed in white Mormon homes hundreds of miles away from the reservation as part of the Indian Placement Program operated by the Mormon Church.

These younger relatives had had a desire to see what America was off the reservation and to experience it for themselves. But the America they were exposed to was not the one my mother and her sister found. It was not a country in the grips of the civil rights movement and the women's rights movement. Many of their younger relatives had been educated at Brigham Young University in Provo, Utah. One of my mom's cousins even toured across Europe with a Mormon Native American song and dance troupe called the Lamanite Generation. They returned to the reservation unwilling to participate in traditional Navajo ceremonies.

This rejection of traditional culture was particularly painful since my mother's parents, like the majority of their generation, could not speak English. Sheltered by a vast reservation, they had successfully maintained, well into the twentieth century, our Diné traditions, intact.

In the 1970s, Native American religious beliefs were legal again after a hundred years, and tribes like my dad's Yankton Sioux Tribe were finally able to practice their spiritual traditions openly. On my dad's reservation, four generations of Christianity enforced by treaty quickly gave way to a return to our ancient Dakota ceremonies. And yet, at the same time, for my mother's family, Navajo culture was eroding due to Mormonism.

The arguments over this, initially fierce at family reunions when I was very small, mellowed by the 1990s as my mom and her siblings entered middle age and some began to re-embrace our traditional culture.

It is true that some loss of culture in my Navajo family would have likely happened nonetheless due to economic forces driving families from the reservation, making transmission of language and culture difficult. Navajo is reputed to be one of the most difficult languages in the world to learn. The efforts of the Mormon Church undoubtedly magnified the loss of culture. For my family, in practical terms, both of these factors, religious and economic, meant we lost something from the 1960s to 2000s. In those four decades, a generation of cultural practitioners grew elderly and died. And due to religion and economics, they were unable to pass on their knowledge to the next generation of potential knowledge keepers to the degree they had expected to do when my mom was growing up on the reservation.

Indeed, instead of the emergence story that connects us to our homeland, the Dinetah, based on our own creation story, what took hold for some branches of the family was an origin story framed by the Book of Mormon as a "lost tribe of Israel," revealed to a white nineteenth-century American named Joseph Smith.

My uncle, describing his visit to Jerusalem, told me of the great joy he felt when upon entering the Holy City, he saw people herding sheep just like Navajos do in the Southwestern United States. He believed he had returned home.

What was happening to my family in the Painted Desert near the Grand Canyon has its roots in a period of American history called the Second Great Awakening. The Founding Fathers, victors in the war to separate themselves from their homeland, drove out the ancient Iroquois nations that had ruled western New York for a thousand years. Growing up amid all this evidence of an ancient civilization that was not in the Bible, Smith started digging for the treasure of lost civilizations as a teenager, a fascination that led him to create a new religion that would eventually rule an entire state.

Today Americans think of the thirteen original colonies as thoroughly settled places in shape and size. We think of them as they are today, but we forget how so much of that territory was new to the colonists. Students are rarely taught that the Revolutionary War was fought to gain access to these lands west of the Royal Proclamation of 1763, which forbade settlement west of the Appalachian Mountains.

When the story of America is told, it is the opening phrase of the Declaration of Independence that is remembered: "We hold these Truths to be self-evident, that all Men are created equal, that they are endowed by their Creator with certain unalienable Rights, that among these are Life, Liberty, and the Pursuit of Happiness." What is forgotten is the Declaration's list of "repeated Injuries and Usurpations" by King George III cited as reasons for dissolving "Political Bands" with Great Britain, which includes this characterization of Native nations: "He has excited domestic Insurrections amongst us, and has endeavored to bring on the Inhabitants of our Frontiers, the merciless Indian Savages whose known Rule of Warfare, is an undistinguished Destruction of all Ages, Sexes, and Conditions."

Smith and his family and countless other European American settlers were able to occupy the western areas once the Revolutionary War was won. My husband's direct ancestor Chief Joseph Brant (Thayendanegea), a Mohawk leader, led the opposition to the colonists, thereby splitting the Iroquois Confederacy. By the time of Joseph Smith's birth in Vermont in 1805, Thayendanegea was dying in Ontario, Canada, on lands provided by the British Crown called the

Six Nations Reserve. The Six Nations Confederacy had lost the hills of western New York in the Revolutionary War, where Smith claimed to have found the golden tablets and transcribed them into the Book of Mormon using typical folk magic of the time. These were the ancient homelands of my own children's Iroquois forebears. The landscape, rich with evidence of long human occupation, must have troubled Joseph Smith and other newcomers, since they had been taught everything had to fit within the history presented by the Bible. This may have led to the fervor of their religious response in what came to be known as the Burned-Over District.

At my grandparents' house in Cameron on the Navajo Nation, I would listen to them and their friends, other elderly Diné, speaking in our language, Diné Bizaad. My uncle would translate for me. The house was lit, as was usual, only by kerosene lamp. Like most other Navajos living in the disputed territories of the Navajo-Hopi land dispute, my grandparents did not have running water or electricity, as land development was frozen while the court case was being adjudicated. The elders, men, and women were all dressed traditionally, wearing turquoise and silver jewelry, hair in buns. These were the clothes they had worked in their entire lives while ranching, sheepherding, planting corn and watermelons. They dressed elegantly and made their lives of hard work seem like the activities of the nobility. My uncle explained to me they were discussing what was in the Bible. They were wondering who these Hebrews were and why everyone wanted them to care so much about them.

Much of America—and the world at large—is a collection of stories. Our lives are framed by these sometimes half-understood, half-remembered tales of our forebears' lives or even the lives of those we choose to ordain as our forebears. Histories and identities form from hieroglyphic images, stained glass figures, or Greek vases, so highly stylized, inviting scrutiny of each scene or iconography. Whether pieced together from cut and colored glass or etched on papyrus or pottery, the characters, symbols, and actions can only be understood if you know the accompanying tale. From my own culture, Navajo sand paintings depict holy people and the proper ordering of the universe. Lakota/Dakota buffalo robes are, in the same vein, a distillation of a past beyond our own reckoning. We can make these scenes and stories—like the great flood in the Bible or the meeting with the White Buffalo Calf Woman—come alive in our imaginations, and they can be taken many ways, literally or metaphorically. However, their perceived truth is taken unquestioningly and acted upon accordingly.

I imagine what it must have been like for Mormon Americans in the early nineteenth century, faced with a vast continent filled with peoples of nations not mentioned in the Bible. Of course, Native tribes must be the lost tribe of Israel and Eden must be in Missouri. For Smith and his adherents and others migrating west from upstate New York in 1830, it may have seemed so. The beckoning continent must have felt as magical and full of potential as anywhere on earth.

It may seem only natural that these competing visions would result in the two major American standoffs that bookended 2016: white men with guns fighting for unfettered exploitation of natural resources and Native Americans fighting for treaty rights. The Bundy takeover of the Malheur Wildlife Refuge and the Standing Rock Sioux Tribe's demand for consultation over the Dakota Access Pipeline may seem as far removed from one another as could be feasible on the spectrum of American politics—one invoking the privilege of white colonial rights to the land and the other a sovereignty that preexists and persists despite colonial invasion.

While covering both of these events, I came to see that examining their historical and philosophical underpinnings could bring clarity to the present American political climate—one that brought us the Trump presidency and an uncertain future for the progressive gains of the civil rights movement once depicted as inevitable. I'm reminded of Martin Luther King's quote, paraphrased from the speeches of the abolitionist minister Theodore Parker: "The arc of the moral universe is long but it bends toward justice." Facing the persisting division of the American electorate, largely defined by race, the future of that arc towards equity and inclusion appears, at this time, uncertain.

In each of the articles I first wrote about both Cliven Bundy and his son Ammon Bundy, I addressed Bundy claims to "original ownership" of the public land to which they claimed unfettered rights to utilize as they saw fit. In the case of Cliven Bundy, his fight for his family's rights to graze cattle on more than half a million acres of public lands seemed to elide some sort of title to the land. The land Cliven does hold title to is a comparatively tiny 160 acres, which in arid Clark County, Nevada, home of Las Vegas, is not enough to sustain a true ranching operation. He pushed to anyone who would listen a specious claim that the title had been transferred to him the moment one of his animals had nibbled on a blade of grass. From that moment, the cattle and horses had transformed the environment into one teeming with flora, fauna, and water. All created by his animals foraging, and thus granting him title to the land they grazed in perpetuity. If this sounds as self-serving to you as the Doctrine of Discovery, you would be correct. Legal jurists were not on his side, and he lost every case but one, finally winning in the court of public opinion. Not the entire public, but a very active, armed, and white contingent.

Ammon Bundy, living in Idaho near Boise, just due east of Burns, Oregon, launched an armed takeover of a wildlife refuge on behalf of the citizens of Harney County, Oregon and their right to profit off the land. He saw a father and son, the Hammonds, ranchers, being sent to prison for standing up for their rights to graze cattle on leased public lands without undo harassment by the feds. Driven by what he sees as another example of federal overreach and the ability of environmentalists who do not live in the county to dictate policy, Ammon's reading of the history of Harney County omits a lot of history and context. Like his father, he ignores the preexisting Indigenous claims to the land. In this case, the Paiute Nation, whose traditional territories extend throughout the Great Basin from Oregon to southern Nevada.

He doesn't reckon with the limits of extractive industries like timber and mining imposed by supply and demand. Ammon's representation of the land use issues for ranchers is also inaccurate. Interviewing ranchers and the tribe, I quickly discovered the existence of a compact that they were all proud to have worked on collaboratively for several years and agreed to in 2013. It's considered the country's gold standard of collaborative use.

In October 2016, despite their armed occupation of a federal facility, brothers Ammon and Ryan Bundy were found not guilty on all counts in Portland, Oregon. They were charged under a Depression-era law of attempting to impede or threaten a federal employee. The jury's decision was astounding to many observers, since their takeover had been broadcast on CNN and Fox News, as well as on social media twenty-four hours a day for everyone to see. Federal employees I spoke to after the trial, who had been threatened by Bundy supporters and had to go into hiding during the takeover and send their children to other school districts, were in shock. Some reconsidered their careers, grappling with the realization there was nothing stopping the harassment and endangerment of their lives.

After two years, Cliven Bundy was finally arrested for his armed 2014 standoff in Nevada by the Federal Bureau of Investigation at the Portland, Oregon, airport where he'd flown to join his sons in their occupation of Malheur. The father and his sons were tried in Nevada for inciting two hundred armed citizens to aim guns at federal employees who had come to remove Bundy cattle grazing on public lands. The elder Bundy had illegally grazed them on a fragile desert ecosystem for twenty years, racking up a million dollars in fines and fees. The area where the cattle wander with little oversight by the Bundys includes Gold Butte National Monument, a place sacred to the local Paiute tribes in Nevada. With Cliven Bundy's supporters aiming guns directly at federal employees, the cattle were returned and are, as of this writing, still illegally grazing on federal lands.

The case against the Bundys collapsed in Nevada due to prosecutorial misconduct, and in January 2018, the judge declared a mistrial and dismissed the case with prejudice. Indeed, one must ask if the Bundys and their anti-federal-government supporters have also won their battle politically, as Trump appointees, including former Interior Secretary Ryan Zinke and his successor, Secretary David Bernhardt, dedicate themselves wholeheartedly to the privatization of public lands.

President Trump granted full pardons on July 10, 2018, for their arson and poaching convictions. That same year, Wyoming property-rights lawyer Karen Budd-Falen confirmed to the press she was being considered by the Trump administration to lead the BLM. Budd-Falen, a former Bundy attorney, is the legal architect of the questionable "county supremacy" ideology, which holds that the ultimate authority in a county is vested in the local sheriff—not the president of the United States or any other official. She was ultimately appointed chief solicitor of the BLM, an agency whose staff she once sued under the Racketeer Influenced and Corrupt Organizations Act, claiming their enforcement of federal laws amounted to racketeering.

In the first week of December at Standing Rock, the camp swelled to an estimated ten thousand strong with the arrival of US military veterans of all races and backgrounds from across the country. Gathered in the face of a winter storm on December 4, they received the news that the US Army Corps of Engineers had revoked the easement for the Dakota Access Pipeline with cheers and celebration. After Trump, a former DAPL investor, took office, one of his first actions was to issue an executive order on January 24, approving the easement for the pipeline. By February 23, 2017, both the Océti Sakówin and Sacred Stone camps had been cleared by the authorities.

While the Bundy cattle remain and the Hammonds are free, the pipeline is now completed and oil flows under the Missouri, a potential threat to the well-being of the Lakota and Dakota communities downriver. These standoffs clearly served their constituents in vastly different ways. The Bundys, although enduring months in jail awaiting trial, were in the end affirmed by both a jury of their peers and the voters who ushered in a new administration to the White House sympathetic to their cause—regardless of its legality. Tribes learned what they had already suspected. Treaties would not be honored even as thousands of their fellow Americans put their bodies on the line to join them in demanding they be enforced. Under Obama, their demands for consultation were ignored until the last possible moment. Under Trump, their hard-won victory was reversed.

I hope this book will provide some basis to understand the 58 percent of white voters who voted for Trump in 2016 versus the broad coalition of Americans who did not. Certainly, the result of the election challenged the concept of exceptionalism and social progress assumed worldwide to be embodied by the United States of America. The country's origins lie in the dispossession of the homelands of extant Indigenous nations, calling into question the moral argument of social progress used to justify the subjugation and removal of those nations.

I often describe the way we see the world as the house that was built for us as a child. It is a house—yet it orients the whole world. We look out the window and think the view that is framed by it to be the same one shared universally. This perspective or house is composed not only from our own personal experience but also through an understanding of history and social circumstances that is passed down in families through a mix of oral history, spiritual teachings, and written texts. The Bundys and the Standing Rock Sioux people both drew from cultural frameworks that shaped their perspectives and values. Family stories, published books, and oral histories from my paternal grandmother's family, including her aunt Ella Deloria, cousin Vine Deloria Jr., uncle Vine Deloria Sr., and cousin Phil Lane Sr., demonstrate a Lakota/Dakota counterpoint to the Bundy family's lore as presented in interviews and the religious and political writings compiled by a Bundy associate in *The Nay Book*.

These two American standoffs, as divergent as they are, illustrate the legacy of colonialism that created our world. On one hand, we have the Bundys' takeovers of public lands and demand for local sovereignty that privileges their rights to exploit the land—an assertion of rights as a colonist. On the other, the Standing Rock Sioux Tribe's demand to consult on the construction of a Canadian company's heavy crude pipeline through their unceded treaty lands—an assertion of rights as a sovereign nation.

That these two fights are with the same federal government through its proxies of federal agencies and state and county governments was not lost on the Bundys. I received confirmation from local Standing Rock Sioux activists that the Bundy family reached out to the tribe and offered to come in support of the camp. They were not welcomed, because the tribe understood that the Bundys, colonists promised benefits from western expansion and opponents of Paiute claims to Gold Butte Canyon, were not true allies. Indeed, Ryan Bundy had participated in an ATV ride over an ancient Pueblo archaeological site with white Mormon county officials in San Juan County, home of the Bears Ears National Monument—a monument supported by five tribes. These two standoffs, defined by oppositional experiences following the invasion of this hemisphere, illustrate part of what the American experiment has wrought.

A major component not touched on sufficiently in this analysis is slavery and the Black experience in America. The harshly imposed color bar is such a defining feature of colonialism in the United States, that it is probably the greatest weakness of this book that the comparison between the Bundys and Standing Rock does not encompass this—although Native Americans face racism, many citizens of Native nations are Black, and many Black Americans stood side by side with Lakota/Dakota people at Standing Rock.

Nonetheless, what this book does examine will hopefully help increase understanding of how this country became the most powerful in the world, a nation that has dominated and shaped the global political and economic reality we know today for 330 million Americans and billions of other people around the world. I will also examine, the colonial engine, "Iya," which the United States has set loose on the world. This, along with the impacts of climate change and the threat of nuclear winter, may have a decisive influence upon the very continuation of human existence on this earth, our mother, as we know it.

The Standing Rock Sioux Tribe understands its history and obligations to its people and its rights as a nation, while constituent groups of disaffected rural anti-government residents, mostly white Americans catalyzed by the Bundys' call to arms, see themselves as sovereign citizens even as they faced off against their own federal government carrying copies of the US Constitution in their shirt pockets. Compelled by divergent viewpoints, both groups are still understood by the majority of Americans through the traditional roles each was assigned in the story of America. The story America tells itself about itself. And so it is, that "cowboys" versus "Indians" still meet in that American story with starkly different degrees of success.

The Stories We Carried: An Ihanktonwan Dakota Family

When I trace the places where I begin as a Dakota woman, I always return to the stories that I was told as a child by my father's family. I suppose other families in the tribe have other stories, but these are the ones that shaped and made me.

I place them here at the beginning of this book, so they can function as a sort of cultural family bible on their own and because they shape my understanding of what happened at Standing Rock and how I view the stories of other people like the Bundys.

Stories are fundamental to our sense of what to expect from the world, the rules we aspire to live by and how we will achieve them. While most people are familiar with the stories the Bundys reference, like the American Constitution and War for Independence or pronouncements from the Bible, they have likely never heard these Dakota stories.

A Boy's (Hoksina's) Vision: Tipi Sapa or Why My Great-Grandmother was Raised at Standing Rock

It must have been a sight that day, told and retold in my father's family, when Saswe (pronounced this way because the Dakota could not say Francois) Deloria, a boy of twelve, fell and lay still on "the handsome inclined plain" described by explorer William Clark in his diary. Called the Big Bend of the Missouri River in present-day South Dakota, some of it has been put underwater by the dam built in the 1950s.

Hundreds of Dakota and Lakota men and boys would have been playing. Numerous bands of the Océti Sakówin gathered in this part of the Missouri to feast and share stories and songs, and arrange marriages. They lived together as one people in this camp of tens of thousands before heading out again, each band to their respective favored hunting grounds and village sites throughout what would become South and North Dakota, Nebraska, Minnesota, Wyoming, and Montana.

In the story, as it was told to me, some players accused the boy of faking an injury. Apparently, that was a thing even then. But his grandfather came forward and said no, his grandson was having a vision. The boy was taken up to the caves above the Missouri River and left to have his vision undisturbed. After checking on him a few days later, his grandfather returned to camp, wailing and ripping at his hair and skin. He had found his grandson in the cave laying still, his eyes closed and covered in snakes. The whole camp joined him in grieving for the boy.

A few days later, the boy returned to camp on his own, unharmed and very much alive. The camp rejoiced, and it turned out his grandfather was right—Saswe had had his vision. My grandmother's cousin, Vine Deloria Jr., recounts it in his book about Saswe's life.

The boy became a great medicine man. As a child, I was told he had on one moccasin the hawk and on the other the owl. When he lifted one foot, a hawk would screech, and when he lifted the other, an owl would hoot. He would demonstrate this to Americans with sticks in his mouth to show that he was not making the sounds. He'd tell them, "I'm showing you this not for entertainment but to show you this power is real."

More than a hundred years later, my dad's cousin, a great-great-grandson of Saswe, was talking to a white farmer who owned land in the Big Bend. When he asked about the caves, the farmer said he knew where they were and had visited them but warned him about snakes in the caves. The snakes slept there huddled together for warmth at night. We surmised that this is what the grandfather had seen, and the boy, still in the midst of the vision, had not moved or realized this is what had happened. By the time he awoke the snakes had left, and he was again alone in the cave.

Later, the vision was interpreted by Saswe to mean his descendants would have to serve in the Episcopal Church for four generations as priests, beginning with his son, the Reverend P. J. Deloria, named Tipi Sapa after four black tipis in the vision. After fulfilling his father's vision and studying for the priesthood, Tipi Sapa was assigned to serve the Lakota community at St. Elizabeth's in the village of Wakpala on the Standing Rock Sioux Reservation. Six feet tall and slim, he arrived to serve Chief Gall and Sitting Bull's people, his dark face visible above the white collar of an Episcopalian vicar, not simply in deference to the demands of invaders to serve their religion—a church, at that time, still led by Queen Victoria in England. When he got off the train he was met by other Yanktons who were living on Standing Rock; they had gathered to see an *itancan*, a chief of their own, arrive, brought there through obedience to the vision his father had as a boy. A vision given to the boy Saswe when our Lakota/Dakota people were still in the sweet last days of the summer of their world, perhaps only a few glimpsing the winter that was to come. A time when all the old songs were still known, all the old stories, the native language spoken on every bit of prairie and river. This is how a Yankton (Ihanktonwan) Dakota family came to Standing Rock to serve its people in a time of significant change, a time when survival was not assured, and our Lakota and Dakota people were still in disagreement as to how to proceed.

To a Lakota/Dakota mind it speaks to the power of *taku skan skan*, that which moves moves. The spirit that is on the land pushes us from one thing to another. Sometimes described as akin to the Christian notion of the Holy Spirit, it is an expression of the power of that great *wakan*, that which is holy, that is not known in any human form, but somehow moves us. Like the wind on the prairie, that unseen but felt power that makes the grass sway like a great writhing living sea, and fills us with the promises of life and of every good thing. Every being that crawls, flies, grows, and lives on the earth, our mother.

What I have learned from my family's telling and retelling of the story of Saswe, is how a boy with a vision, shepherded by a powerful culture that informed his grandfather's actions, gave my ancestors a path, and how present-day Lakota/Dakota people turn to the spirit world for these very same answers. And what it meant when even our allies did not respect that communication.

The story of my family always begins with the story of a boy—well two boys, really. Both about twelve years old it seemed, not quite out of childhood but ready to be called by the mysterious forces of the land itself, the spirits that dwelt upon it, to take their part, play their role in the deep and vast spiritual life of the Great Plains and its peoples. A mystery that was as deep and real as the prairie's roots, roots that were several feet deep and slept undisturbed, and anchored our lives until the pioneers came and plowed them up and then the dust blew and nature turned against them.

The Last Sighting of the White Buffalo Calf by the Yankton

This second story about a thirteen-year-old boy often told in my dad's family was about the last time we saw a real white buffalo calf. It is a story that ends not only with the usual *hechetu ye* (this I speak is the truth), but with an admonition that our family must tell the story so that the people will not lose hope. It was told to me orally by my Lala, Phil Lane Sr., and I can tell it precisely in the same cadence. My Lala and his wife, Grandma Bow, were the nearest living relatives we had, and I was lucky to be the recipient of his stories when I was young. Such words can shape and alter your very understanding of your own story and how you came to be through the struggles of your own people and their relationship to the wakan and the tragedy that lay before them in the coming decades with the arrival of the Americans.

My Lala was a retired engineer and had been raised as a cowboy on the Standing Rock Sioux Reservation. He met Grandma Bow at Haskell Indian School in Kansas when they were both students there. He was lean with a cauliflower nose, from his Golden Gloves boxing days, and he favored dressing as a cowboy in a cowboy hat, western shirt, and boots. In his retirement in Walla Walla, Washington, he raised cutting horses using the methods he had learned as a boy from Lakota cowboys in the early twentieth century.

He would say, "Now *takoja*, there was a horse no one could tame—a bay horse. And a boy named Mato Gi (Brown Bear) went to his grandfather and begged him to let him tame this horse. Now, for reasons, no one knows why the grandfather agreed to let this boy try to tame this horse no one could tame." I asked Lala why the grandfather did this, and he explained to me that people didn't ask direct questions like that in those days. It was considered impolite, so they had to wait until the person chose to tell them. The grandfather never did explain to anyone why he let the boy take on such a dangerous task, but now that I'm older, I can see the story itself explains why the grandfather allowed it. So, the boy tamed the bay horse. Once again, no one knows how he did it.

Shortly after this, a herd of buffalo was seen near our village at White Swan. Between Lake Andes, the town where my father was raised, and the tribe's Fort Randall casino, is a place which was a buffalo run alongside the Missouri River. Today, locals call the hilly area of grassy scrubland near it "the tundra." The boy joined the men riding the horse no one could tame. Our band could field about one hundred hunting scouts, and as the men approached the herd, they could see a white speck in the very middle. The buffalo herd was a mile wide. My Lala explained to me how the buffalo bulls would be on the outside facing out in a defensive position, the females behind them, and on the inside were the calves. What made this herd unusual was not its size, which was usual at that time, but the white buffalo calf at its very center. Seeing this, the men broke rank and began to race towards the calf.

My Lala explained how the western painters got the scenes of the buffalo hunt all wrong. They would not shoot their arrows and hit the buffalo just anywhere. They would aim for the heart. As they were running, the goal was to hit the area exposed by the left foreleg. It sounds like an impossible task, but this is what he told me.

As the horses raced forward one by one, they fell away until there were only two horses left, the bay and a black horse. Suddenly, the black horse's nostrils filled with foam, and his rider pulled back. This was a ceremony and had to be done without injuring the horses. The rider, a grown man, shouted to the boy, to "go and do it." So, Mato Gi and the bay rode on alone. As he approached the calf, he raised his spear in his left hand (here my Lala would often point out that most men in our family are left-handed—indeed, my father was), and he threw it and hit the calf.

As the calf fell, the men came forward, weeping and tearing their hair, as if for their loved one. They built a scaffold and put the calf on it on a bed of sage, and they put sage in its ears. They carried the calf on the scaffold for four days and four nights. On the fourth night, they camped, and no one knows what they did with the calf. When they returned to our village, all of the headsmen from up and down the Missouri River were there.

They placed the boy, Mato Gi, on a bed of sage and put a crown of sage on his head. The bay horse was brought forward, and a headsman threw a necklace of eagle claws over its head. An elder asked, "Who knows the name of this horse?"

It is said it was Struck by the Ree who stood up and said, "Eagle Claw, his name is Eagle Claw," and that was the name of the horse. In this way, the horse was honored and given a name, and the boy was honored. It is said that later he was regarded as a great counselor, and it was him, Mato Gi, that Crazy Horse sent for on his last night alive.

This white buffalo calf was seen as a message that a winter of our people was coming, and, as I mentioned before, it was for my family to tell the story so our people would not lose hope in that winter: that they would know that spring will come again for our people. My Lala was invited to see the new white buffalo calf Miracle that was born in 1994. When I asked him about it, he brushed it away, saying, "Pink eyes, pink ears, pink nose, pink hooves, *that's* a white buffalo calf." Miracle, with his black eyes and nose and ears and hooves, was not, according to him.

I once told this story at a sundance on the Navajo Nation. The children asked me why the buffalo calf was killed. It's funny—I never thought to ask that question. Without a doubt, my Lala was a more compelling storyteller than I am. Although I asked him a lot of questions over the years, I don't know the answer to that. Perhaps the reasons are made clear by the story. As a child, I was always deeply moved by the scaffold-bearing and the naming. But even more so by the admonishment to tell the story so our people would not lose hope. I always swore silently to myself that I would tell the story, but I rarely have told the story. Perhaps it seems too heavy of a story to launch into with people I do not know well. Telling it within the family seems more comfortable because it is part of who we are, the fabric of our collective experiences.

The Story of Dependable Woman

This story my family tells came from the Hunkpapa people, Sitting Bull's people, a story that of course came from our time, forty years living with them. It is the story of a girl, and when I think of the power that our people once possessed, the qualities our great leaders once had, this is my touchstone. Sometimes, insight into who we are or were is not published in any book (although members of my dad's family have published many). This is a story I heard only orally, and I believe this is the first time it has been published. But it is this story I carried with me when I went to Standing Rock in 2016. I thought of it often, like a stone one carries, caressing it in my mind, like a prayer for the future and what our ancestors had to teach us.

When my grandmother's cousin was a boy growing up in Wakpala on the Standing Rock Sioux Reservation in the early decades of the twentieth century, he observed an elderly woman who walked with a limp. When she stood up she made the sound "hu huh hey"—it was something commonly said by the elderly as they experienced the aches and pains of later life.

Being a curious boy, my Lala (this is what he insisted I call him) wanted to know why she limped and what was the cause of her pain. So, he went to his grandfather, the Reverend P. J. Deloria, known to the people as Tipi Sapa, and began sweeping his grandparents' house and trying to be helpful in every way. Finally, observing this behavior, his grandfather told him, "Okay, I know you want something. Why don't you just tell me what it is?" My Lala then asked about the elderly woman who walked with a limp and said "hu huh hey" every time she stood up. His grandfather looked at him sternly and said, "Now *takoja* (grandson) you know you aren't supposed to ask about things like that. If she wants you to know she will tell you."

My Lala said he acknowledged this was true. In our Lakota/Dakota traditions it is extremely bad manners to demand such knowledge. If you are meant to know you will know. Still, his grandfather conceded to his curiosity just this one time and explained the source of the grandmother's injury.

When the Hunkpapa were fleeing from the US Army and making their way to safety on the other side of the Canadian border, this elderly woman was a girl of thirteen years. She had an older sister who had a two-year-old daughter and a newborn. This was a serious violation of Lakota convention, which held that parents should space their children four years apart.

Believe it or not, it was considered the height of manliness for

Lakota and Dakota men to be able to control their sexual drives. I know, it's hard to believe today, living in the heteropatriarchal society that frames the basis of our world.

The shame would be shouldered by the older child if their parents broke this rule. The older child would be called a "killed child," because it was assumed that their parents were so unhappy with the child they sought to replace it by having another too soon. This term was the exact opposite of a "child beloved." A child would be given this honorific after a ceremony where many gifts were given to the community by their family, and would be allowed to wear the red ochre in their hair part. This shame of being a killed child would, like the honor of being a child beloved, be carried by the older child for the rest of their life.

My great-great-aunt Ella Deloria, a Lakota/Dakota ethnologist and Tipi Sapa's daughter, recalled once interviewing an elder who admitted to being a killed child. She thought this was extraordinary because the shame was so great that few would ever admit it later in life.

As they were fleeing, the older sister could only really carry one child, the infant. It fell upon the younger sister to carry her two-year-old niece on her back. While they were escaping, the younger sister was shot in the leg by the soldiers. But she persisted and carried her niece all the way to the Canadian border on her back with a bullet in her leg.

When the Hunkpapa arrived in Canada, the first thing Sitting Bull did when they set up camp was set up a bed of sage and install the young aunt on it. He told the people that it was because of young people like her that the Hunkpapa people would survive. My Lala would always make a point to say that Sitting Bull did not honor any of the warriors. He honored this girl, and this shows the true love and respect our culture had for women. In fact, the name for wife is "most beloved woman." And Sitting Bull gave the girl a name: Dependable Woman.

<<>>

Soldiers vs. Warriors

I often think about the fundamental differences between the culture of my own people and that of the colonizers who made their way across the ocean from the Old Feudal World. When I was sundancing, elders would talk to us about the Lakota concept of being *ikce wicasa*, a free, ordinary man. It was a concept that took pride of place in our egalitarian culture and stands in contrast to the feudal system with the lords on top of the pyramid and the multitude of serfs on the bottom. Their description of ikce wicasa reminded me of a story my grandmother's uncle Vine Deloria Sr. used to tell about Yankton chief White Swan and the difference between being a soldier and being a Dakota warrior. Soldiers follow orders, in contrast to our warriors, who were truly ikce wicasa. We didn't build great monuments or enthrone a few in gold, but we lived authentic lives as people, and I believe that is the secret of our success as Dakota and Lakota human beings.

Here is the story "Soldiers versus Warriors" recounted in full, as told by Vine Deloria Sr. from *Remember Your Relatives: Yankton Sioux Images, 1851 to 1904* by Renee Sampson Flood and Shirley A. Bernie:

> You know... after the Minnesota Sioux War [in 1862]... a lot of refugees [the Santee] came to live among the Yanktons [my dad's tribe]. The government had issued orders to General Sully to visit the Yanktons and remind them of their Treaty obligations. He was to tell them that since the [United States] government was an ally of the Yanktons, the refugees should be treated as enemies.
>
> General Sully held a council with the Yanktons and told them, "I'm going to be gone about four months. When I return I want you to tell me that they're gone." The Yanktons told themselves that these refugees were their relatives. Why should we drive our own people out, they thought.

Later, Sully came back and said, "Well, did you drive them out?" The Yanktons told him they did not. Then General Sully told them, "Well, I'll tell you what I'll do. I think that the President [Lincoln] is asking too much. I'm going to be gone again, so during that time if you shoot one of these refugees, I'll report that the Yanktons are allies. They have killed the Isanti."

Struck by the Ree came to my (great) grandfather (Francois des Lauriers) and asked him if he would do this. My grandfather said, "Yes, I suppose. I've killed two Sioux and this will make a third. I had that in a dream. I saw four purification lodges in my vision. At the end was a great big, black hawk. And on the side was a big, white owl. And they stood there. They told me that by passing those purification lodges, I was going to kill four of our own people. I've killed two and here is the third. I'll kill him." So, he did.

When Sully returned, he came with two mule teams and a driver. He sat up there on the back. He said, "Well, did you shoot one?" Struck told him at had been done. Then, Sully asked, "Who shot him?" Struck told him Deloria had shot the man. Sully told him, "Oh, I meant for one of you full bloods to do it. Deloria is half French. I'm going to go back and bring my soldiers to attack you."

White Swan walked up to him. He said, "Tell this monster to get down." So Sully got down. "Sully," said White Swan, "You're a fighting man and I'm a fighting man. When your boys go into battle, you're on top of a big butte back there with your field glasses on, riding the fastest horse. When there are enemies coming, I go without asking anybody to join me. And my warriors look at each other and say, 'Get on your horses. That darn fool will get himself killed.' So they come thundering from behind.

When your soldiers are getting beat, and they try to run,

you have them shot. When some of my warriors get scared, and run, that's alright. Maybe they'll be braver some other time.

So you select any gun, any weapon that you want and give me fifteen paces, and with these two knives, I'll dodge you all the way, and chop you allll up."

Then Sully told him that he didn't mean anything by what he had said and White Swan said, "I don't know how you meant it!" White Swan bluffed Sully down. THAT was White Swan.

The authors add the following description of Chief White Swan "After the war ended, White Swan expressed his concern about what would be done with the captured Minnesota tribes. When visitors came to his lodge, he kept them up half the night talking about current national events such as the Civil War. Many of these people, both Indian and white, came away from their visits with him impressed by his keen intelligence and wit."

My dad served in the army but had no love for it, reserving his true dedication and love for us, his family. He was a lot like White Swan, who was the head man of the village our family was from, a place that was later put under water by the dam at Fort Randall. I took my children there and with their cousins they played in the water by the shore of the dam. Life goes on; our people persist.

CHAPTER ONE

FROM MALHEUR TO STANDING ROCK

When I go around America and I see the bulk of the white people, they do not feel oppressed. They feel powerless. When I go amongst my own people, we do not feel powerless. We feel oppressed. We do not want to make the trade. We see the physical genocide they are attempting to inflict upon our lives and we understand the psychological genocide they have already inflicted upon their own people ... that this is the trade-off they want us to make for survival, that we become subservient to them, that we no longer understand our real connection to power, our real connection to the earth.

—John Trudell, Santee Dakota, We Are Power speech, 1980

Here beyond men's judgments all covenants were brittle.

—Cormac McCarthy, *Blood Meridian: Or the Evening Redness in the West*, 1985

In December 2016, the Océti Sakówin camp was blanketed in snow, with temperatures so cold the simple act of taking my hand out of my glove—just for a minute to adjust my camera—was punished with exquisitely painful pricks, harbingers of frostbite, all over my exposed flesh. The pain immobilizing my hand served as a reminder of the unforgiving nature of life at this northern latitude. I thought about my ancestors, who had endured countless winters here in skin tipis and buffalo furs. These products of their ingenuity also attested to the importance of their all-encompassing relationship with the Tatanka Oyate, the Buffalo Nation that made life itself possible.

This starkly beautiful landscape, known as the Great Plains, is the homeland of my father's people, the Dakota (known in the western dialect as Lakota). It was serene and powerful and quite capable of killing us all. It is a place of exceptional beauty, but a place that—hand stripped even for a moment of a humble glove—will remind you of your mortality. Or as they say in Lakota, of our pitifulness when we stand alone and our need for help, *unsimala ye*, whether from divine intervention or fellow human beings. Life here was made possible by our traditional culture of sharing based on kinship and responsibility. When stripped of the protection of these life-sustaining relationships, we would not survive.

The glove I wore was the product of western capitalism made in a factory in far-off China, and the gloves and clothing my Dakota and Lakota ancestors would have worn 160 years ago would have been the product of those relationships. A buffalo or a deer hunted by a male relative became the property of his female relatives by their industry—

the tanning of the hide, the butchering and preserving of the meat, their overseeing the sharing of that food, and the sewing and decoration of buffalo robes, moccasins, deerskin dresses covered in quills and, later, trade beads. And, of course, the humble glove.

When I walked through the camp, I could hear muffled by the snow the sounds of human industry. The sun beamed down and made the blanket of white glisten but offered little warmth. Cars and trucks entered the camp, driving by accompanied only by the muffled, crunching sound of the snow beneath their tires as they proceeded almost silently down flag row.

Even now, I can still hear the tinny music played over the PA system at camp and the quiet echo of the hammer as white men from Vermont worked on the frame for a straw bale house. Sometimes, when I talk to others who had been there at camp, there is a moment when the longing for that place makes their voices crack; but how can you go back but in thought, pictures, old social media posts, friendships? Most at the camp hoped it might last forever. The Océti Sakówin encampment was for a moment the dream realized, the dream that the organizational principles of our traditional camp circle societies might once again have a place in the world.

Our traditions cannot just be intellectual concepts, written about in academia or social media posts, they must be lived and afforded space in the real world. Capitalism has introduced the idea that without serving a profit motive that benefits the captains of industry life, ways like ours should not be given any space to exist. At the root of it, this is what is at stake with yet another pipeline.

Through the end of the standoff at Standing Rock, Unci Maka—our mother—seemed to slumber beneath the snow. Perhaps she only heard us in her dreams and when we were praying in *inipis* (sweat lodges). Or when our young people and elders were being sprayed down by water cannons in the cold North Dakota night as temperatures went below freezing. Maybe it was then she heard us. But on the main road of the camp, I sensed her thoughts were turned to the coming spring, new life, fertile ground for a new order—and the greenery of spring oblivious to the agony of whoever lost this battle on the shores of the Mni Sosa, our beloved Missouri River. Or more correctly, now the human-made Lake Oahe, our wild river, turned into a giant pond.

When I returned a little over a year later in January 2018, it was all gone. No sign remained to show that a camp holding over ten thousand souls was ever there. Well, one sign remained. A blue and white "No Trespassing US Government Property" sign.

My friend Desiree, a fellow journalist, took me to a small bridge off of North Dakota state highway 1806, where there had been a confrontation between water protectors and law enforcement. I was there on assignment, reporting on the upcoming trials of several water protectors charged with felonies, each facing fifteen to thirty years in prison. Here, a car had been set alight, and the two sides had been at a stalemate for several hours. We looked again for signs that anything had ever happened here. Beyond some recent tagging on the bridge, there was once again nothing.

As I gazed off the bridge to the north, I saw a young bison emerging from a small herd, and with an intense look of curiosity, he loped towards me. He was young, and his dark fur was tinged with orange. He kept coming closer and closer. I remained still. The rest of the herd was foraging further up the dry creek bed. I don't know how close he would have come if I'd stayed there, but I lost my nerve and turned and went back to the car. As I got in, another older member of the herd chased after the yearling and insisted he rejoin the rest. Suddenly, looking scared, the younger *tatanka* turned, and they both galloped away, occasionally kicking up their heels behind them as they ran. But as we were getting ready to leave, I saw the young one again perched on a rise that afforded a view of our vehicle.

I had begun the year covering the 2016 Bundy takeover of the Malheur Wildlife Refuge in Oregon, which ended tragically with the death of Bundy follower LaVoy Finicum. Oregon State Police shot him on a lonely road in the empty, snowy expanses of a vast forest in the American West. In his last moments recorded on a compatriot's cell phone, the Arizona rancher exits his vehicle, boldly marching at law enforcement like an angry father thinking he can talk to them man-to-man even as they have their rifles trained on him. He was still fully invested in his role as the cowboy, presumably the good guy, protecting civilization and the "good people of America."

I went to the refuge when it was reopened exclusively for the media for a guided tour in April of 2016, a few months after the take-over of Malheur had ended. By then, Ammon and Ryan Bundy and their accomplices were in jail awaiting trial in Portland, Oregon.

The Bundys and their followers had not camped on the land as our people had. They stayed in the stone buildings of the refuge offices. They had not made the land itself their home. Albeit, there were fewer that joined the Bundys than answered the call of the Lakota people. At most, thirty to forty occupied the refuge. However, white men with guns immediately commanded twenty-four-hour news coverage on every major news channel. Even when supporters at Standing Rock swelled to an estimated ten thousand, it was difficult to get news coverage, and never equal to that of the Malhuer takeover.

The sense we got from our guides, a mix of local ranchers and Fish and Wildlife Service employees, was overwhelming relief that the natural order of the refuge could be reasserted after the mess the occupiers had created. An enthusiastic Bundy follower had commandeered a backhoe they had found on-site and dug trenches for latrines, inadvertently digging up Paiute graves and artifacts. Human feces were found in the pit they left behind. In contrast, at Standing Rock, the tribe paid about a thousand dollars a day for chemical toilets and dumpsters to minimize the impact of their supporters, arriving from around the world, on the land.

The two camps, one in Oregon at the Malheur Wildlife Refuge and the other in North Dakota just north of the Standing Rock Sioux Reservation, represent in a single crucial year, the year of Trump's election, conflicting visions for America's future. Both were challenges to federal, state, and county authority arising out of vastly different experiences with western expansionism that led to demands at odds with one another—yet both manifested as standoffs with law enforcement. Although both received worldwide coverage, they are both still, four years later, mostly a puzzle, an aberration, in the minds of most Americans.

Before the year was out, Donald Trump had won the presidency of the United States. It appeared the progress the country had voted in with the election of Obama eight years earlier had been snatched from the coalition of voters representing a multi-racial future of America, a coalition forged in the civil rights movement and tried by the pushback of the Reagan/Bush years that had found its way to the ballot box and to a more thoughtful American exceptionalism.

It had been defeated by a solid phalanx of white support of a candidate who had run his campaign via Twitter and was caught on tape gloating to a TV host about how his celebrity status meant he could grab women "by the pussy," and who crowed that he was so popular he could shoot a man on Fifth Avenue and get away with it.

His election did nothing to bring his actions into line with what would be called a normal presidency. Trump's control over the Republican Party became absolute in 2020 when he was able to avoid impeachment in the Senate, corralling the votes of former "Never Trumpers" with his popularity among their voting base and the very real threat of being driven from office by his supporters in their states.

Throughout Trump's first term in office, his approval ratings by Republican voters remained above 80 percent, dashing the hopes of Beltway players that the administration of the American empire would return to its normal two-party quagmire.

As Trump assumed power, executive orders streamed out of the Oval Office. Photos appeared nearly every day of the president holding aloft yet another letter he had signed, as a child would a drawing for a parent to admire. On February 6, he restored the permit for the Dakota Access Pipeline that the Army Corps of Engineers had revoked just a few months earlier. Another pipeline victory for Lakota/Dakota people, the Keystone XL Pipeline, was also announced to be back on track. And there was talk of a pardon for the Bundys as Cliven Bundy's former attorney was being considered for the position of head of the

Bureau of Land Management, the very federal agency Cliven Bundy had defied in an armed standoff in 2014 in Bunkerville, Nevada.

Trump's new secretary of the interior, Ryan Zinke, took office declaring open season on public lands and a refocus of priorities from his predecessor, Sally Jewell, a former REI CEO whose careful balancing of stakeholder interests now devolved to a free-for-all for mining and extractive industries. The former congressman from Whitefish, Montana, rode to his first day of work at the Department of the Interior, which oversees not only public lands, but Native nations, and announced that the plundering of national monuments and parks was necessary to meet the new goal posts, which were not simply for energy independence anymore but energy dominance.

It seemed perhaps the Bundys were not as much the outliers many had presumed. The strange groups they drew to their cause included militia members, Sagebrush Rebellion and wise-use stalwarts, and the odd sovereign citizen. These groups were still fringe in their actions, but they were the tip of the iceberg of some larger component of the body politic that considered itself "white." A large segment of the country, large enough to put Trump into power, supported specific underlying ideas these groups espoused, if not their particular methods for doing so. The Empire and its beneficiaries—that is, those whose interests it privileged due to race or, in the case of corporate interests, capacity for colonial exploitation—had indeed struck back.

When Ammon Bundy charged into the Malheur Wildlife Refuge near Burns, Oregon, he declared he was going to return the land from an overreaching federal government to its "original owners." He was certainly not thinking of the Burns Paiute Tribe. He quickly admitted he knew very little about the Paiute people and to tell the truth, neither did I.

I live in Oregon but had never visited that part of the state. Burns, Oregon, the Harney County seat, is closer to Boise, Idaho (about a three-hour drive), than to Portland where I live (over five hours away).

Harney County has a population of more than seven thousand people occupying 10,229 square miles—that's larger than New Jersey and less than one person per square mile.

The forty-one-day takeover never attracted more than forty supporters to the refuge, but it immediately received twenty-four-hour news coverage. How could it not? After all, it featured the already famous Bundy family and the spectacle of armed white men and women in a mix of army surplus and western gear draping themselves in the American flag.

The mainstream media showered Ammon and Ryan and fellow occupiers with coverage despite the media banishment of their father, Cliven. In 2014, he had ruled the news cycle after Bureau of Land Management agents arrived at his ranch in Bunkerville, Nevada, to impound his cattle that had been grazing illegally on federal land. The Bundy paterfamilias had refused to pay his grazing fees for twenty years and, with penalties, they amounted to more than a million dollars. An aggressive federal agent assaulted a Bundy aunt, and Cliven's son Ammon was tased while reacting in anger to seeing his aunt body-slammed. All of this went viral on social media, and a call for help went out and drew hundreds of supporters. Many came to the Bundy family's aid in full cowboy attire and on horseback, looking for all the world like the heroes in a climactic scene from a John Wayne western, where order is restored by a western code of honor, community, and hard work.

Cliven was soon holding court on sympathetic news outlets like Fox News, dropping bon mots like, "I don't recognize the United States government as even existing."

But the rancher and melon farmer brought an abrupt end to media coverage of his anti-government crusade with an infamous interview where he claimed, "I want to tell you one more thing I know about the Negro...They abort their young children; they put their young men in jail because they never learned how to pick cotton. And I've often wondered, are they better off as slaves, picking cotton and having a family life and doing things, or are they better off under government subsidy? They didn't get no more freedom. They got less freedom."

But Ammon Bundy, despite wholeheartedly supporting his father's interpretation of his "Constitutional God-given rights" to land and liberty, proved to be a very different media figure. A stout, bearded man who, like his father, kept a cowboy hat on his head at all times, he had a calm demeanor and a quiet approach that belied his calls for armed support. The media, eager for another replay of high viewing ratings, trained their cameras on him and his followers. CNN, Fox News, and many others sent journalists and satellite media trucks to make the trek out to the wilds of Harney County for more than a month in the middle of winter.

Very little of the reporting that emerged from this media spotlight included the perspective of the Burns Paiute Tribe. As I saw the news break from the opposite end of the state, I wondered if there was a tribe in the area and what their perspective was. As a Native woman, I know that even the most remote areas are not empty—they are someone's homeland. As a journalist, I wanted to know who they were and share how they were handling the convergence of a bunch of armed white men on their homeland (undoubtedly not for the first time). And yet, like Ammon Bundy, I knew next to nothing about the Paiute people. So, I reached out to the Burns Paiute tribal offices and was immediately put on a conference call with their entire tribal council.

They quickly got me up to speed.

Ammon had arrived in Burns, Oregon, a town of about 2,700 about an eleven-hour drive from his hometown of Bunkerville, Nevada, just days after the New Year, to march with locals in support of the Hammonds, a local ranching family. The father and son, Dwight, seventy-three, and Steven, forty-six, had been recently resentenced to serve five-year mandatory prison sentences for illegally burning hundreds of acres of public land in 2001 and 2006 and endangering the lives of firefighters.

After the march, which had attracted over a hundred supporters of the Hammonds, Bundy made a speech announcing his goals were "getting ranchers back to ranching, getting the loggers back to logging, getting the miners back to mining." He identified these groups as the "original owners" of the land. Who are these owners? Without a doubt, he meant recent European American arrivals like himself.

But in fact, it is the Burns Paiute Tribe and other northern Paiute tribes who lived for thousands of years in the area that are the "original owners" and possess the most substantial and senior legal claim to the land. Particularly since the wildlife refuge, which Ammon Bundy described as "destructive to the people of the county and to the people of the area," was once part of their former reservation. The Malheur Indian Reservation, a 1.78-million-acre reservation, was opened to white settlement after the Paiute and another tribe, the Bannock, facing starvation, rose up against settler depredations.

Almost exactly 173 years before Ammon's takeover of the refuge, five hundred Paiutes were force-marched, knee-deep in snow, some shackled in twos, about 350 miles northward to the Yakama Indian Reservation in what is now the state of Washington. It goes without saying Bundy didn't know the history of the refuge, much less the tribe, and had no idea his takeover was effectively commemorating this tragedy.

A grandmother, wearing reading glasses, her short black hair peppered with gray, Burns Paiute tribal chairwoman Charlotte Roderique addressed the media and had stern words for Ammon: "We don't want people who have no interest at all ramrodding themselves into the discussion. I understand Mr. Bundy is going back to Las Vegas. He can give back land to the Paiute there. For those who don't know, our tribe ranged all over Nevada, Utah, and California and southwestern Idaho. We are all interrelated. We all speak the same language, some variation in dialect, but we can understand each other. I think it is important that these people know they are not just affecting the Burns Paiute."

Indeed, both the Malheur Wildlife Refuge in Oregon and the land that the Bundys have been illegally grazing cattle on in Nevada were never actually ceded by treaty to the United States. The Northern

Paiute signed a treaty with the United States government in 1868, but Congress never ratified it.

The treaty process represents the US government's recognition of the preexisting sovereignty of the tribes over the lands they wished to acquire. Also, under international law, a sovereign nation cannot treaty away its existence, so the implication that signing a treaty extinguished the political existence of any tribe in the United States is a false one. Tribes are still sovereign. It is only the power of the US military that limits and suppresses the exercise of that sovereignty. This suppression amounts to an ongoing military occupation of Indian lands in Harney County, Oregon, and Clark County, Nevada, where the Bundys' ranch is located, and in Morton County in North Dakota, where the Standing Rock Sioux Tribe lives.

After the Northern Paiutes' Trail of Tears, some tribal members did find their way back to Burns, Oregon. However, they were landless and considered outlaws, surviving for decades on the edges of town, finding odd jobs working for the white ranchers who had taken their land. Finally, in 1928, the Egan Land Company gave them ten acres of land just outside the city of Burns. It was the old city dump, the first patch of land they had to call their own in nearly half a century.

"The one thing I'm really proud of is the tenacity of our people," Chairwoman Roderique said. "Four hundred twenty people are descendants of people who were able to get back here from Yakama."

By 2016, the tribe had regained federal recognition and boasted about 420 members. The population for just their band that lived around Malheur before the US Army declared war on them in the late 1860s was about 2,000. They still have not recovered in number, but the tribe oversees over twelve thousand acres. One thousand of which is held in trust, but ownership is so fractionated that Roderique notes, "It's hard to develop or do anything with the land when you have to get permission from fifty-eight other people. Those lands are pretty much in limbo and are administered by the Bureau of Indian Affairs."

"They have rights as well," Bundy opined when asked about the Burns Paiutes. "I would like to see them be free from the federal government as well. They're controlled and regulated by the federal government very tightly, and I think they have a right to be free like everybody else."

Roderique responded humorously, saying she was "trying to compose a letter for when they return all this land to us."

Ammon Bundy, a former truck maintenance fleet operator (it is unclear what his profession is now beyond anti-government activist) with less than a year of college, is like most white Americans, utterly unaware of the existence and sovereignty of tribes, even on lands where their families have lived for generations. This is the result of a long history of clouding Native American peoples' very real political status as sovereign nations and subsequent claims to the land. Native nations are sovereign, which means they have a political status higher than that of states, and yes, a higher standing than the county governments Bundy wishes to "restore" the land to.

The United States presents itself as an arbiter of fairness, a moral force on the international scene, the world's policeman, standing up to dictators and standing for the oppressed. Yet, at the same time, the same country disingenuously pursues a policy of denigrating Native American title to their lands, and legalizes this theft in Constitutional law, so as to hide the theft outright. Under US Constitutional law, a papal bill written in 1454 by Pope Nicholas V, which holds that only "discovering Christian nations" can have title to the land, is still the law of the land—the Doctrine of Discovery. It was cited as recently as 2005 by the US Supreme Court in *City of Sherrill, NY v. Oneida Nation* in a majority opinion authored by Justice Ruth Bader Ginsburg: "Under the 'doctrine of discovery'... fee title (ownership) to the lands occupied by Indians when the colonists arrived became vested in the sovereign—first the discovering European nation and later the original states and the United States."

The United Nations Permanent Forum on Indigenous Issues has rightly called the Doctrine of Discovery "the foundation of the violation of their (Indigenous people) human rights."

This violation will continue until the US renounces this doctrine and Americans comprehend the weak legal claims they have to the land they live on under international law. Americans will only resolve this by demanding their government honor the treaties made with tribes (even returning the land). Until this happens, white men like Bundy will continue in their folly and their ignorance, perpetuating injustices against the Native American nations.

In 2020, there are 574 federally recognized tribes. Scratch the surface of any land issue in the United States, and you will find the original owners—and they won't be from Europe.

So who are the Hammonds, and why were they being tried for arson under a terrorism statute?

After the 2001 fire, three hunters testified they saw the Hammonds poaching deer. Their party was endangered by the fires allegedly set by the Hammonds. D. H. "Dusty" Hammond, the grandson of Dwight and nephew of Steven, testified against them in court. He claimed he was given matches by his uncle and ordered to "light the whole countryside on fire" to burn any evidence of illegal hunting.

In 2012, the father and son were convicted on two counts of arson on federal land. Initially, the judge sentenced Dwight to three months and Steven to a year and a day. He claimed the mandatory sentence of five years "would shock the conscience." This breaking of the mandatory sentencing statute was challenged by US Attorney for the District of Oregon Amanda Marshall, who affirmed on appeal that the five-year sentence was required under the law.

These charges brought against the Hammonds, under a law that had the word "terrorism" in its title, predictably outraged right-wing pundits. The idea of white "all-American" cowboys being convicted under a "terrorism statute," which they assumed was meant to protect

America from Middle Eastern terrorists, seemed wrong to conservative sensibilities. Not only that, but conservative commentators saw it as yet another example of a federal government drunk on power and bent on depriving rural white men from the heartland of their liberty and constitutional rights.

A closer look at the statute section 844(f) that the Hammonds were charged under reveals the law was ratified as part of the Antiterrorism and Effective Death Penalty Act of 1996 (AEDPA). And this part of the bill had nothing to do with terrorism. It had been bundled by House Republicans led by Newt Gingrich in what amounted to an omnibus "tough on crime" bill sure to pass the House after Timothy McVeigh and Terry Nichols detonated a bomb on April 19, 1995, in Oklahoma City, Oklahoma.

Minimum sentencing guidelines were in vogue at the time with Republican leadership and contributed to a massive rise in incarceration rates of Black Americans. This law resulted in some of the highest rates of imprisonment of any country in the world.

The Hammonds, rural white Republican landowners, had been caught by a statute created in response to white male terrorism in the heartland and passed by a party they voted for.

"The case of the Hammonds could have been a victory for fixing laws long regarded as broken," reads a blog post from Oregon Wild, a conservation organization based in Portland. "Instead, it became something worse: vindication."

Indeed, at town meetings in Oregon during the standoff at Malheur, the state's very liberal senator Jeff Merkley announced it was time to take a closer look at "mandatory minimums that can sometimes produce more injustice than justice."

A year later, all three Democrats representing Oregon in Congress, Senators Ron Wyden and Merkley, and Rep. Earl Blumenauer, asked President Obama in a letter to review the cases of Oregonians serving mandatory minimum sentences for nonviolent offenses in federal prison.

The sole Republican member of Congress from Oregon, Rep.

Greg Walden, resorted to blaming President Obama on Twitter for enforcement of a law passed by his party in 1996. None of the Oregon delegation, including Republicans, voted for AEDPA. Walden's district, which encompasses two-thirds of the state of Oregon, includes Harney County.

As the Hammonds' court case proceeded, Ammon Bundy began receiving requests to help the Hammonds from his followers and his father Cliven, who had read about their case and felt the two ranching families shared a common cause.

Ammon had sold or closed his truck maintenance shop (poorly rated on Yelp) in Phoenix, Arizona, after the 2014 standoff at Bunkerville, and purchased a home with several acres and an orchard outside Boise, Idaho. In late 2016, Ammon was living with his family just a hundred miles due east of Burns, Oregon, closer to Harney County than most residents of Oregon who live around Portland. His neighbors in Boise included the Republican governor of Idaho. It is unclear how, without any apparent income, he could afford to live in this neighborhood. He had previously received a five-hundred-thousand-dollar Small Business Administration loan and perhaps the funds to purchase the house and land had come from the sale of his business. It is striking how, despite a refusal to recognize the existence of the federal government, the Bundy family and followers like the Finicums (who made their income primarily as foster parents, not by ranching) depended on federal dollars to underwrite their lives. Interestingly, the home had been previously used as the mailing address for the Republican Party in Boise.

In December 2015, the younger Bundy solemnly announced on YouTube that he had been praying, and God had told him that he needed to go and help the Hammonds. Ammon claimed in his videos that the FBI had threatened the Hammonds, both father and son, with longer prison sentences and further prosecution if they continued speaking to him.

On January 3, 2016, as the march for the Hammonds concluded, Bundy announced—without prior warning to the march organizers or local community members or even the Hammonds—his plan to occupy the wildlife refuge. A handful of marchers followed him. Most present, including the Hammond family, disagreed with this tactic and remained in town.

"This will become a base place for patriots all over the country," Bundy announced in a video posted to the Facebook page of Sarah Dee Spurlock, a local Burns, Oregon, supporter. "We're doing this so the people can have their land and their resources back where they belong...We need you to bring your arms."

Although Ammon Bundy appeared to know very little about the Paiute, his father's 160-acre parcel in Bunkerville, Nevada, is also on Paiute land. Mah'ha-Gah-doo, or in English, Gold Butte, is a 350,000-acre swath of land on the northeast side of Lake Mead, just south of Mesquite. It is the home of ancient native petroglyphs and other artifacts located on federal land managed by the Bureau of Land Management. Cliven Bundy's acreage is located south of Interstate 15, but the public lands he once held grazing permits for extend into Gold Butte, which was declared a national monument by Obama in the 2018 executive order that also created the Bears Ears National Monument in Utah.

More than two and a half years before the monument was established, the day after Earth Day in 2016, representatives of Nevada's Paiute tribes and preservation supporters held a "culture walk" through Gold Butte. What they found was dismaying. Ancient petroglyphs had bullet holes through them. Some had been defaced with graffiti. Many burial and campsite artifacts were trampled or stolen. And a Joshua tree used as a marker by hikers had been chopped down. Although BLM agents are supposed to patrol the area, the agency had scaled back enforcement after the 2014 Battle of Bunkerville.

Annette Magnus of Battle Born Progress told journalists she has been threatened for simply writing about dead cows she has found on the side of the road. These are some of the same cows the federal agents tried to impound in 2014 due to Bundy's nonpayment of grazing fees. After armed Bundy supporters escalated the situation—some were even photographed stationed as snipers on an overpass with BLM agents in their sightlines—the cattle were returned to celebration and cheers from the Bundys and their compadres.

Magnus noted the cattle were emaciated and dying, failing to live off of the meager forage available in the desert. She noted the animals did not enjoy "liberty" but abuse at the lack of care by the Bundy family.

Cliven Bundy is fond of claiming that ranchers know what is best for the land. He claims they know better than the bureaucrats or biologists or specialists from the federal government. His claim to ownership of the public land his cattle range and attempt to stay alive on, some six hundred thousand acres between Gold Butte and Lake Mead, is based on something he likes to call "preemptive rights." These rights transfer actual title to the land to him when one of his cattle nibbles on a blade of grass. He alleges the minute this happens he has improved the land and water begins to flow, the desert blooms, and this is all due to his animals foraging on it.

I grew up taking care of cattle. My parents kept a small herd on a farm we purchased in Washington State when I was a child. We had (and still have) water rights to the Yakima River, adjudicated in the courts by the state of Washington. I mention that because Cliven Bundy likes to use the term "adjudicated" as well regarding his rights. He has lost every single case in the courts; my parents won theirs.

My Navajo grandfather was also a cowboy and my mother's family ran cattle on the Navajo Nation in the Painted Desert near the south rim of the Grand Canyon. As a child, I participated in round-ups on horseback with my extended family in a desert environment similar to that around Bunkerville or the "Virgin Valley," as Cliven refers to it.

I also tended to cattle on our small farm in Washington State. My sisters and I and our parents would drive them into the squeeze chute of our corral and administer shots and spray red powder in their eyes to prevent pink eye. We made sure they had maple salt licks to indulge in and bags properly suspended so they could powder their backs. My dad set up wheel lines to water our bright green fields of alfalfa and clover with water pumped from the river and once had to bring in the vet to puncture one steer with a straw—the steer had gotten bloated from gorging himself on the rich grass. We grained them in winter. I know what it is to take care of cattle. I guess I was a cowgirl. So were my mom and her sisters, so were my sisters and my grandmother and my great-aunts.

I remember feeding the yearlings fermented apples, and how they ran through the field kicking up their heels as if drunk on the fruit. I remember my dad telling us, his voice breaking up and choking, how he found forty head of Black Angus dead on our farm after an ice dam broke on the frozen Yakima and traveled for a mile inland destroying everything in its way. I looked at a photo of it later. Our fields were white in winter and littered with their bodies.

The business of raising cattle is death, but it is also about animal husbandry. Watch old film footage on YouTube of a Navajo grandmother with her grandchildren and her sheep and you will see that the relationship was one of caretaking. But senseless killing? That is not something any people who take care of animals as their way of life can understand. Even several years later as a teenager, I saw my grandparents and their siblings, all traditional Navajos who normally spoke softly and wore turquoise, the women with scarves tied around their faces and velvet tops and full skirts, spit out the name of former Bureau of Indian Affairs Commissioner John Collier. In the 1930s, under his orders, federal agents shot and killed half of their herds of horses, cattle, sheep, and goats right in front of them as part of an erosion control plan. They spoke his name, their voices full of pain, the same way they said Kit Carson's name. In 1864, Carson rounded up several thousand Navajos and marched them off to a concentration camp to die in eastern New Mexico.

All this is to say, I wonder what kind of cowboys Cliven Bundy and his sons are that they would leave their livestock out there to die. To be honest, I don't wonder—I can guess. I understand fighting against the taking of animals—certainly my family has felt that pain with Collier's livestock reduction plan—but I don't understand how Cliven Bundy can call himself a true rancher.

My mom used to tell us our traditional Navajo grandparents' bank account was out there in the desert walking around on four legs. Despite his poor ranching practices, Bundy still sold cattle (some without brands, so his ownership is uncertain) at auction after 2014, bringing in over one hundred thousand dollars. His cattle have been reported seen near Lake Mead, on the roads thousands of tourists take each year. Under state law, if a driver hits one, even if the driver dies, their estate has to pay Cliven Bundy.

"We are exercising our constitutional rights," Ammon Bundy told reporters as he stood in front of a cluster of news microphones with the white snow-blanketed Malheur Wildlife Refuge behind him. "We won't leave until these lands have been turned over to their rightful owners. More than one hundred ranchers and farmers used to work this land, which was taken illegally by the federal government."

It is Representative Walden's job, as the solitary Republican member of Oregon's congressional delegation, to represent these diminishing numbers of ranchers and farmers in the US Congress. In the solidly blue Pacific Northwest, it is the sparsely populated eastern side of Washington and Oregon where the Republican Party holds sway. Sometimes there is talk of these vast sagebrush-covered areas, in the rain shadow of the Cascade Range, seceding from their more urban and progressive western sides to join Idaho, which shares their ideological perspective.

"But what people don't understand is the culture, the lifestyle, this is a great American West," Representative Walden said just six days after the occupation began in an unscripted speech on the floor of the House of Representatives in what amounted to a spirited defense of Ammon's motives. "I understand and hear their anger...how do you have faith in a government that doesn't ever listen to you?"

His conclusion reinforced Ammon Bundy's narrative, which the media was relaying with nonstop coverage of the armed takeover. Walden stressed that the real problem in America was not militia members with guns occupying federal facilities, but "how we manage our lands and how we're losing them." The "we" in the sentence was referring not to the American people who allegedly own these public lands, nor the federal government that administers them on their behalf, nor even the Native nations who had them taken by American expansion, but individuals, primarily white, who wish to make use of these lands as they see fit.

Yet, Walden's speech ignored the work of actual ranchers, his constituents, in Harney County. (Ammon Bundy is not his constituent.) They had helped create a Fifteen-Year Comprehensive Conservation Plan (CCP) for the Malheur National Wildlife Refuge. Founding board members of the High Desert Partnership (which brought together different interest groups to develop the plan) included ranchers Gary Marshall and Mike Bentz along with Dick Jenkins and Chad Karges of the Malheur National Wildlife Refuge. Partners also included the Burns Paiute Tribe. Chairwoman Charlotte Roderique stressed to me how the collaborative process the CCP entailed proved a significant step in healing divisions in the community that went back five generations to the Bannock Wars.

The ranchers, the tribe, and the refuge had worked for ten years to create a management compact they were all proud of, and they wanted the media to write about it. They failed, however, to catch the interest of the national press, and Bundy's mischaracterization of what was actually a successful compact rules much of the public's imagination to this day.

Georgia Marshall, a Harney County rancher for sixty-four years with husband Gary Marshall, who has grazing permits on both BLM and Malheur Wildlife Refuge lands, opposed the stoking of animosity between ranchers and federal agencies.

"Let's not destroy what we're doing because we think we have to make a stand for everything that's happened," Marshall said at a community meeting in Burns a few days after the Bundys occupied the refuge. "I'm pissed as hell right now. And my boots are shaking. But I'm not going to let some other people be my face. I am me. This is my home."

While Ryan and Ammon Bundy have attempted to start various businesses, they are not ranchers; I heard actual ranchers around Malheur refer to them as "lost souls."

Even as Representative Walden implored Congress to listen to the Bundys, their anti-public-lands agenda was enshrined in the Republican Party platform, which called for Congress to pass legislation to "convey certain federally controlled public lands to the states"—language echoing that of Ammon Bundy in his takeover of the Malheur.

When Ammon's brother Ryan Bundy was questioned about the rights of the Burns Paiute Tribe to the wildlife refuge, which was part of their reservation prior to the Bannock Wars, he said, "We also recognize that the Native Americans had the claim to the land, but they lost that claim. There are things to learn from cultures of the past, but the current culture is the most important."

If the Bundys' "current culture" is one epitomized by cowboys and ranching, it constitutes a tiny minority of Americans today—and many "ranchers" are not simple rural folk trying to make a living or maintain a way of life. Fifty percent of grazing leases on public lands are controlled by billionaires like the Koch brothers, the Hilton family, and even a Hewlett-Packard heiress.

Local ranchers like the Marshalls are more willing to come to the table because they operate on smaller margins. What brought many into the compact was the desire to prevent the listing of the sage grouse on the endangered species list, which would have required changes to their cattle operations. Large ranches owned by billionaires or corporations would not be financially impacted in the same way and also have the political influence to fight listing of endangered species in the halls of power.

<><>

Public lands advocates will often counter the Bundys' and other wise-use proponents' demands to privatize or localize control of those lands by asserting that they are actually owned by all the American people. However, both the Malheur Wildlife Refuge in Oregon and the six hundred thousand acres of federally owned public land the Bundy family illegally grazed cattle on for nearly three decades were never ceded by treaty to the United States. The Northern Paiute did sign a treaty with the United States in 1868, but Congress never ratified it. In light of the fight over the Standing Rock Sioux Tribe's right to consultation on unceded treaty land that would follow later in 2016 during the protest against the Dakota Access Pipeline, this is significant.

Because only sovereign nations can sign treaties under international law, the treaty process, by definition, represents the US government's recognition of the preexisting sovereignty of tribes. The popular notion that by signing a treaty tribes commit political suicide is inaccurate. On the contrary, entering into a treaty is an expression of sovereignty. The only rights that are given up—to land or the use of hunting grounds or fishing sites—are those explicitly stated. Any rights not mentioned in the treaty are called retained rights.

The limited exercise of sovereignty tribes experience now is due, frankly, to the military power of the United States. When America speaks of itself and its subjugation of Native nations "from sea to shining sea" it is always couched in the language of morality, of rightness, progress, and providence. The manifestation of the United States is described as the apex of human evolution, of self-government and human freedom. Yet, continued suppression and use of Native homelands was not only accomplished militarily in the nineteenth century and the age of Manifest Destiny, but continues to this day. It is the way everyone who is not Native American is able to go about their lives, purchase real estate, and build their futures. It is all incumbent on a continued military threat. Wounded Knee and Standing Rock were two recent incidents on Lakota homelands where that military-based landholding became visible.

Most Americans are unaware that Mount Rushmore, billed as "America's Shrine of Democracy," is also located on unceded treaty land. The Black Hills, the oldest mountain range in the United States, are considered sacred by tribes in the area, including the Lakota and Dakota. Many Native people regard the carving of these sixty-foot-tall sculptures of US presidents as the defacement of a living mountain.

Lieutenant Colonel George Armstrong Custer's demise at the Battle of the Little Bighorn in 1876 is celebrated by the Lakota and their allies and considered tragic by Americans, but few know that in 1874, he led an expedition into the Black Hills looking for gold. Gold was found and led to a massive gold rush, sparking conflict with the Great Sioux Nation.

Custer's expedition was a clear violation of the Fort Laramie Treaty of 1868, signed after the victories of Red Cloud forced the Americans to negotiate for peace. The treaty forbade white settlement of the Black Hills. The Océti Sakówin's sovereignty between the North Platte River and Yellowstone River had already been recognized by the United States government in the Fort Laramie Treaty of 1851.

In 1980, the Supreme Court of the United States in the case *United States v. Sioux Nation of Indians* upheld the Great Sioux Nation's right to the sacred Black Hills under the same treaty. The Supreme Court agreed with a lower court ruling that found the 1877 act seizing the Black Hills from the Océti Sakówin was a violation of the Fifth Amendment. The court sought to remedy this not by returning the land but by purchasing it at 1868 prices (with interest). Totaling over one hundred million dollars, the money was deposited in the accounts of the Bureau of Indian Affairs, a US federal department. With that, the US effectively had paid itself for the land, and the matter was considered resolved. The tribes have refused to touch the money, and it has now grown to some 1.5 billion dollars. The Lakota and Dakota people want the land back—all of it.

The route the Dakota Access Pipeline ended up taking—crossing the Missouri River north of the Standing Rock Sioux Reservation—runs through forty-five miles of unceded territory under the Fort Laramie Treaty of 1868.

"I have a nephew, Jonathan Edwards, who is very active in things around Standing Rock," Virgil Taken Alive, aka Lakota Soulman, an elder who wears his hair in a gray ponytail, tells me. He's now retired, but was a DJ for KLND radio in 2016 when community meetings began that led to the creation of the huge NoDAPL camp north of the reservation. "On February 12 of 2016, a Sunday, he talked to me about DAPL. I didn't know anything about it."

In the summer of 1990, Virgil and Alex Looking Elk had a dream of starting their own radio station that would serve their reservation. It took a few years, but in 1997, KLND 89.5 opened its doors and broadcast its first show. It now serves not only Standing Rock but the surrounding communities and streams worldwide online, as well.

A grandpa, Taken Alive is open that he's opinionated and so didn't last long on the tribal council. But this quality may have made him a perfect ally for the young people on Standing Rock who sought to rouse the community to action to realize the danger the pipeline posed and to fight it.

At this time, a group of young parents and adults and youth including Edwards, Honorata Defender, Bobbi Jean Three Legs, and Waniya Locke emerged as community leaders. The initial meetings were held at an old movie theater in the community of McLaughlin, on the South Dakota side of the reservation. These meetings were entirely grassroots efforts, potluck meetings, and did not yet involve the tribal council.

"A new grassroots group going by the name of Čháŋté t' íŋza uŋ nažíŋ po—Očhéthi Sakówiŋ (Stand with a strong heart—the Seven Council Fires) has begun to hold meetings throughout the reservation area," read a post on the Facebook page of the reservation's local newspaper, the *Teton Times*. This is probably the first media coverage of the movement to stop the pipeline, a movement that would capture the attention of the world.

The group began to make their case to the community at these meetings, warning other tribal members that the pipeline would cross spiritual sites, burial grounds, hunting lands, and sources of drinking water not only on Standing Rock but other Lakota and Dakota reservations. They raised concerns over the probability of a line breach in the future, and were already using a call to action tagline that more Americans would become familiar with in the months ahead: "It is not if the line will leak, but when the line will leak."

All concerned community members were encouraged to attend and to help with outreach to other tribes, groups, coalitions, and individuals. With each session, the meetings were gradually moving north, going from community to community, and it was the meeting held at Fort Yates that LaDonna Brave Bull Allard attended.

The 3.8-billion-dollar Dakota Access Pipeline was being built by Dallas-based Energy Transfer Partners to carry five hundred thousand barrels of heavy Bakken crude oil to Illinois. The pipeline would cross the Missouri River just a mile north of the community of Cannon Ball on the reservation and threaten the community's primary water source, the river. The pipeline's original route had crossed north of Bismarck, but was scrapped after the white community had expressed the same concern that it would endanger their water source. DAPL was then rerouted to endanger a Native community instead.

Even in the February meeting announcement on the *Teton Times* Facebook page, there was already mention of discussions within the group to have a "Spirit Camp" where they would "seek to gather as many people together, along with any possible alliances made, to camp along the Cannonball and Missouri Rivers to pull attention to the concerns of the people."

They envisioned this Spirit Camp as a place to teach the participants how to demonstrate nonviolently through prayer circles, sign making, and contacting various departments within federal and state agencies.

At the meeting Allard attended, held in late March, there was further discussion about having the Spirit Camp in the Cannon Ball district, which was the closest reservation community to the pipeline's Missouri River crossing. LaDonna Allard, in her sixties with a striking streak of white through the front of her hair, was a tribal employee on the tribe's planning commission. She offered her land for the camp. Joye Braun, a Cheyenne River Sioux tribal member and activist who is usually sporting a beret, was invited to oversee establishment of the camp. Braun had previous experience establishing a resistance camp along the Keystone XL Pipeline a few years earlier in South Dakota.

As a member of the tribe's planning commission, Allard had attended meetings between the tribe and DAPL representatives in 2014. In the meetings, tribal leaders learned more about plans to put the pipeline eighty-two feet down into the bed of the river. This aroused concerns as to whether this was deep enough, because the waterbed was not stable. Tribal members at the meeting recalled a bridge in Bismarck that was buckling.

When I interviewed Allard in 2014, she said that construction would disturb a burial ground near where the pipeline crossed an island. Tragically, she had lost her own son and buried him on her family's property overlooking the river.

"I walked up to a young woman who was from Dakota Access," LaDonna told me, "and I said, 'Remember me, I just looked at your maps. I'm the closest landowner. Remember my face. I will stand there even if I stand alone. You cannot put this pipeline next to my home.'"

On April 1, Allard's land, just south of the Cannonball River, became the site of the first NoDAPL encampment, which would become known as Sacred Stone Camp.

Another meeting was held at Cannon Ball to get the community's input and permission. They had a good turnout of Cannon Ball residents who accepted the idea of a resistance camp, and it was decided there would be a ride on the reservation from Fort Yates to Cannon Ball to create awareness. Tribal members came to help clean up the area where the camp was to be.

"Didn't want, even for our local governments, we didn't want to be a burden," Taken Alive told me. They wanted to be independently funded and grassroots.

It was a cold day on April 1, when forty to sixty horseback riders left from the front of the Standing Rock tribal headquarters and rode to the camp to officially open it. They chose the first of April, April Fool's Day, because the Army Corps of Engineers were slated to make the decision whether to issue a permit for the pipeline to cross the Missouri River on April 14. The organizers wanted to have the camp set up before that date to make their opposition to the proposed pipeline clearly visible to the federal agency.

The camp's name was decided at the Cannon Ball meeting by elder Sissy Goodhouse. She shared her memories and knowledge of the days before the flooding of her community by the Army Corps of Engineers when the dam was built. The community had been rebuilt at a higher elevation. It had gotten the name "Cannon Ball" for the round basalt stones that were created where the river emptied into the Missouri, called in our language Mni Sose, "Turbulent Water." In Lakota, the Cannonball River was known as Inyan Wakan Kagapi Wakpa—a place where the stones were made in a sacred manner.

When I came to the camp, I stopped, as many did, at the convenience store on the road to Cannon Ball that was owned by the tribe's chairman at the time, Dave Archambault II. In the parking lot a couple of the stones were displayed. With the damming of the river, these sacred stones are no longer created by the churning whirlpool of the two formerly wild rivers merging.

On his Facebook page, John Eagle Sr., elder and tribal historic preservation officer for the Standing Rock Sioux Tribe, wrote on August 14, "When the US Army Corps of Engineers dredged the Cannonball River and altered its course, the rivers quit making those stones. That Federal Undertaking had an adverse effect on an area of

Religious and Cultural Significance to our people. We will never again see this. When man changes the land, it is changed forever."

The US Army Corps of Engineers didn't even bother to tell the Lakota people the dam was being built to provide hydroelectric power to the white neighbors. It wasn't until the water came that the Lakota realized their community was flooding. It was the same story for my grandmother's community of White Swan further south on the Missouri on the Yankton Sioux Reservation. In fact, the Army Corps began charging White Swan residents rent to live on their own land in the late 1940s. They did not receive payment for their land for decades, and unlike Cannon Ball their community was not rebuilt on higher ground. The Dakota people of White Swan were homeless, bunking with relatives on other parts of the reservation until tribal housing was built near Lake Andes in the 1960s.

The displacement of Lakota, Dakota, and further north, Mandan, Hidatsa, and Arikara communities that knew the Missouri like a relative and farmed the river bottom left behind a deep spiritual wound that our communities and families feel to this day. We lost traditional foods, medicine, and our independence. These were all things those intact river ecosystems provided us. Now our communities are plagued with diabetes, heart disease, obesity, and meth use. The price we paid to bring electricity to white communities—where the transmission lines marched from our river shores—was high. The price was our very lives and the supportive community we might have known.

For the Lakota and Dakota people of Standing Rock, the land between the Cannonball River and the Heart River to the north of the reservation boundary is sacred. Historically, it was a place of commerce where enemy tribes could camp peacefully within sight of each other because of the reverence they held for the sacred nature of this place. Native people came to the area around the sacred stone to pray for good direction, strength, and protection.

Tribal historian Tim Mentz later documented in a court filing for an injunction on the pipeline construction how the construction route of the pipeline threatened sites of religious and cultural significance.

We were a People who followed the buffalo; wherever they roamed there is evidence of our ancestors' existence and connection to everything in creation. This cultural evidence extends as far west as Wyoming and Montana, north to Canada, as far east as the Great Lakes, and as far south as Kansas. The construction corridor of the Dakota Access Pipeline crosses this entire region. Who knows the extent to which ancestral graves and sacred sites were disturbed or destroyed utterly?

"For our relatives traveling to Standing Rock to pray with and support the Hunkpapa," elder John Eagle Sr. admonished, "remember, you are on sacred land. Respect each other, watch over each other, be good relatives to each other."

Bobbi Jean Three Legs, a young mother and runner from the Standing Rock community of Wakpala on the South Dakota side of the reservation, organized a run to Mobridge, about a twelve-mile journey. After that, Three Legs and Waniya Locke, also from Wakpala, began to organize another run, this time to Omaha, Nebraska, to the office of Colonel Henderson, regional director of the Army Corps of Engineers. However, they had no funds for the run. Hearing this, Taken Alive did a blanket dance at a powwow he was emceeing to honor graduating youth, which raised $367.00. Bobbi Jean was reportedly overwhelmed and deeply touched over the generosity of her people and wept. Tall and beautiful, she would find even more support for her cause including from Hollywood stars like Shailene Woodley. The runners were able to leave the next morning.

As the runners went through Standing Rock, they received enthusiastic support from the community despite it being a windy, drizzly day. Some of the people who joined the relay came from the neighboring Cheyenne River Sioux Tribe, including Jasilyn Charger and Danny Grassrope, who would become founders of the International Indigenous Youth Organization, which provided youth leadership at camp. As the runners clocked mile after mile following the Missouri River south to Omaha, they passed through Lakota and Dakota communities—including my father's tribe, the Yankton Sioux Tribe—and garnered more runners and support in the form of food, donations, and places to stay.

Social media played a significant role in getting the word out. The youth were adept in using it and were also calling into the tribal radio station. The day the runners got to Omaha, elders had such limited resources they had to borrow a vehicle to bring them home. But still, the organizers were very emotional knowing they had done all this with heart, not money.

"I said on Facebook at the time," Virgil told me, "that these young people would be uniting the Očéti Sakówin. And that really came true."

When the five-hundred-mile spiritual relay (called Run for Your Life: NoDAPL) reached the Army Corps of Engineer's Omaha district office, the runners delivered a petition requesting the corps complete an environmental impact statement for the pipeline crossing near the confluence of the Cannonball and Missouri Rivers. The agency had signaled it was planning to rely on a less rigorous environmental assessment for the easement approval and would only conduct an environmental impact statement if there was a finding of significant impact. The fact the tribes were telling them there was one was not considered convincing or significant enough.

It wasn't until the run to Omaha that the tribe got involved with the activities opposing the pipeline and began to hold meetings with the grassroots organizers. After accompanying the runners in his dad's van, Jonathan Edwards helped organize a motorcycle ride and another run at the tribe's Grand River Casino. They were there in force at the casino to register their opposition when Army Corps head Colonel Henderson came to visit the reservation. The tribe held well-attended awareness meetings about the pipeline the next day at both casinos.

Lakota, Dakota, and Nakota[1] speakers are all members of the Očéti Sakówin. The dialects are distinct and arise from the large

---

1. A linguistic term describing a dialect where N is substituted for D or L. This usually occurs in the latter half of the word, not the first, and so they call themselves "Dakota."

geographic area from the Great Lakes to the Black Hills, which the different council fires (*oyate*) call their homelands.

The people of Standing Rock are famously the people of Sitting Bull and Gall, leaders who were headsmen of the Húnkpapa band, and the present-day tribe also includes Ihánkthunwannaa (Yanktonai Dakota) and Sihásapa (or Blackfoot Sioux) Lakota bands.

According to the territory agreed upon in the 1868 Treaty of Fort Laramie ratified by the US Senate, the Great Sioux Reservation comprises nearly sixty million acres—the same size as England. The existing nine reservations are remnants of that territory that would include all the land west of the Missouri River in South Dakota and a good chunk of southwestern North Dakota.

South of and adjacent to Standing Rock is another even larger reservation belonging to the Cheyenne River Sioux Tribe. Together, these two reservations are equal in size to El Salvador or Israel, spanning two states and constituting the largest single continuous land area left to the Océti Sakówin. They both border the Missouri River and are at risk of a pipeline spill, as are four more Lakota/Dakota reservations downriver on the Missouri. This archipelago of Sioux reservations is all that remains of their homelands, much of it now in the hands of often hostile state governments.

In July, the Standing Rock Sioux Tribe sued the US Army Corps of Engineers in federal court after the USACOE had granted the final easement permit for the Dakota Access Pipeline. However, on August 24, Judge James E. Boasberg of the US District Court from the District of Columbia delayed a decision on the tribe's request for an injunction that would have halted the project. He promised a decision before or on September 9.

The news was met with disappointment by the two thousand supporters camped near the crossing of the Missouri River pipeline construction site. Thousands more who were now following the protest via social media registered their concern using the hashtags #NoDAPL and #RezpectOurWater.

Despite the unprecedented size of the encampment and intertribal unity, there was very little mainstream media coverage. This was especially notable when compared to the 24-7 coverage on Fox News and CNN of the Bundy family's armed standoff with federal authorities that had garnered countless news reports within hours of their occupying Malheur with only a dozen supporters and no valid legal argument.

By August, local support had snowballed, and the Sacred Stone Camp, located on a narrow butte, was too small to accommodate a bus full of supporters from the Cheyenne River Sioux Tribe. The organizers had expected a small spiritual resistance camp of at most forty to fifty people.

In response, the Standing Rock Sioux Tribe negotiated with the USACE to allow them to begin a new overflow camp off the reservation north of the Cannonball River. The new camp would be located on a flat plain prone to flooding on land claimed by the Army Corps of Engineers after the building of the Oahe Dam. According to Allard, it was a location with a tragic history for the tribe, which retains an oral story about a Dakota camp of about three hundred horses being swept away by a flash flood in the nineteenth century.

This camp, Océti Sakóẃin, was destined to become home for the thousands of supporters. This was the camp seen in photos of the NoDAPL camp at Standing Rock. At its middle road was the famous "flag road," with flags representing some of the six-hundred-plus Native nations who would eventually come to the camp to support the Lakota and Dakota people.

"What I see is the healing of Native nations," Allard told me in an interview in early August. "What I see is an amazing event that I could never have imagined in my whole life."

On August 12, Standing Rock Sioux tribal chairman Dave Archambault II and councilman Dana Wasinzi (Yellow Fat) were arrested at the Dakota Access Pipeline protest at the barricades surrounding excavating machinery and taken to the Morton County jail. There the elected head of state of a Native nation was unceremoniously strip-searched—this for standing up to threats to the drinking water of his people. The consultation promised under the treaty with the federal government had not broken down; it had not happened. Treaties may be "the supreme law of the land" according to the United States Constitution, but that meant nothing to Morton County sheriff Kyle Kirchmeier. Harsh treatment for demanding consultation, essentially the mildest invocation of the tribe's rights under the terms of the Fort Laramie Treaty.

Eleven days later, the *New York Times* finally covered the story of the NoDAPL camp (the arrest of a tribal leader did not rate coverage) with an article that ran under the headline "Occupying the Prairie: Tensions Rise as Tribes Move to Block a Pipeline." Still the venerable gray lady got it wrong and Lakota and Dakota opponents of the pipeline objected to the *Times* headline, which they felt cast them as "occupiers" in their own homelands.

Elders at the camp released a response addressed to the *New York Times*, saying, "We are Protectors, not Protesters. Our camp is a prayer, for our children, our elders, and ancestors, and for the creatures, and the land and habitat they depend on, who cannot speak for themselves."

Most of the water protectors would come to be camped just north of the border of the Standing Rock Sioux Reservation at what began as an overflow camp when the Sacred Stone campsite, up on the bluffs overlooking the river, proved too small. The new camp, on a flat plain along the Missouri north of the Cannonball River, was named Océti Sakówin for the Seven Council Fires, the name for the Great Sioux Nation. It grew quickly and would reach a breathtaking size of more than ten thousand supporters by December. The camp was located off the reservation but within boundaries of unceded treaty territory, under the terms of the 1868 Fort Laramie Treaty, which extends to the Heart River that flows through Mandan near Bismarck, the capital of North Dakota.

In late August, Navajo Nation president Russell Begaye and Vice President Jonathan Nez arrived at the Océti Sakówin camp. They planted their nation's flag in a line of flagpoles representing hundreds of Native nations. The Navajo Nation is the largest tribe in the United States, with about 360,000 citizens and a land base the size of Ireland.

When asked by a reporter if he thought Energy Transfer Partners' decision to build the pipeline just north of a Native community was evidence of racism, President Begaye said, "Of course, because they could put this further north, but they are not going to do that because the population up there is not Indian."

The Navajo Nation leader compared the pipeline to the Gold King Mine spill in the Animas River the year before, which harmed the crops of at least two thousand Navajo farmers downriver.

On September 1, 2016, the Standing Rock Sioux Tribe announced that 188 tribes from across the United States and Canada had declared their support for the Lakota/Dakota people's fight to stop the 3.8-billion-dollar Dakota Access Pipeline.

Acts of nonviolent direct action began to garner more support and notice on social media. On September 2, Iyuskin "Happi" American Horse, a twenty-six-year-old Sicangu Lakota man from the Rosebud Reservation, was arrested after he had locked on to a digging machine for six hours. Images of him with his hands encased in PVC pipe and a red bandana quickly become memes and created more support for the cause.

"In our Lakota language, we use the word *Mni Wiconi*, which means 'water is life.' Protecting the water is equal to saving the world," Happi's mother, Cheryl Angel, told the media, which was beginning to cover the arrests. "I honor that, Happi honors that. Everyone standing with Standing Rock understands that no one can live without water."

Despite the peaceful nature of the encampment, North Dakota governor Jack Dalrymple, a Republican, Lieutenant Governor Drew Wrigley, and Morton County sheriff Kyle Kirchmeier characterized the water protectors in both statements to the media and internal communications as being violent and unlawful. The sheriff claimed during a press conference that water protectors were armed with pipe bombs.

Observers, including those from the United Nations, substantiated none of these claims. The governor received a letter from the ACLU threatening legal remedies for state and county First Amendment rights violations of the nonviolent demonstrators.

Chairman Archambault, after his arrest, was hit with a temporary restraining order requiring him to stay away from the construction site. He issued a statement critical of the governor's inflammatory language, noting that the only pipes at the camp were canunpas, traditional pipes used for smoking čhaŋšáša (which can include a mix of red willow bark, tobacco, and other herbs) to offer prayers.

The United Nations Permanent Forum on Indigenous Issues called for a "fair, independent, impartial, open and transparent process to resolve this serious issue and to avoid escalation into violence and further human rights abuses." In late August, Amnesty International called on the US government to protect the protectors' human rights to freedom of expression and assembly.

The fight to stop the 1,168-mile pipeline from extending across four states from North Dakota to Illinois began to catch on and to unite Native Americans of all walks of life in a way not seen since the occupation of Alcatraz by Indians of All Tribes in 1969. Many compared it to the second Wounded Knee in 1973 when the American Indian Movement led an armed standoff with the FBI at the village of Wounded Knee on the Pine Ridge Reservation. Veterans of those previous events began arriving at Standing Rock in 2016; they had been young people in the 1960s and '70s and now came as elders to provide guidance and encourage and honor the youth who had begun the NoDAPL fight.

"In the beginning, I camped at the big camp, the overflow camp," Virgil Taken Alive recalled months after the camp had been riven by internal divisions. "We saw the number of people who showed up. Amazing."

Following the original Wounded Knee in 1890, when US soldiers massacred unarmed Lakota women, children, men, and elders—

members of Big Foot's Miniconjou band—under a white flag of peace, my grandmother's uncle, the Rev. Charles Cook, returned from Pine Ridge to live out his last few years of life with her grandparents and father (who was still just a small child) on the Yankton Sioux Reservation. He was the first man from our tribe to become an Episcopal priest to his own people. My grandmother's grandfather, the Rev. P. J. Deloria, honored at the National Cathedral in Washington, DC, as the first, was actually the second. Her uncle had been assigned to serve the Pine Ridge Reservation. During the massacre, working with another young Dakota man, Dr. Charles Eastman, he turned his church, decorated for Christmas with pine branches and a banner that read "Peace on Earth, Goodwill to Men," into a hospital. For days the Dakota men, the first generation of their people to graduate from college and pursue professional careers, rode out into the blizzard searching for anyone who might still be alive and bringing them back to the makeshift hospital.

I had never heard of him until I was at my grandmother's house and she brought out a large old rolled-up daguerreotype portrait of a handsome man. She told me this was her uncle and how after ministering to the Lakota people at Wounded Knee, he had returned home and died a few years later of, as she put it, "a broken heart."

An Episcopal missionary publication memorialized her uncle: "It was he who, after the massacre of Wounded Knee—that final outrage perpetrated by the military upon disarmed and defenseless captives— went down upon the stricken field to succor the wounded and count the dead. It was he who tore the seats from his church to use as stretchers, and made it a hospital for the suffering."

Charles Eastman's wife, Elaine Goodale Eastman, who described my great-uncle in her autobiography as "an able and singularly attractive man," wrote, "I can never forget Mr. Cook's incredulous horror when he came upon the poor creatures in their bloody rags… too stunned in their culminating misfortunes to utter a sound until the torture of fresh movement wrung from them screams of agony.

The horses had been taken out and the helpless prisoners left alone in darkness and cold, while army surgeons were busy with their own wounded."

It was a tragic event that signaled the end of our world and extinguished any hope that our people could live as they once did. As Lakota holy man Black Elk is quoted as saying, "A people's dream died there. It was a beautiful dream."

Yet the US Army called the massacre a "battle" and awarded twenty medals of honor, its highest commendation.

"The action of the Commanding Officer, in my judgment at the time, and I so reported, was most reprehensible," General Miles wrote in 1917. "The disposition of his troops was such that in firing upon the warriors they fired directly towards their own lines and also in the camp of the women and children, and I have regarded the whole affair as most unjustifiable and worthy of the severest condemnation."

Three years later, Miles wrote to the commissioner of Indian Affairs in support of a compensation bill for Wounded Knee survivors and the need for the nation to atone. This time his words were even stronger, calling the affair a "cruel and unjustifiable massacre of Indian men and innocent women and children."

And yet, on the shores of the Missouri River, 126 years after Wounded Knee, we were witnessing the resurgence of a nation. The dream was not dead. The dreamers were still here.

It is questionable whether the United States, its government, and citizenry that identify as white have ever atoned as General Miles hoped they would a hundred years earlier.

Native people calling themselves water protectors were being arrested, regardless of status, chairman or not, and regardless of what band or reservation. The name of the main camp, Océti Sakówin, emphasized the reorientation of Lakota and Dakota people's understanding of themselves as a single nation. This was the first time in 140 years when all seven council fires of the Océti Sakówin had camped together—not since before the Battle of Greasy Grass (known to Americans as the Battle of the Little Bighorn) in 1876.

In 2020, Rep. Deb Haaland (D-NM) of Laguna Pueblo, one of the first two Native women to be elected to Congress in 2018, sponsored a bill to rescind the medals. She cited her experience at Standing Rock as her inspiration to run for office.

The Missouri River tribes, like all tribes, with variations of place and time, have a painful and challenging history with the US federal government—and with the Army Corps of Engineers in particular. In the mid-twentieth century, the corps built a series of dams up and down the Missouri River as part of the Pick-Sloan Plan that flooded almost exclusively tribal lands. Over ten years, hundreds of thousands of acres of prime farmland were flooded, affecting twenty-three tribes and displacing more than one thousand Native American farmers. This was after a hundred years of trying to force the Dakota and Lakota people to take up the plow and be farmers.

The tribes lacked the political capital that their white neighbors possessed in the halls of power in Washington, DC, and at the state capitals, so the new dams primarily benefited white landowners and communities while decreasing the financial stability (such as it was) of reservation families. Federal funds for infrastructure to bring the new cheap electricity and irrigation canals did not find their way to serve tribes, only whites.

One of the most striking images that came out of the Pick-Sloan era of the damming of the Missouri is a photo of Three Affiliated Tribes council chair George Gillette wiping away tears as he is signing away the river-bottom land on his reservation, where 80 percent of the tribe lived, and consigning communities like Elbowoods to flooding and their people to relocation.

Standing in camp and looking out at the Missouri, the mantra I heard again and again from tribal members at Standing Rock seemed more prescient than ever: "It's not if it leaks, but when."

In North Dakota, the tribe had counted two-hundred-plus pipeline breaks, including the Keystone Pipeline spill in 2011 that released 400 barrels of oil and a 2010 leak from Enbridge Line 2 that discharged 3,784 barrels of crude oil, of which only 2,237 barrels were recoverable.

"Right now, because oil spills are happening north of us," LaDonna Allard told me, "we're pulling fish out with tumors and sores and some really bad things coming out of the river."

The Standing Rock Sioux Tribe estimated it would take less than two minutes for a pipeline break to bring heavy crude oil downriver to a tribally-run Head Start building and less than five minutes to reach an elementary school. From there, it would take only fifteen minutes to reach the tribe's water intake.

"We get all our water from the Missouri River, and we will be without water. And I keep asking who is going to come to help us? Who will come when we have no water?" asked Allard. "You go down and ask the Diné people who came? They have had no water since it [the Gold King Mine spill] destroyed their water system. Who is helping them? You have to remember our bodies are 70 percent water, everything in the world is water; water is life."

For months, the state of North Dakota maintained a blockade on Highway 1806, the main road used by tribal members to reach Bismarck, North Dakota, for shopping and to get to jobs in white communities like Mandan.

Driving to camp in October, I was confronted with heavy concrete partitions, which created a zigzag maze that was maintained by the National Guard. Traffic that had been speeding along this two-lane country highway at fifty-five-plus mph slowed to a crawl as each car was stopped and uniformed officers leaned into car windows and asked drivers for proof of identity and where they were going. Tribal leaders criticized this checkpoint as an undue burden on the tribe, and that it, in effect, constituted a de facto embargo of the tribe by the state.

By the end of the year, the tribe's Prairie Knights casino profits were down by millions of dollars. The eight million dollars per year gaming brought the tribe provided crucial funds that were used for social service programs for tribal members, including heating and assistance to the elderly and the poor. Even after the camp and state blockade were gone, the casino income had not recovered by the end of 2017.

This standoff on the shore of the Missouri River by the descendants of Sitting Bull's people has been described by the late Vine Deloria Jr., prominent historian and Standing Rock tribal member, as both prayerful and political. Deloria saw this as a function of the origin stories of "the people" (as most Native nations call themselves). He wrote, "Religious events such as the coming of a primordial holy person who gives ceremonies, rituals, and prophecies, contribute to tribal identification as a distinct people." It was this notion of peoplehood that gave even "the idea of the treaty," which Europeans saw as merely a legal, political instrument of international law, a basis in the sacred life of the Lakota and Dakota peoples.

"Opposite is the Ihanktonwan camps, my people's camps, and on the Cannon Ball side, we have the Mandan camps ... there are also ceremonial sites and burial sites and medicine rocks and origination of people sites," Dave Archambault II, the chairman of the Standing Rock Sioux Tribe, said. "They are the center of who we are. Our footprints in the land. Our hearts are in that land. We can tell you the history of all of these sites, who put them there, how they got there, why they are there, why we go there to pray."

I, too, brought these stories, both passed down to me orally and written down by members of my dad's family over the past hundred years. The story of the hero boy Mato Gi and how he tamed the bay horse no one could tame. The story of Saswe Deloria's vision, also as a young boy, that led to my grandmother's family's dedication to the Episcopal Church, and to his son Tipi Sapa, later the Rev. P. J. Deloria, to his assignment to tend to the church in the community of Wakpala on the Standing Rock Sioux Reservation. My great-great-grandmother Mary Sully (Akicita Win) served by his side for forty years and my great-grandmother and her siblings were raised there, only returning to the Yankton Sioux Reservation to marry or after their grandfather had retired to a home built for him at White Swan.

"He convinced his listeners through his tingling, thrilling language," the Standing Rock historian Josephine Waggoner (who worked with my great-great-grandparents at St. Elizabeth's in Wakpala) wrote of the sermons Tipi Sapa gave in Lakota. "From indifferent, apathetic expressions, from their depressing onerous unsatisfactory condition, he roused their interests, their ambitions, their energies."

I used to stand up on "Facebook Hill" where the media tent was and where a signal for my cell phone could be got, the constant buzz of the aircraft sent to surveil us over my head, and gaze out at the hundreds of tents and tipis and yurts and RVs gathered in the meadow before me. The blue of the sky, the golden yellow of the grass, the curve of the river. The sounds of a community working, building, cooking, singing. That energy was thrilling to see, the rousing once again of a People.

CHAPTER TWO

ORIGIN STORIES

The ultimate aim of Dakota life, stripped of accessories, was quite simple: One must obey kinship rules; one must be a good relative. No Dakota who has participated in that life will dispute that. In the last analysis every other consideration was secondary property, personal ambition, glory, good times, life itself. Without that aim and the constant struggle to attain it, the people would no longer be Dakotas in truth. They would no longer even be human.

—Ella Deloria, *Speaking of Indians*, 1944

Does the United States have a homeland? Is it truly a nation? Or is it still just a colony that exists to exploit the homelands of other peoples? The federal government presently recognizes 537 tribes within its claimed territory. This number is continually growing and doesn't include state-recognized tribes and Indigenous people lacking any political recognition. Although homelands can be shared, this extreme example of nations within a nation plainly describes an occupation, not a country, and therefore, an ongoing colonial endeavor.

If the United States is still a colony, it could be described as a colony without portfolio—that is, without a homeland. It broke with its homeland, Great Britain, during the Revolutionary War in 1776, and now occupies sans terra firma the homelands of other countries, our nations—Native nations.

How can you tell if something is a colony? How can you determine if it never stopped being one despite vigorous marketing? Well, examining how it operates can be enlightening. We can begin with: What does a colony do? What is its definition? The Cambridge Dictionary defines a colony rather simplistically as "a country or area controlled by a more powerful country." I would go further and describe how it operates, how it functions. A colony extracts resources and wealth from other nations and sends the profits gained from that enterprise back to the ruling elite of its home country—its 1 percent. In a colony without a homeland, as I propose the US is, that 1 percent, that ruling elite, is corporations.

This should come as no surprise when you remember that corporations founded the United States. The Hudson's Bay Company, the Massachusetts Bay Company, and the Virginia Company, among others. These joint-stock companies were formed to meet the high risk and vast costs of exploration and colonization. Expenses that even the monarch, the Crown itself, could not afford. The French ancien régime discovered this after losing its colonies in America and funding the English colonies' Revolutionary War against King George III, which became a factor in precipitating the French Revolution.

In exchange for the capitalization of colonial aspirations and the assumption of risk, these early corporations were given rights by the Crown not only to lands and markets but also to government powers. In India, of course, the East India Company's role evolved over the seventeenth century, from trading to ruling large parts of India in the eighteenth century, which culminated in India's British rule.

In 2015, I had the opportunity to attend the hearings for the proposed Keystone XL Pipeline held by the South Dakota Public Utilities Commission. There, I met a coalition of Native activists and leaders and white farmers and ranchers from South Dakota and Nebraska who called themselves the Cowboy and Indians Coalition. Before attending the all-day hearings and embedding with the coalition in their rented house in Pierre, the state capital, I had not spoken to white landowners opposed to the pipelines. As we sat around a dining table after a long day of testimony, they described their outrage and shock when they discovered the US government had given TransCanada (now TC Energy Corporation), a foreign corporation from Canada, governmental powers of eminent domain over their lands. These landowners were faced with the hard choice of either giving in to the corporation's demand for right-of-way and risking a pipeline leak that could damage their operations, or fighting an expensive and protracted legal battle with the pipeline company and its army of attorneys—a battle they would surely lose.

Looking into these incredulous white men's faces, the first thought that ran through my mind was, "Don't you know history? How do you not know the history of this country?"

In my high school history class, I learned about the founding of the earliest settlement in Jamestown and the role the outlandishly named Virginia Company of London "adventurers" played in it. A company (it's in the name) started the state, the Commonwealth of Virginia.

Who can forget watching Richard Attenborough as Lord Burghley tartly informing Cate Blanchett's Queen Elizabeth I that she had to marry because she was inheriting a bankrupt country with no army. The Virgin Queen lacked the funds to embark on such a risky endeavor as exploration and colonization on her own. She relied on the piracy of "Sea Dogs" like Sir Walter Raleigh to replenish her coffers, which technically made her a pirate queen.

All of this illustrated to me why a clear understanding of this blend of corporate and governmental power was necessary to explain not only the invasions of our homelands, but the role this fundamental dynamic plays today: How this dynamic dictated past outcomes and future ones, too. How the "Age of Discovery" was funded. How the English came to be in what they called the "New World," and which my ancestors called "Our World." Each of these factors play a role in our relationships to this day. This powerful and fruitful engine, the modern corporation and its relationship to governance and domination, is why the interview I conduct with the white landowners four hundred years later is in English. It's also why this book was composed in English. Most farmers in South Dakota are of German, Scandinavian, or Czech descent. English is not their native tongue either.

All people have origin stories; however, there is a distinct difference between the origin story of a colony and that of an Indigenous nation—that is, the creation of a "real people."

Origin stories operate not merely as history lessons, but as algorithmic functions structured by the nature of the relationships the origin story details. Algorithms are "a set of rules that precisely defines a sequence of operations."[2] The rules, or "original instructions," origin stories describe function like directions given in a recipe and, when followed, produce specific outcomes.

In the case of a colonial algorithm, the pervasive rule is the demand of profitability free and unbound by Malthusian limits to growth. In a country, particularly an island nation like Britain, these limits were real and created by a set limitation on arable land. The end run around these limits is colonization, that is, the domination of other peoples' resources. Applied to the "New World," this has culminated in a powerful engine of consumption whose endgame appears to be the present specter of catastrophic climate change.

The United States' origin story begins primarily with a financial incentive driven by colonial interests that are evident in the corporate origin of many of the colonies and in the land speculation that fueled the revolutionary furor of the Founding Fathers.

In contrast, an Indigenous origin story encodes a set of rules that produces vastly different outcomes. A People's story begins with transformative contact with a spiritual being and the agreement or original instructions that are made with the being, who is a manifestation of the land itself.

When we compare the colonial origin story or algorithm to that of the People, as Native nations often call themselves, a distinct difference in orientation presents itself. Sometimes Indigenous peoples will call themselves the "real People" as in the case of my mother's people the Diné (or Navajo). In the context of the Bundy worldview versus an Indigenous one, the two narratives can be labeled by political outcomes desired by protagonists in these respective movements: sovereign citizen vs. sovereign nation. These are part of a broader analysis comparing the Bundy takeovers of public lands, an expression of the

2. Harold S. Stone, PhD, *Introduction to Computer Organization and Data Structures*.

sovereign citizen movement, to Standing Rock, an assertion of an Indigenous nation's sovereignty as a People.

Depending on the dialect, *Dakota* or *Lakota* means "allies" or "friends." This meaning emphasizes the relationships that define them as a People and, consequently, as a nation. This is exemplified (and reinforced) by the way my father's people end their prayers with the phrase *Mitákuye 'Oyás'iŋ,* "we are all related."

Lakota/Dakota origin stories (stories of us becoming a distinct people) begin with the meeting with the White Buffalo Calf Woman (Pte San Winyan) and her gift of the canunpa, the sacred pipe, and the seven sacred ceremonies. My Lala, Phil Lane Sr. (my grandmother's cousin) used to say, "Before we met the White Buffalo Calf Woman, we were not Dakota. We were something else. After we met her, we became Dakota." It was in this meeting with her, a sacred being who was a manifestation of the Great Plains itself and the Buffalo Nation (Tatanka Oyate), that we became Dakota. It is our origin story as a People.

"My people, the Dakotas," my great-great-aunt Ella Deloria recalled in her 1944 book *Speaking of Indians*, "understood the meaning of self-sacrifice, perhaps because their legends taught them that the buffalo, on which their very life depended, gave itself voluntarily that they might live."[3]

It is said that the meeting with the White Buffalo Calf Woman took place while the people were camped near the Pipestone Quarry in Minnesota. This soft claystone bed was the sole source of the red stone (now called Catlinite to honor the white American painter George Catlin) used in our sacred canunpa. They say the rock is red because it is the congealed and fossilized blood of our ancestors who died in the great flood. Until 1928, the quarry was part of the Yankton Sioux Reservation of my father's tribe, who were its traditional protectors in the Océti Sakówin.

This demonstrates how, for us, the land itself is sacred. When we traverse it, our mother's body, we are reminded of the stories that

---

3. Deloria, E. C., & Deloria, V. (1998). *Speaking of Indians*. Lincoln: University of Nebraska Press (p. 21)

recall the myriad ways we have experienced a sacred relationship with the land, with our mother, Unci Maka. It is a relationship necessarily built on respect, awe, and gratitude. An interdependency that is not only the core of our identity as a People but also defines and frames the experience of our very humanity. When we travel across our mother, we are reminded of this agreement we made with her. Because the moment we became a People, we became her people. The responsibilities we agreed to obey are imbued with the honor that kinship implies.

This relationship is something the Dakota Access and Keystone XL companies (Energy Transfer and TransCanada, respectively) can never understand as corporate entities with origin stories dependent on a colonial imperative. The colonial relationship is not contained by boundaries, only the calculus of profit—more rightly described as plunder, because the real costs are never deducted from the taking. The original colonial instructions are not bound by a specific place on earth, like the Great Plains, or, for my mother's people the Dinétah, our homeland between the four sacred mountains and the four sacred rivers. Without boundaries, the corporation does not have to pay for the consequences of its moneymaking ventures. It merely moves on to somewhere else when the oil field runs out.

Even as thousands took a stand at Standing Rock to prevent a pipeline, an oil by rail pipeline was quietly completed beneath Lake Sakakawea on the Fort Berthold Reservation. The tribe already has over four thousand miles of pipelines crisscrossing its reservation. The Mandan-Hidatsa-Arikara (MHA) Tribe also had the opportunity to stop the DAPL in 2015 and refuse Energy Transfer Partner's right of way on fee land the tribe owns and uses as a buffalo ranch a couple of hundred miles north of Standing Rock. The tribal council ultimately chose not to fight a losing battle over eminent domain in the courts.

The MHA is a tribe with over sixteen thousand members, their million-acre reservation encompassing fully one-third of the Bakken oil fields. The tribe, also known as the Three Affiliated Tribes, issues leases for hundreds of fracked oil wells on their reservation, which pump out the same fracked heavy crude oil the DAPL is transporting, and have brought the tribal treasury and individual tribal members who are fortunate to have oil-rich land (not all do), more than two billion dollars in oil revenue since 2009.

"We are of the firm belief we will become more sovereign by the barrel," former MHA tribal chairman Tex "Red Tipped Arrow" Hall declared in a 2011 speech before the North Dakota legislature. Hall was later embroiled in a murder-for-hire scandal by a business associate, covered by the *New York Times* in 2014 with the headline "In North Dakota, a Tale of Oil, Corruption, and Death."

In 2013, after several years of an oil boom, MHA tribal members on the Fort Berthold Reservation worried the tribe was not putting money aside like they had promised to do for tribal members without mineral rights. Despite not all tribal citizens profiting equally, they still paid the price in a reduction of quality of life created by fracking. One tribal member I spoke to was concerned about his parents driving to the grocery store due to increased danger from numerous water trucks driven on their rural roads to supply the fracked wells. In addition, there was an increase in sexual assaults as nearby camps filled with oil workers.

The fracked wells also produced uranium waste and irradiated commercial detritus with little oversight of the waste's disposal and storage. Yet Tribal Chairman Hall testified before Congress opposing federal Environmental Protection Agency oversight, claiming it violated tribal sovereignty. At the same time, he gutted the tribe's environmental program.

Many MHA tribal members told me they could foresee a future where, having trashed their reservation, they would need to buy a new one. These are not concerns corporations have to concern themselves with since the capital they represent is not constrained to any homeland. Many corporations, like Peabody Coal and other mining companies, have a history of declaring bankruptcy to avoid paying for cleanup. Their investors and owners then structure capital to form new corporations, like a bad spirit or monster in possession of a new body.

The MHA tribal council passed a resolution in 2016 supporting the Standing Rock Sioux Tribe in its fight against the pipeline. Chairman Mark Fox brought the MHA flag to be flown on flag row with other tribal nations in support of the opposition to the DAPL.

Native studies scholars will tell you the Lakota or Dakota people originally came from the East Coast and that we may have relatives in faraway Virginia. They say there are/were tribes of people that spoke our language. Sometimes, these linguistic and even genetic ties are used against Indigenous peoples to invalidate our land claims. At the 1974 Wounded Knee trial in Lincoln, Nebraska, William S. Laughlin, the dean of American Bering Strait scholars, gave testimony on academic speculation regarding our migration across a land bridge, now gone, that may have made travel between North America and Asia possible. After hearing his testimony, white audience members left the court concluding that Native people, like themselves, were merely earlier immigrants and had no greater claim to the United States than their own. But these theories are not relevant to how we understand ourselves. For the Lakota/Dakota, who we are as a People begins with the White Buffalo Calf Woman and the gifts she gave us. Today, that identity is mixed with pain, as I imagine it is for any of our co-linguists anywhere on this continent who still retain an identity as a People.

Perhaps now, for the Dakota, our story begins in 1862 on the day after Christmas, when thirty-eight Dakota men were hung in Mankato, Minnesota, in the largest mass hanging in US history. President Lincoln signed the order for their deaths just days after he signed the Emancipation Proclamation. The Dakota rose up against the Americans. What did they have to lose? They were facing starvation, consigned to a narrow strip of land after signing treaties and losing their hunting grounds. They were utterly dependent on treaty provisions, which never arrived. The uprising was precipitated when Dakota men confronted a trader suspected of stealing treaty supplies. He allegedly told them to feed their hungry children grass or dung. Little Crow, a Dakota headman, called a war council and decided to go to war to drive the Americans out of their lands. There is no official account of the death toll from the war. In his second inaugural address, President Lincoln claimed eight hundred had been killed. Little Crow and his son were killed by a white homesteader seeking the bounty. Little Crow's skull and scalp were displayed in St. Paul, Minnesota, and remained on display until 1971.

For the Lakota, our western cousins, the moment when the door shut on the past and the present epoch became inevitable was undoubtedly the 1890 Wounded Knee Massacre. The shock of these events impacted both Dakota and Lakota, for we are and were one People, despite living scattered across five states on separate islands of reservation land left after the storm.

"The web of inter-relationship among the various tribes of the Sioux Nation is very intricate and extensive," an anonymous minister wrote to Secretary of War Redfield Proctor just weeks after Wounded Knee in January 1891. "The fact that at the recent engagement at Wounded Knee, a number were killed has deeply affected all tribes, as they consider the killing of women and children an unpardonable offense."

As a child, I heard stories from my dad's family that gave me a personal perspective on how my ancestors viewed and experienced both of these events. I first heard about the Dakota 38 incidentally, while reading a book published by my dad's tribe called *Remember Your Relatives* that my grandmother had sent to us. The story was a transcribed oral retelling by my grandmother's uncle, the Rev. Vine Deloria Sr., which recalled a shocking deed committed by his grandfather Saswe Deloria.

He begins the story explaining how the Santee Dakota became refugees and fled Minnesota after the uprising. They came to our people, the Ihanktonwan Dakota, seeking refuge. We took them in, because how could we not? They were our relatives. The Yankton were told by the army they had to fulfill their treaty obligations by killing a Santee. If they did not, the soldiers would attack them all, Santee and Yankton. After discussing this all night, the headmen were at a stalemate. No one wanted to do it. At that point, Saswe announced he would because he'd had the vision of the four black lodges as a boy and had been told they represented the four men of his own people he would kill. So, he killed one Santee to save the rest and our people from mass slaughter. It was a decision that, despite the vision, haunted him for the rest of his life. After the killing, he announced he would sit, unarmed, for four days and nights on a hill, and any relatives of the Santee he killed who wanted retribution could come and kill him and that there would be no retribution. He sat for four days and nights, and no one came. The Santee Sioux Reservation is across the Missouri River from ours, in Nebraska.

The second story is of my grandmother's uncle mentioned in an earlier chapter, the Rev. Charles Cook, the mixed-blood Yankton Dakota Episcopal minister at the first Wounded Knee in 1890. I have only seen his story portrayed once, in the HBO movie about Charles Eastman's life. In it, my grandmother's handsome young uncle is characterized as a balding, middle-aged white man. Eastman is more accurately depicted by First Nations Saulteaux actor Adam Beach. Still, the notion there could be two college-educated Dakota men working together for their people in 1890 was obviously a story beyond the imagination of white television screenwriters and casting directors more than a century later.

But getting the story right has always been a challenge. Toward the end of his life, Vine Deloria Jr. tried to produce a more accurate retelling of the life of Saswe. The family had been unhappy with a book written by Sarah Olden in 1918 called *The People of Tipi Sapa* about Saswe and his son Tipi Sapa, the Reverend P. J. Deloria. Deloria's *Singing for a Spirit*, published eighty-one years later, was an attempt to correct the record. While I appreciate Vine's effort, I miss the cadences of the spoken word, the oral stories told to me by his father and Phil Lane Sr. that I heard as a child. These stories, even told in English, captured for me something that I have yet to see duplicated in print.

That old intimacy of familial, first-person storytelling has been given new life in the twenty-first century via the internet. Social media carried over Wi-Fi connections have obliterated the challenges of time and space that once hindered transmission of cultural sharing. Yet, despite this great interconnectedness within our communities and families, what is newsworthy to Indian country hardly ever makes it into the mainstream news—and, yes, we Indian people are used to it. We never expect the issues near and dear to our hearts to be covered twenty-four hours a day on CNN or to trend on Twitter or be gossiped about on BuzzFeed. Yet, a few years ago, I felt more connected than usual, perusing my social media feed.

As we entered the holiday season, it felt good to see, on my Facebook and Twitter feeds, hundreds of posts, videos, and retweets hailing the Dakota 38 plus two memorial riders (the plus two refers to two more Dakota men who were hung after the thirty-eight). Dakota people were posting images of the riders, descendants of the Dakota men hung by Lincoln, as they began their 330-mile trek in early December. Following the dream of an elder, they were starting from Sisseton, in northeastern South Dakota. Some of the Dakota survivors of the Dakota uprising in 1862 had been moved to this reservation after being driven out of Minnesota. Updates kept coming as the riders made their way down snowy roads, from Sisseton to the Lower Brule Reservation in South Dakota and then east to Mankato, Minnesota, where the Dakota 38 had been hung. Their goal was to reach the site the day after Christmas to commemorate the Dakota men executed for rising up against the Americans for not honoring the treaty by which they gave up twenty-four-million acres. President Lincoln, who at first glance appears to be the villain for signing the order to hang the Dakota 38, can also be credited for reducing the number of executions requested by the military commission: 303 souls. How many of us

Dakota would not be here today if he had not spared some of our forebears' lives?

Reportedly, some of the money owed to the Santee was reallocated by Congress to cover the costs of Mary Todd Lincoln's redecorating the White House. In addition to that stolen through years of graft by Indian agents, the money would have prevented Dakota children from starving. Andrew Myrick, a trader who refused to release any food from his stores without payment, is said to have instigated the uprising, saying, "If they are hungry, let them eat grass—or their own dung." Myrick was the first white man killed in the rebellion, and his body was found days later with grass stuffed in his mouth. General Jon Pope was then dispatched to Minnesota to defeat the insurgency. Pope's assignment was, in part, a demotion for losing the Second Battle of Bull Run against the Confederacy; he wrote, "It is my purpose utterly to exterminate the Sioux if I have the power to do so."

In December Lakota/Dakota people have another ride commemorating the Wounded Knee Massacre of 1890. Native people fill social media with posts decrying the murder of hundreds of defenseless Lakota, mostly women and children, by the US Army on the December 29 anniversary each year. Commemoration of this tragedy occurred just three days after the Dakota 38 riders reached Mankato bearing gifts of reconciliation for the town. To be a Native person on social media during the month of December is always tinged with sadness. Images show a group of horse riders, bundled in winter parkas, their faces barely visible under caps and sometimes cowboy hats, led by a lead rider holding aloft a medicine staff strewn with eagle feathers. They ride relentlessly, bravely, on a background of white, showing us that we have more to celebrate in that holiday season than a countdown of shopping days. We are still here, we remember, and we carry that knowledge with intent, with our ancestors guiding us.

One year, a tweet with the image of the burial of the frozen victims' bodies was retweeted hundreds of times with my Twitter handle attached to it. All day long, my Twitter stream became filled with that painful image and caption repeated ad infinitum: "123 years ago today, 150 #Lakota men/women/children were massacred by the US 7th Calvary @ #WoundedKnee H/T @jfkeeler." Each time someone retweeted, it showed up again on my timeline. Even though I clicked on the image only once, the long rectangular hole dug for mass burial with the bodies of Lakota people strewn inside it kept reappearing before me. Over and over again, I saw it. Our people, our ancestors, lying frozen in the ground while white men pose, holding guns or with hands at their hips as if for a job well done—and I am a descendant of someone who was there.

That photograph is filled with all those things that, as Native people, we cannot name. It remains a symbol of all the ways in which we are not allowed to be ordinary Americans merely living our lives in the most powerful nation in the world. December 29, 1890, is the date when we became a marginalized people denied the comfort of being part of a country that recognizes our experiences and commemorates them with us. We live out our American lives in a twilight existence where the only way other Americans, our compatriots, remember us is as we were then—when we were truly separate from them and each of us a member of our own nations, not theirs. Then they dress up like us with feathered headbands made in China and cheer for their sports teams on weekends named to "honor" us. The people of the United States do not acknowledge us as we are today—as our encounter with America has made us. But still, after all this time, we are different because we remember Wounded Knee, Mankato, the Long Walk, and every broken promise that we must, for our own good, put aside to live in our new country, the United States. It only makes it harder that citizens of a country that claims us and all we possess do not join us in this, the pain that is their legacy in our lives. This blithe disregard makes what we lost, the millions of acres, the lives of our loved ones, feel cheapened and unappreciated and forgotten, and makes present-day ignorance of us even harder to bear.

As we Native people mourn and reflect upon these painful events in our history, we do so very much apart from the rest of the country. There is no national news coverage of the Dakota 38 riders. No one is following their journey down icy roads and freezing temperatures except for us—we look for updates on their Facebook event page and watch their YouTube interviews, creating our own piecemeal media coverage that does not exist elsewhere. Instead, on that Sunday, the 123rd anniversary of Wounded Knee, a Washington Redsk*ns football game was on TV.

Seeing photos of Redsk*ns and Chiefs and Braves fans dressed up in fake eagle-feather headdresses, I think of a photograph of Owl Man, my great-grandmother's grandfather. In it, he stands with a delegation of Yankton Dakota headmen at the White House in Washington, DC, to sign the treaty with the United States in 1868. A diminutive President Andrew Johnson stands in a frock coat on the balcony above the Yanktons, flanked by the Miami Tribe's delegation, who tower over him in turbans and eagle-claw necklaces. My ancestor is easily identifiable since he is the only one wearing the full eagle-feather headdress. What would he have thought of all this? Each feather is said to have represented the confidence the people had in the leader. It was something very precious, but it came with a great deal of responsibility and accountability to the people. When the headmen returned home, the women chastised them for signing away the salt mines, which they needed to preserve meat. Even then, there were no good deals to be made in DC. The people were focused on securing their survival. They were focused on living, to protect and raise the young, and yet sometimes, like at Wounded Knee, even that was an impossibility.

Looking at this image of Wounded Knee, I want to run—run like the Ihanktonwan man my dad used to tell us kids about around the dinner table when I was growing up. He told of a Yankton man who was at Wounded Knee just visiting, and despite being shot through the middle of his body, he ran all the way across the state of South Dakota to our people.

We kids would pepper our dad with questions. "How could he run all the way across the state with a gunshot wound in the middle of his body?" "They were just tougher back then." "But why did he do it?" "Because he thought our people really needed to know. It was important to the people."

I want to run like that man and keep running, carrying the story with the pain still lodged inside of me, the worry and the doubt eating me up. And only by putting my feet to the ground and feeling the tempo of my movement, a heartbeat upon the body of my mother, Maka, can I shake loose the overwhelming despair the specter of the assault on our people brings up in me.

I suppose a lot of Native people feel this way, and this is why we share our stories with each other on social media—because these things are terrible and the country we are supposed to be part of cares not at all, or it cannot care without assuming guilt, and it is unwilling to do that because of its enduring belief in Manifest Destiny. In their minds, it was all for the greater good, the creating of this country, a necessary evil that led to nations being buried in the snow, bodies left in the cold.

When they share the images with each other, they use the photos of our ancestors' bodies for shock value and feel no shame in doing so. They share those images thinking, perhaps, that it will change America, and yet it never does because the algorithm doesn't allow for it. The only way change will happen—real, lasting change—would be to change our origin story, to change the algorithm itself. And so we live in a country where Wounded Knee and the Dakota 38 do not receive the same amount of broadcast time as does a perpetually losing NFL team, its fans sporting redface and doing tomahawk chops, failing weekly on the field in every way they possibly can.

Even as we mourn publicly for the first time in a long time, we are confronted by those who tell us to "get over it" on social media sites like Twitter. They refuse to see that we cannot do so as long as our concerns remain shunted off to the side of our daily American experience. We are mourning the dead, but also the death of our own centrality in the story of our lives. We are surrounded by stories of white men and boys overcoming obstacles and triumphing in their quests—to get the woman of their dreams, to save the world, to become rich—on TV, in films and books.

One white guy felt compelled to respond to the tweet of the photograph of Wounded Knee by saying it was okay because Indians were not "noble savages" after all, and did far worse to each other, so we should stop remembering or feeling bad about what happened. In rejecting one stereotype, he had embraced something even worse. The notion that unless Native people are better than any other people in the world they do not deserve basic human rights is the most dehumanizing thing anyone can say to alleviate white guilt.

Does he mean that we, having fallen off our pedestal, must endure any atrocity? Even the murder of unarmed women and children, and even infants? In his myopic attack on the "noble savage," this man has returned full circle to the mindset that initiated the genocide on this continent in the first place.

I'm reminded of Colonel Chivington's words to his soldiers before the Sand Creek Massacre. "Kill them one and all; nits make lice."

To Americans like this gentleman, Indigenous people and our tragedies are annoying reminders of the actual price paid for this land, reminders that must be silenced.

In her blog post, "On telling Native people to just 'get over it' or why I teach about *The Walking Dead* in my Native Studies classes," Cutcha Risling Baldy explains why Native people cannot just "get past" these experiences. She compares the trauma felt by her ancestors, survivors of the wholesale slaughter that took place in northern California at the hands of the forty-niners, to the characters depicted on the television show *The Walking Dead* after a zombie apocalypse.

Professor Baldy describes the miners and pioneers celebrated in California's history books and an NFL team as "hungry for your scalp and your head. They had no remorse. There was no reasoning with them. And there were more of them than there was of you." And yet, she notes the atrocities were committed not by monsters, but by white people.

Jim Miller, the Dakota elder who had the vision for the memorial ride, has said that part of the ride's purpose was for the Dakota to be the first to apologize for their role in the historical tragedy. Another

Dakota organizer, Peter Lengkeek, a veteran, explained, "We're trying to reconcile, unite, make peace with everyone because that's what it means to be Dakota."

On YouTube, you can see a video of Redbone, the Native rock band, singing in 1973, "We were all wounded at Wounded Knee for Manifest Destiny." I'd take it a step further than "wounded." Even if your tribe had no runners present to bring them the news, that was the day that, as Black Elk said, the tree was cut.

I always feel the contrast between what we lost after those terrible events and how little white America appreciates or even comprehends that loss. On social media, white men are busy telling Native people to "get over it" or carrying on about how terrible it would be to give up their team's racist mascot. Meanwhile, the genocide and how we survived it burns within me. Choices made by my ancestors to revolt, take in those fleeing American domination, dance the Ghost Dance, and tend to those shot by the US Army were not made for the benefit or comfort of these white men. It was all for me, for us, for their descendants. We are the reason they did these things and made these hard choices and survived. It was for the hope that we would be alive, living today, and loving life—loving the beauty of the sun on our faces, and even the blistering snow of the Great Plains, our homeland, on a long ride, as we remember them and all they sacrificed for us.

I write down these family stories in an attempt to preserve the dignity of our ancestors' actions because no one else will. No one in the American media cares as much as we do about these things. And, ironically, it is because social media provides these communal spaces to grieve and remember and to take courage in these Indigenous-led acts of reconciliation, like those of the Dakota 38 riders, that I feel even more the vast, yawning distance between my experience as a Native woman and mother, and my experience as an American citizen. I wish the two were closer together. The distance is part of the pain, and being told to be silent about it makes me think others know this, too.

<><>

The stories told by my father's family have taken on a life in the past century that extends beyond our immediate relations. They have traveled beyond the confines of White Swan, an Ihanktonwan village located on the Missouri, from which we derived our primary kinship relationships and resulting responsibilities as relatives, leaders, and even dreamers. Guided by these visions and driven by a desire to restore our people's well-being, my father's family tree is full of writers, more than is usual for an American family, and unique in Indian country.

Books and articles written by Delorias, Bordeauxs, and even a Keeler, provided me with breadcrumbs to understand myself. The privilege of possessing my ancestors' perspectives on the history that had placed me, a child of Relocation, outside of the *hocoka* of my own people helped me to arm myself in this war—and make no mistake, it is a war. Not just a cultural or a metaphorical war, but one with a body count that can be seen in the high rates of death by suicide and murder of Native people to this day. We have not just high rates, but, consistently, the highest rates. These terrible statistics are nothing to brag about, but they are a measure of the war that the US continues to wage against Native people with our pesky land claims that won't go away until we do. This ongoing body count is the real price our women, children, elders, and men pay every day for the continued existence of the United States. These are small daily massacres—the body count did not end at Wounded Knee in 1890.

Members of my dad's family undertook this writing decade after decade. Each generation was doggedly trying to understand, frame, and find solutions to our predicament. Their writing finally found a broader audience in the 1960s, beginning with the book *Custer Died for Your Sins* by my grandmother's cousin Vine Deloria Jr. Growing academic interest by Native scholars in the '80s and '90s led to the publication of manuscripts written decades earlier, like *Waterlily* by my grandmother's aunt Ella Deloria and *With Mine Own Eyes* by her great-aunt Susan Bordeaux Bettelyoun. These books helped to lay the philosophical basis for a Lakota/Dakota response to an ongoing occupation of our lands. This Lakota/Dakota philosophy was dealt a deathblow after the first Wounded Knee, but was reborn in defiance at the second Wounded Knee in 1973. This made Standing Rock a powerful moment not only for our own Lakota/Dakota people but for Indigenous people across the world engaged in a life and death struggle with their occupiers.

Both of my paternal grandparents were enrolled members of the Yankton Sioux Tribe (my maternal grandparents were Navajo), as were all four of my paternal great-grandparents, but only five of my paternal great-great-grandparents were Ihanktonwan Dakota. The others were Lakota, French, Pennsylvania Dutch (German), and English.

These Dakota and Lakota stories my father's family carried both on paper and orally were shared with me when I was very young. These stories were primarily accounts of how my ancestors once lived and survived through the war with the Americans that led to the end of our way of life. These stories, coupled with my mother's Diné family stories, forged my perspective for comprehending the world in which I found myself. The European stories were understood only in the broadest strokes. These great-great-grandfathers became part of a Dakota family and community, not the other way around.

The primacy of these stories, often introduced by a family member as counter to what I was learning in school, makes me wonder how my worldview would have been different had I fallen prey to US programs bent on separating Native children from their families. In 1977, a study presented to Congress found 25-35 percent of Native children were being removed from their homes by the government and placed with white families. In 2011, NPR reported that the state of South Dakota was still removing Native children at an incredibly high rate and profiting from it.

The stories I was lucky to receive from my parents include the origin stories of my parents' Peoples, Dakota and Diné. Even as I appreciate how fundamental these stories were in providing me with the tools and perspective to fight back, both intellectually and emotionally, against a colonial system that seeks to deny my humanity, I realize the extent to which a Native child raised by a white family would be at a distinct disadvantage. I try to imagine myself with parents whose worldview is shaped by an origin story based in white supremacy and exploitive principles and I cannot imagine I'd be the person I am today. The stories of colonizers are imbued with the negation of the relationship to the land that defines the very identity of an indigenous People. The colonizer wants the land, but their relationship is no longer tied to it per se, but to how they can profit from it. Without profit they cease to have legitimacy as a human being. They become "white trash." Being non-white, I could never be white trash even as I could never fully enjoy the benefits of being a colonist when whiteness is the ticket for full membership in the club.

A "humanness" based in profitability absent a relationship to the land can be traced to the closing of the commons in England (beginning in the Tudor period). The old Anglo-Saxon link to "the bounty of the land" was largely severed then and the right to live was now conferred by employment. It is provided by the "job," which is now necessary to stave off starvation, homelessness, and vagrancy, all criminalized as the commons were enclosed, even as privatizing public lands caused them. It also led to the definition of persons who did not own land or possess jobs as "waste." This term could be applied to the majority of people from the British Isles who were transported to America, and later, Australia. In this New World, the term "white trash" was coined to refer to white people who were poor and uncouth.

This is a fate the Bundys seek to prevent by owning land—or at least by maintaining a right to privatize public lands or "the commons" primarily for their use.

Even as a large segment of the population in England was consigned to the status of human waste, the colonial rulers promulgated abroad a self-serving legal status so that Native people, who did not "improve" the land, did not possess rights to the land. This is still the law of the land in the United States. In an 1823 Supreme Court ruling, Chief Justice John Marshall solidified a fledgling nation's claims (and future claims) to the land it occupied by claiming that Indigenous peoples had no title to the land they had lived on for thousands of years beyond that of occupation and use—similar to the title animals possess.

The case, *Johnson v. M'Intosh*, was brought before the Supreme Court to settle a dispute between two white men in Illinois—an area then still the frontier and largely Indian territory—who each held titles to the same plot of land. In 1775, Thomas Johnson, while still a British citizen, purchased title from the Piankeshaw (now the Peoria Tribe of Indians of Oklahoma). William M'Intosh's more recent title had been sold to him by Congress. In that opinion, Marshall claimed Indian nations' "rights to complete sovereignty, as independent nations, were necessarily diminished, and their power to dispose of the soil, at their own will, to whomsoever they pleased, was denied by the original fundamental principle, that discovery gave exclusive title to those who made it."

Within the context of invasion and conquest, this ruling gave all Native nations' land to US settlers, who derived basic control over the land from the "Doctrine of Discovery" that Marshall's ruling first articulated.

Johnson later became a Supreme Court justice and the suit was brought by his heirs, while M'Intosh, a fur trader and Scottish immigrant who ostensibly won the suit, had heirs who were, according to one account, left destitute after his death, unable to inherit any of his land holdings. M'Intosh had lived with a former slave named Lydia and had several children with her. This legal victory was not for the Black M'Intoshes, nor was it for Indigenous nations that had survived invasion because the precedents set by cases related to any tribe, a category of constitutional law called federal Indian law, applied to all federally-recognized tribes, even those not yet subject in 1823 to US domination.

Also, the Doctrine of Discovery implied the existence of a wasted land, an entire continent that required the supremacy of Europeans to reach the best use of its resources. This perception can be seen in the name for the Bureau of Reclamation, a federal agency established in 1902 whose goal is saving "wasted" water through large-scale projects like hydroelectric power generation, and which flooded many Native communities.

Europe's unequal social structure was also perpetuated by the idea of the frontier as a wasteland for a waste people. Many of the earliest colonists were sent to America under a system of indentured servitude and headrights. Later, the term *pioneer* was borrowed from the French military. It was a term used for peons who were sent ahead of the regular army because they were considered expendable.

The extent to which the Doctrine of Discovery informs the Bundys' belief system probably lies not in actual knowledge of this early nineteenth-century Supreme Court ruling, unknown to the majority of Americans, but in the principles it expresses, which are central to the origin story of the colonizer.

The Bundys' philosophy received a full airing on national media during their standoffs with the Bureau of Land Management in Nevada and at the Malheur Wildlife Refuge in Oregon via round-the-clock coverage on CNN and Fox News. Mainstream outlets like BuzzFeed featured Cliven Bundy's YouTube videos, where he shared his fringe legal theories on the absolute power of the county sheriff. This "county supremacy" theory is based on an ahistorical concept of feudal Anglo-Saxon society and a debunked reading of the US Constitution denying the federal government's right to own any land outside of the nation's capital and military forts.

In contrast, there is only one video on YouTube of Phil Lane Sr., my grandmother's cousin, who taught me our family stories. It is titled "The Man From Wakpala" and made by his grandson, who captures so well his storytelling style. Great storytellers like him exist in a family chain of storytelling, passed down because the stories are not merely stories of long ago. The passing down of the stories is for us, younger relatives, a living expression of our ancestors' love. I think often of what he gave me, a child growing up in the sagebrush of eastern Washington State, where he and his wife, Grandma Bow, had already made their lives.

People think these stories are only on the reservation, but I've found them everywhere because our people are everywhere. It is a manifestation of the Lakota/Dakota concept of the great holy, the *wakan*, as *taku skan skan*, that which moves moves. We are a people whose lives and movement over the land were not governed by an uncaring authoritarian government, but by a supernatural force that directed us in unexpected ways across the face of Maka, our mother. So it was that when we moved to this strange place in Washington State, our stories had preceded us and were waiting for us in the person of my Lala.

For a long time, the oral stories were the only ones I knew, despite my father's bookshelf filled with books written by members of his family. Many of his tomes were quite old, first editions from the early twentieth century. There was, of course, the first Dakota dictionary written by his great-aunt Sophie Williamson's father-in-law, the Rev. John Williamson, in 1902. The Dakota Episcopal hymnal *Wakan Cekiye Odowan*. There was also a tattered first edition of *Speaking of Indians* written by his great-aunt Ella Deloria in 1944; my mother kept it in a plastic freezer bag since it was falling apart. There was *Conquering the Mighty Sioux*, written by his grandmother's cousin William Bordeaux in 1929. On that shelf he also had a signed first-edition copy of *Custer Died for Your Sins* by my grandmother's cousin Vine Deloria Jr. He also kept a copy of the *Cleveland Plain Dealer* magazine that included a book review of *Custer Died for Your Sins*. The photo of the man on the back of the book looked like a version of my dad: the black curly hair, five o'clock shadow, meaty hands, large eyes, and glasses.

As the years went by, the shelf grew to include recently released books by my dad's great-aunt Ella, called simply Aunt Ella by his siblings and my grandmother when the family would reminisce about her in the family home in Lake Andes. She had taken care of her nieces and nephews and been a constant beneficent force in their lives. Both my grandmother and her cousin Phil Lane Sr. grew up motherless, their mothers (her sisters) having died in childbirth or shortly afterwards, and she was not insensitive to this. When my grandmother was a young woman, her aunt had obtained for her a paid position as her assistant in the field through Columbia University. Going through my grandmother's things after she died, my father and I came upon the paystubs. Aunt Ella had begun her career as an ethnographer in 1916 while a student at Columbia Teacher's College, translating George Sword's (Oglala Lakota) narratives for Franz Boas, the "father of American anthropology." She collected ethnographic interviews of Lakota and Dakota elders throughout the twentieth century and the body of her work is invaluable to Native scholars today.

Aunt Ella's numerous unpublished manuscripts were released in the 1980s and '90s after her death. These included her well-regarded ethnographic novel, *Waterlily*. As each new book was published, my dad would purchase them and give them to me for my birthday or Christmas. Each book had an inscription from him in his distinctive handwriting, which consisted of tight, perfectly formed capital letters he had learned in engineering school that suited his left-handedness. His missives generally included the date and a stern reminder to read these stories and remember my family.

I only skimmed the books until I went to college and was assigned to read them in Native American studies classes. There, I read them in classrooms filled with white, privileged, young Ivy League men. When we read *Waterlily*, these young men, headed to Wall Street to take part in financial machinations that would culminate in the 2008 financial crisis, bristled at the notion that Lakota/Dakota society could have been so perfect. My professor, Elaine Jahner, who had been a student of my great-aunt's, assured them that everything was as Aunt Ella had written it. This reply was met with open scorn by these future masters of the universe.

I read my aunt's books in a lonely place, in the dark woods of New Hampshire far from the open vistas of the West that was my home. It is a state with no reservations, no extant Native communities. Surrounded by hostile, unbelieving white people, I saw in her books, when I finally read them, that lost community where I would have been entirely accepted, wholly a part, and fully loved. I remember lying in my bed covered in my grandmother's star quilt. I had rented a small house with another Native student, near a creek that, although in the center of town, lay in an empty woods and gave me the sense of being far from that campus filled with fraternities and self-satisfied expressions of whiteness. As I lay beneath a giant star created by pieces of triangular fabric, I felt home.

My grandmother had made the star quilt for me and given it to me at my graduation from high school. I spent many a night in my dorm room at college studying all the colors of it and the careful construction of it, making out every hand-stitched thread. She kept a massive quilting loom upstairs in her house on the reservation. She would always greet me with a warm smile, her eyes shining, calling me "my girl."

She grew up in the vicarage that was built for her grandfather, the Rev. P. J. Deloria (also known as Tipi Sapa, Black Lodge), when he retired from serving as the Episcopal priest on the Standing Rock Reservation. It was next to the old White Swan church, which had been moved to Lake Andes after the Fort Randall Dam was built in the 1950s. St. Philip's was the church where I was baptized. She pointed at the square single-story house next to the white clapboard church and would tell me about the *winyan omniciye* (women's meetings) held every Wednesday, when the women would quilt together. I wondered if this quilt had been finished on such a Wednesday and examined the hand stitching to see if I could find slight differences in the length of stitches that might be the signature of each hand that had touched it.

Despite all the oral stories and books written by family members, there were things that did not get passed on. In the introduction to the 1998 reissue of Aunt Ella Deloria's book *Speaking of Indians*, her nephew Vine recalled:

> Strangely, Philip's [Reverend Deloria, Tipi Sapa's] mother, and several older family relatives lived to be quite old, so Ella knew many things from the very olden times. I tried one time to get her to talk about these things, but she grew very angry and told me that these things were so precious to the old people that my generation would not appreciate them and should not know them. They should not be talked about by people who cannot understand, she argued, and so when she died, an immense body of knowledge went with her.

Tipi Sapa's mother, although enrolled by the Americans on the Yankton Sioux Reservation, was Minneconjou Lakota. Because of this, he was born in 1853 with her people near present-day Mobridge, South Dakota, across the Missouri River from the Standing Rock Reservation, and just south of what would become the NoDAPL Océti Sakówin camp in 2016.

So, when I arrived at camp, I felt that force, that taku skan skan, that had led my people and brought us back to this place where we had made our agreement with that manifestation of the land, Ptesáŋwiŋ, White Buffalo Calf Woman.

Perhaps a part of me is always standing there at that Océti Sakówin camp with its tribal flags, brought by tribal leaders or by proud tribal citizens, flapping in a row like a fluttering heartbeat. Many hearts were left at that camp or carry some spark from it with them forever. The Americans knew what they were doing when they separated us in square homes far apart from each other. Being reconstituted at the Océti Sakówin camp as a camp circle society, as my great-aunt Ella called it, was a more powerful experience than we could have ever known—and once given, it must be sought again and again. We know what is right for us. It truly was, as Aunt Ella said, "a way of life that worked."

As I walked through the camp in winter, the snow swallowed up the sound. The muffling gave me a sense of purpose, carrying my camera with its shotgun mike as I interviewed those who remained in the yurts and tents.

In October, just a few months earlier, the camp had been bathed by the warmth of a hot yellow sun as I watched people from the Cheyenne River Lakota camp trucking over tipi poles I had purchased from them for a tipi cover I had found lying abandoned on the ground in the Yankton camp. After we tied the poles together with assistance from members of the Lower Brule camp, I was astounded to see what was painted on the tipi cover, not visible to me before, folded up as it was. In orange and black and red, there they were—the Seven Council Fires, the Océti Sakówin. It seemed at that moment like we were in the grips of prophecy, of something that was beyond us, wakan, serendipity, that which moves moves us across the prairie, across the world.

Yankton elder Faith Spotted Eagle was there. She had been driving up regularly from Lake Andes, South Dakota, my dad's hometown, on the Yankton Sioux Reservation. This wasn't her first camp. She had told me the story a few years earlier while we were at the local powwow, a small community *wacipi*, as they are called in Dakota. It is held each year outside Lake Andes in the tribal housing community of White Swan, named for my grandmother's band's village that was put underwater by the Army Corps of Engineers while building the Fort Randall Dam.

"Your grandmother and another elder came with us to the camp at the Point—you know, where White Swan was before the dam flooded it." Spotted Eagle runs the Brave Heart Lodge located on the main street in Lake Andes. She is an energetic woman in her late sixties, her long gray hair is in a bun, and her usual uniform is a ribbon skirt and T-shirt that celebrates cultural events and initiatives in the community.

"Then a young man, just a young thing, a park ranger, approached these grandmas and told us we couldn't go to the camp. And your grandmother"—Faith laughs—"she held up her hands and said, 'What are you going to do, arrest me?'"

The camp at the North Point Recreation beach is near where our underwater village of White Swan lies under Lake Francis Case, created by the Fort Randall Dam. Fort Randall is one of several dams that put thousands of acres of Indian farmers' land underwater to bring power to white North and South Dakota farmers. In 1999, the Army Corps of Engineers lowered the water, and bodies of family members buried in the old cemeteries and ancient burial sites that dotted the riverbank came up. They had not been moved like the corps had assured my grandmother and other former residents of White Swan. These were her relatives coming up, and she joined her niece, Faith Spotted Eagle—who had grown up at White Swan with her father, Henry Spotted Eagle—at the camp to prevent the corps from raising the water again before reburial could take place.

Seventeen years later, I arrive at another camp on the shores of another human-made lake, Lake Oahe. To the south of the Océti Sakówin camp on a ridge above the Missouri River are the Dakota and Lakota survivors of another drowned village called Cannon Ball on the Standing Rock Reservation. The ridge is separated from the plain upon which these tipis stand in this new Lakota encampment by a small tributary of the Missouri, also called Cannonball. Before the dam was built, the whirling eddies created when the Cannonball emptied into Mníšoše formed perfectly round stones. The Americans called these stones "cannonballs," hence the name for the river and the town. But the Húŋkpapȟa (Hunkpapa Lakota) and Iháŋktȟuŋwaŋna (Ihakntownan-Yankton Dakota) call it Íŋyaŋ IyÁ Wakpá, the name derived from the sacred act of the creation of these stones. The initial camp was named Sacred Stone in honor of this. Once the dam was built and the fast-running river became a lake, the stones ceased to be produced.

The Army Corps of Engineers inundated the original Cannon Ball community and much of its river-bottom farmland. The federal claim to the crossing of the Missouri arises from this violent and traumatic taking. The Pick-Sloan Missouri Basin Program, authorized by the Flood Control Act of 1944, was a compromise of two plans. One by Lewis A. Pick, director of the Missouri River office of the United States Army Corps of Engineers, and the other by William Glenn Sloan, director of the Billings, Montana, office of the United States Bureau of Reclamation. The plan passed by Congress made sure the five dams would flood mostly Indian bottomland, which constituted each tribe's most fertile farmland and valuable timber. The members of Congress were well aware that after the Tennessee Valley Authority flooded thousands of acres of white-owned land, white farmers would not allow their property to be flooded, even if it meant electricity and irrigation for dryland farming. These were the same sorts of calculations that some eighty years later led to the Dakota Access Pipeline being rerouted to protect white communities, leaving Native communities with the costs of the cleanup if the pipeline failed. Tribes, including my dad's tribe, lost 90 percent of their timber and 75 percent of the wildlife. Vine Deloria Jr. said "the Pick-Sloan Plan was, without doubt, the single most destructive act ever perpetrated on any tribe by the United States."

When will this end? When will our own origin stories no longer dictate these outcomes? Can America ever live up to its narrative of exceptionalism?

When I give lectures about how the US is still a colony, I often say to my audience, mostly composed of well-meaning white Americans, "You consider yourself a good person, a moral person, and yet, you are a colonist. These are not your homelands. You occupy them by force of arms. That raises the question, what would ethical colonialism look like?"

I think this is where the answer lies. As impossible as it sounds, an oxymoron. How do we marry the two algorithms? That of a real People and that of colonists?

CHAPTER THREE

DESERET VS. OCÉTI SAKÓWIN

Thousands of floating islands between which flow narrow channels that are endless in their windings. The main body of the lake is still a mile beyond the place where the spring branch enters the tule jungle. The tules grow from eight to twelve feet high, so that when one enters the mass, he has no landmarks, unless, perchance, he can read signs in the heavens above.

—William L. Finley's account of Malheur Lake from *The Trail of the Plume-Hunter*, 1910

The name Malheur comes from the River au Malheur, a name given to the river on a map drawn by a fur trapper with the Hudson's Bay Company. Derived from *rivière au malheur*, it means "River of Misfortune." But this is not the name the Burns Paiute people call themselves. They call themselves Wadatika (*waada*-eaters) from *waada*, a plant that grows around the lake.

The lake is home to thousands of birds who stop here to nest and is part of the western flyway that spans the entire hemisphere. On August 18, 1908, it was protected by a proclamation by President Theodore Roosevelt after a market for feathers for women's hats in the early twentieth century led to egrets and other waterfowl being threatened with extinction.

The lakes within the Malheur National Wildlife Refuge provide a crucial habitat for over 320 species of migrating birds and is a significant stop on the Pacific Flyway for hundreds of thousands of waterfowl. Within the refuge, the smaller Harney Lake can by itself support more than three hundred thousand migrating ducks with its abundant aquatic bed habitat filled with pondweed, watermilfoil, coontail, white water buttercup, bladderwort, and widgeon grass. Archaeological digs document that both Malheur and Harney Lakes have been major foraging and nesting habitats for thousands of years on the West Coast. In addition to shorebirds, these lakes once supported 58 species of mammals, including large numbers of muskrats, beaver, and mink.

"As a little girl, we'd go along the river in the marshes and gather waterfowl to eat in the spring," former Burns Paiute chairwoman Charlotte Roderique says. "We'd make our little tule baskets. I was told if there are three eggs, take one. Leave the other two. One's going to grow up and fulfill its life. One is going to be taken by predators. So you never just go and throw all the eggs in your basket, you only take one. That way, there was a continuation of the species. Our people have been doing that for thousands of years, and those are the things that are taught."

The name "Burns" appended to the tribe's name comes from the name of the white town of Burns, Oregon. The small rural community was named in honor of the eighteenth-century Scottish pre-Romantic poet Robert Burns whose work championed the culture and musical language of the ordinary people of Scotland. It's his version of the old Scottish ballad "Auld Lang Syne" that is sung in English-speaking countries around the world on New Year's Eve.

In January 1879, knee-deep in snow, five hundred Paiutes were force-marched over three hundred miles northward to Fort Simcoe, on what is now the Yakama Indian Reservation, and to Fort Vancouver, both in Washington State. Some of the men were shackled together two by two. All in all, the survivors of the Bannock War of 1878 crossed two mountain ranges and the Columbia River.

Despite this, over the years that followed, tribal members found their way back home. The Burns Paiute Tribe website's history section describes how returning Wadatika swam back across the Columbia, some holding on to their horses' tails. Although they were in their homeland, they were landless and considered outlaws after the Bannock War. The returnees eked out their lives on the edges of the town of Burns. Some found work as cowboys for the white ranchers who had taken over their land. In 1928, the Egan Land Company took pity on them and gave the remaining tribal members the old city dump. It was just ten acres of land outside of Burns, but tribal members cleaned it up and drilled a well and built their homes there.

Over many decades the tribe managed to get the federal government to agree to put more than 13,000 acres into a trust. They rebuilt their tribal government and became one of the larger employers in the county. They also developed a strong working relationship with the US Fish and Wildlife staff who ran the 180,000 acres of Malheur Wildlife Refuge that had once been part of their former reservation.

On a cold winter day on January 2, 2016, standing in a parking lot of the local Safeway in downtown Burns, Ammon Bundy, son of scofflaw Nevada rancher Cliven Bundy, appeared. He addressed a crowd that had turned out to support the Hammonds, a local ranching family facing prison time for arson. It's time for supporters, he told them, to take a "hard stand" at the Malheur National Wildlife Refuge.

Two years earlier, his family had been joined by hundreds in their face-off with the Bureau of Land Management in Nevada. Living due east of Harney County, in Emmett, Idaho, Ammon had heard about the plight of the Hammonds. He had not heard of the Burns Paiute. In an interesting turn of fate, Ammon Bundy's takeover of Malheur took place almost 137 years to the month of the Paiutes' Trail of Tears. Certainly, Bundy had no idea his takeover of the refuge was effectively commemorating this tragedy.

Harney County is vast, one of the country's largest counties, and unlike Clark County in Nevada, where Cliven Bundy is "the last rancher standing," it contains no large urban centers like Las Vegas. While Cliven blames environmentalists and the desert tortoise for making ranching impossible, he rarely mentions the city that bills itself as the Entertainment Capital of the World, famous for its mega casino-hotels.

Here in the open sagebrush steppe, local ranchers worked for years to create a comprehensive management plan with the US Fish and Wildlife Service, the tribe, and environmental groups like the Audubon Society. The younger Bundy had closed his truck fleet maintenance shop in Phoenix, Arizona. Like his father, he had not been averse to public funding for private ventures and had obtained a $525,000 federal small business loan.

<><>

Ammon was joined by his older brother Ryan Bundy. The Bundy brothers arrived on the scene dressed in cowboy hats, western shirts, jeans, and cowboy boots. Ryan even sported a buttoned-up shiny leather vest like the one worn by Gary Cooper in *High Noon*. Their costuming—neither brother is a rancher like their father—and old-timey phrasing of their "speechifying" evoked powerful visual and verbal cues of the American mythos of expansion and individualism promulgated by the Wild West shows of the nineteenth century and Hollywood in the twentieth century.

Patriotic cowboy images emerged from this remote corner of rural Oregon, despite the anti-government stance of the occupation, and were shared worldwide by media and social media. These included images of occupier Duane Ehmer on his horse Hellboy. It was hard to miss the iconic images of the Irrigon, Oregon, resident riding in the snow that blanketed the refuge, carrying the stars and stripes and wearing a cowboy hat and jacket with another smaller American flag on his back. In 2017, Ehmer was tried and convicted in a US District Court of digging a trench on the refuge and disturbing artifacts and burial sites of the Burns Paiute Tribe. On Facebook, after his sentencing, Ehmer continued the show, announcing he would ride Hellboy while carrying the flag to turn himself in to serve his time in a federal prison in California.

Along with this performance of cowboy identity, the occupiers demonstrated a talismanic attachment to the Constitution that recalled not so much the age of reason that produced the document, but the traditional folk magic of Europe's pre-modern era. Tiny Constitutions in the front pockets of the Bundys and their followers could be conspicuously seen. The US Constitution was held in the same regard as the Bible and Book of Mormon, religious texts. This transformation of a document, regarded by many as ushering in a new age of government based on secular human rights precepts, seems an unlikely turn of events at first glance. Yet much of the philosophical underpinnings of the Bundy movement are based in another time, or at least an imagined reinterpretation of it.

Even Cliven Bundy's claim of his right to maintain unfettered access to more than half a million acres of public lands has echoes of that preindustrial world. Although he couches his demands in words like "liberty" that gained currency during the eighteenth-century revolutions in America and France, he uses this terminology to assert his right to the "commons." When phrasing his fight for what amounts to privatization of US public lands in language used to fight against the commons' enclosure, he is using the language of Robert Burns, the eighteenth-century Scottish poet—after whom Burns, Oregon, and the Burns Paiute were named. Burns's poetry condemned the closing of the commons, which drove rural people off the land in Britain in the years leading up to the Industrial Revolution.

The Jolly Beggars; or, Love and Liberty: A Cantata
Robert Burns, 1785

A fig for those by law protected!
Liberty's a glorious feast!
Courts for cowards were erected,
Churches built to please the priest.

Bundy also invokes his own peculiar reading of English common law of that same era. When he explains to the public why he appeals to the county sheriff to join him in defying federal agencies, Cliven asserts the sheriff was elected by the ordinary people of the county and holds absolute power in their name that exceeds that of any government in the world. This county supremacy doctrine was developed by Karen Budd-Falen, an attorney who represented Cliven in the early 1990s—since then, Budd-Falen and her doctrine have emerged as the legal backbone of rural "sagebrush" dissent in the West, despite courts and legal scholars finding this interpretation to have no substantive validity.

In 2018, Budd-Falen announced she was under consideration by the Trump administration to lead the Bureau of Land Management, a federal agency she had relentlessly sued in the courts and denied had any legitimacy. It is also the very same agency her former client faced off against in Bunkerville, Nevada, in 2014 when BLM agents impounded his cattle. If Bundy's attorney was chosen to lead the BLM, Bundy would win his battle against the federal agency entirely.

And there is the issue of the Bundy family's Mormon roots. Early on, while reporting on the Malheur occupation, Oregon Public Radio reporter John Sepulvado tweeted "weird coincidence, but the state of Deseret's borders in Oregon would be right where the #bundymilitia is now," with a link to a Wikipedia article on the State of Deseret.

Deseret is described as "a provisional state of the United States, proposed in 1849 by settlers from The Church of Jesus Christ of Latter-day Saints (LDS Church) in Salt Lake City. The provisional state existed for slightly over two years and was never recognized by the United States government. The name derives from the word for 'honeybee' in the Book of Mormon."

Deseret encompassed nearly all the land between the Sierra and the Rocky Mountains ceded to the United States by Mexico under the Treaty of Guadalupe Hidalgo in 1848. This vast area extends over nine present-day states and includes the cities of Los Angeles and San Diego and the entire Colorado watershed north of the Mexico border. It also encompasses nearly all the Great Basin land once occupied by the Paiute and Ute people.

This de facto sovereign nation existed for two years before statehood. It was in the tradition of the Plymouth Colony, a theocratic state. But unlike that colony, which existed under the authority of the British Crown, the State of Deseret had no formal acknowledgment by the United States. The Latter-day Saints (the Mormon Church calls its members "saints") escaped from persecution, and subsequent migration en masse to lands in the West coincided with the start of the Mexican-American War. Their travel was funded in part by their service in the famous Mormon Battalion that served in the war and was the only religiously based unit in United States military history. Five units were assembled, and they saw just one battle, the Battle of the Bulls, literally a shootout with wild bulls. The battalion's wages were used by the church to finance the westward travel of other church members. Despite this service, the US was still distrustful of the church, and to this day, the cannons above Salt Lake remain as they were then: aimed at the city, not in defense of it.

The symbol of the beehive, representing Deseret, the church's aspiration for sovereignty in a temporal world, remains the symbol for the state of Utah and can be found on the state seal and on the steps of the state capitol building, which boasts a giant bronze hive emblazoned with a single word: Industry.

"So now we have created them [rights], and we use them, make beneficial use of them, and then we protect them," Cliven Bundy told the *New York Times*. He was explaining his legal rationale for taking up armed resistance against the federal government. "And that's sort of a natural law," he said, "and that's what the rancher has done. That's how he has his rights. And that's what the range war, the Bundy war, is all about right now, it's really protecting those three things: our life, liberty, and our property."

The promise of America, for colonists, has always been marked by the phrase penned by Founding Father and slave owner Thomas Jefferson in 1776 in the US Declaration of Independence about all men having inalienable rights to "Life, Liberty and the pursuit of Happiness." A phrase and sentiment undoubtedly inspired by John Locke's "life, liberty, and estate" found eighty-seven years earlier in his *Two Treatises of Government*.

Much is made of Jefferson's choice of "happiness" over "estate." It is seen as an improvement because it makes happiness the goal rather than more base needs like property. But it clouds the real nature of American wealth; the property was mainly human beings. And the stolen "estates"? Indigenous land upon which these stolen lives must toil for the happiness of their master.

Of course, Jefferson is writing this for a new country where he legally owns the mother of his children, Sally Hemings, and will raise their children in bondage. Jefferson apologists claim he kept his children as his legal property to keep them close and to oversee their education or training in skilled jobs that may have been difficult to obtain elsewhere. Their father granted them their freedom as adults by presumably looking the other way when they ran away or through manumission upon his death. (Sally was given "her time" by his white daughter upon his death, a sort of pensioner status for slaves.)

If that's truly the best a thoughtful person—which Jefferson must have been to pen the Declaration of Independence—could hope to do for their children, it is a condemnation of a system that was vicious and immoral to the extreme.

Jefferson's admirers are silent on the subject of the families sold and separated upon the great man's death to pay the debts his extravagant lifestyle left behind. Totaling more than one hundred thousand dollars, a considerable amount for the time, the debts took his heirs until the end of the nineteenth century, several decades, to pay off. Jefferson pursued the lifestyle at Monticello and is held up as an American achievement of genius and graceful living beyond the means of even one of the country's top one percent.

The calculus of what society gained by indulging a single wealthy planter who owned thousands of acres while forcing other human beings to spend their lives, and their children's lives, working with little reward, has been regarded by most Americans as worth it. We will never know what philosophical thought, what excellence in the arts and sciences any of those he owned could have achieved and what was lost to us all by even a single life enslaved, much less the millions held in bondage by the laws of the United States. In light of this direct correlation between the right to pursue happiness and the status of keeping human beings as property, it is clear the two, happiness and property, were never genuinely separate from one another in the eighteenth century or even now, almost two hundred years after Jefferson's death.

The Bundys and their followers invoked the importance of land ownership in their social media posts and statements to the press during the two standoffs with federal law enforcement and afterward at their trials and public appearances. They rely on catchphrases derived from Jeffersonian and Lockian words and concepts to express these "God-given" rights encoded in what Cliven Bundy calls "natural law." Natural law may seem undefined and pliable, that is, whatever Bundy may need it to be. Still, it does have central tenets that he repeats—often while referring to himself in the third person.

To understand these planks of Bundy philosophy, some examination of the history of inequality and land rights of the real homeland of Bundy, Jefferson, Locke, and the United States is necessary. As you may have guessed, their real homeland is not America or in this hemisphere, but is a tiny island nation called England.

In the period leading up to the thirteen colonies rebelling against King George III, there was tremendous upheaval in Britain. The English forebears of both the Bundys and of Jefferson would have emigrated just after enduring the tumultuous years of the English Civil War from 1642 to 1651. This war was the first successful challenge to absolute monarchy in English history and ended with the Parliamentarians (or Roundheads) defeating King Charles I and his supporters, called Cavaliers. Today, we cannot fully appreciate how shocking the king's beheading in 1649 was in what was still primarily a feudal society, or how unthinkable it would have been just a few years earlier.

It may come as a surprise that some of Harvard's first students returned to England to join the Parliamentarians' fight and serve in Oliver Cromwell's New Model Army, which brought down the king.

The name New Model Army refers to the Roundhead army's use of a meritocracy system where officers were chosen not by social standing, but by demonstrated leadership skills. This meritocracy was a notable departure from the ancient custom that reserved these roles for the noblemen regardless of military capability. This system had evolved out of feudal tradition in which nobles were required to fulfill their feudal duties to raise a military force for their liege lord to one where command went to those, mainly gentry, who had the connections and funds to purchase an officer's commission.

Also returned to England from Massachusetts was the radical minister Hugh Peter, the fourth pastor of the First Church of Salem. His fiery sermons in London were credited with energizing the common people to commit regicide. In 1660, after the monarchy was restored under King Charles II, the Puritan was executed for high treason and sentenced to be drawn and quartered, as traitors were in those days. After being drawn on a board by horse to the Tower of London, Peter was hanged almost to the point of death, emasculated, his entrails removed and shown to him, and beheaded. His body was then chopped into four pieces (quartered). His remains would have been displayed across the country in prominent places like London Bridge as a warning to the king's other potential enemies.

In America, the English Civil War is depicted by romanticized stories of dashing aristocrats in lace collars with long-flowing curls and ladies in beautiful dresses. It is recalled as a glamourous social order beset by religious fanatics in ugly, plain attire who bring about a gray, boring new reality. Despite playing well on screen and in romance novels, this framing obscures the political stakes being fought over, including freedom of religion and the right to vote. These were the key political arguments that laid the groundwork for the American Revolution. The political outcomes of the English Civil War also laid the foundation for the expectations vis-à-vis the Crown, henceforth based not in a doctrine of absolute power given by God, but in a constitutional monarchy empowered by Parliament.

As progressive as that political development may have been, what drove English colonists to these shores seeking opportunity and a reprieve from inequality remained a factor in most of the population's lives. The issues that drove the English people to revolt against their king were not just religious, despite the Puritan leadership, but were based on rights to the land on an island nation. The land rights movement that fueled the civil war can be seen in the campaign and eloquence of the digger movement in rural England.

The diggers of Warwickshire issued a proclamation in 1607: "Wee, as members of the whole, doe feele the smarte of these incroaching Tirants, which would grind our flesh upon the whetstone of poverty, and make our loyall hearts to faint with breathing, so that they may dwell by themselves in the midst of theyr heards of fatt weathers [herds of fat castrated rams]."

This ancient social history of inequality and landlessness is encoded in the meaning of the Bundy surname itself. While watching television interviews with Cliven Bundy conducted in the living room of his humble ranch home during the 2014 Battle of Bunkerville, I spied a plaque hanging on the wall that reads, "Remember what the name Bundy means." I am unclear as to what the Bundys believe the meaning to be, but one meaning given for the surname Bundy is that it comes from the word *bond*, as in the oaths given by bondsmen to their liege lords. The name Bond, as in James Bond, also has this root meaning. In Anglo-Saxon England, a man's bond was his promise to obey the lord of the manor in exchange for the right to farm a portion of the lord's land. After 1066, under Norman rule, this is alleged to have become serfdom, and Bundy came to mean "bound servitude."

A chief feature of this system was the lack of freedom of movement. A serf could not move to another county or a town or city without his lord's permission. The lord of the manor also had to be consulted before a serf could marry, change occupation, or sell personal items of any value. He was truly a bound man, a bondsman, unable to leave the plot of land that he was bound to by birth and an oath that may have been taken generations before by a distant ancestor. In contrast to Bundy's romanticized vision of this past filled with rural English yeoman farmers, their common law rights to the land, and representation through the sheriff, this was a form of ownership of his person that came with ownership of the land. The likelihood of escape was low. Freedom from the bond was possible only through manumission, enfranchisement, or escape.

So when a lord inherited the land, they inherited Cliven and Ammon Bundy's ancestors. The land and the Bundys were one. Both were regarded as the personal property of the lord, not property owners.

I present this surname history mindful of the limitations of knowing with certainty the history of many surnames that arose in a mostly pre-literate era. I offer this primarily to illustrate the genuine (and changing) constraints feudal systems in England (and Europe) placed upon liberty and, by extension, the potential of their citizens to own property (or estate, as Locke puts it, or happiness, as Jefferson later elegantly rephrases it).

Even in this system, certain rights were recalled from more ancient times and may be asserted as a matter of extralegal custom (or manor law). One of these rights included the right to use common land to graze animals, gather kindling or herbs, and raise vegetables. Access to the commons allowed peasants some measure of economic security and even limited financial independence from their betters, the landowners who ruled their lives.

> They hang the man and flog the woman,
> That steal the goose from off the common;
> But let the greater villain loose,
> That steals the common from the goose.
> —English folk poem, ca. 1764

Preceding the dawning of the Industrial Revolution, the commons came under attack as large landowners sought to remove rural tenants and replace them with more profitable sheep. The closing of the commons and resulting homelessness also coincidentally served to help to drive rural people to the new industrial cities like Manchester and Liverpool, where cheap labor was in great demand. Many peasants, given a choice, would have preferred to remain in villages their ancestors had lived in from time immemorial rather than go to work in dangerous, monotonous factories for meager wages. The economic support provided by farming on strips of publicly shared agriculture land and access to traditional gathering sites and places to graze the family cow had been just enough to keep poor families alive for generation after generation, and allowed free time for a village life that included holidays and socializing. Jobs, on the other hand, often meant working under dangerous conditions for long hours with very little social safety net.

Like later initiatives to "kill the Indian to save the man," closing the commons was often framed as a way to free the rural poor from a subsistence life that made them lazy, unproductive, and unmanageable.

"Our Forests and great Commons (make the Poor that are upon them too much like the Indians), being a hindrance to Industry, and are Nurseries of Idleness and Insolence," said John Bellars, a Quaker economic thinker and close friend of William Penn

The privatization of the commons transformed rural England. Many hedges tourists admire today when they tour the quiet rural lanes of the English countryside were planted at this time and cut off access to what had been for centuries public lands. Parliament passed over 5,200 laws to enclose more and more land, culminating in the Enclosure Act of 1801. Village after village was leveled as enclosure spread across the countryside. It was both impractical and expensive to fence the narrow strips granted to individual villagers to farm, and so the law favored the wealthy who could afford to build fences or to plant massive hedges around large areas. All told, it is estimated some 6.8 million acres were enclosed.

A leader of the fight against enclosure during the reign of King James I, John Reynolds was fantastically nicknamed Captain Pouch. He would not have been out of place at the Bundy occupation of Malheur, graced as it was by the presence of a Captain Moroni. According to records from the time, he attracted huge crowds—three thousand protesters in Warwickshire, and five thousand in Leicestershire. Reynolds was called Captain Pouch because of the large leather pouch he wore, which he maintained had a magical power that would defeat all opposition.

In June 1607, he led a thousand protesters, including women and children, who gathered in Newton to stop an enclosure in Rockingham Forest in the county of Northamptonshire. A local nobleman, Thomas

Tresham, was enclosing the Brand, a part of the forest that had been historically held in common for use by the community. Emboldened by Pouch's claims that he had the authority of the king and the lord of heaven to destroy all enclosures and that the contents of his pouch would protect them, peasants began to pull down hedges and fill in ditches. After local militia refused a call-up, noblemen were forced to arm their own servants to put down the revolt. A royal proclamation from the king was read twice, ordering the end of the riots, and a pitched battle ensued that ended with forty to fifty of the rebels massacred. The leaders (including Reynolds) were hanged and quartered. It was one of the last times the peasantry and gentry were in open armed conflict in England. The infamous pouch was recovered after the battle and was found to contain only a piece of cheese.

Without access to the commons, not only did the peasants starve but shopkeepers and skilled laborers like smithies, dependent on villages to sustain their businesses, suffered. As if this was not enough, people who had lived on the land since time immemorial lost their homes, which were demolished by wealthier landowners. Their resulting homelessness was criminalized as vagrancy.

Even to this day, the ruins of these villages can be seen in the English countryside. However, there is some evidence this land privatization scheme increased farmland productivity in England. Wealthy landowners, with even more land at their disposal, utilized crop rotation, so fewer acres had to lay fallow each year. Villagers farming strips, as they did in the commons, did not possess that luxury; they had to plant to eat every year.

Faced with starvation and Poor Laws that criminalized poverty, former villagers found themselves convicted of vagrancy and sentenced to workhouses. Workhouses, in turn, could hire out entire families to factories at minuscule wages. What emerged from this confluence of laws and greed was the world of workhouses that Charles Dickens documented so vividly in novels like *Oliver Twist*. This was a world he knew firsthand—as a child, his father was sent to debtor's prison, and the twelve-year-old future author was farmed out to work in a shoe-blacking factory, which became the basis of the fictional Murdstone and Grinby's in *David Copperfield*. The correlation between landlessness and a growing industrial workforce is not simply a modern reading of events—it was apparent to observers at the time.

"Manufactures [factories] are founded on poverty," Benjamin Franklin said. "It is the multitude of the poor without land in a country and who must work for others at low wages or starve that enable undertakers to carry on a manufacture."

The entrapment of formerly rural folk in low-paying, repetitive factory work was spun as a way to save them from the evils of idleness, and the country's ruling class profited as labor fueled Britain's economic engine and growing world preeminence. Enclosure proved to be a great boon to the Industrial Revolution as much as coal, the steam engine, slavery, and the raw materials from the empire's colonies.

Jobs, a word once used to describe crooked criminal enterprises, was now used by the new workforce to describe what kept them occupied. When I cover stories like the Dakota Access Pipeline protests in North Dakota or the creation of the Bears Ears National Monument in southern Utah, I often hear the white population of these states counter tribal concerns about sacred sites with the refrain, "But what about jobs?" While tribal people are concerned about protecting their historical, cultural, and sacred connections to the land, colonists' obsession with jobs, once a mark of a new low of peonage by their ancestors, demonstrates how the descendants of English peasants have forgotten their own severed connection to the land. Or have come to believe the spin given by the ruling class because it is all they were allowed to remember.

Four hundred years later, there is still no memorial of the standoff between the diggers and levelers that took place in the small village of Newton in 1607, when fifty men and women were "poleaxed like pigs." Sheep graze over what remains of the land they fought and died for, and the village they fought for is long gone, replaced with serene green fields. The commoners could expect no help from the county sheriff, whose office had been passed down for a century in the family of Sir Thomas Tresham of Rushton Hall, considered "the most odious man in the county." His cousin Thomas Tresham of Newton was later found guilty of the enclosure of four hundred acres and the destruction of nine farms in Newton, displacing all of the residents. In all, royal commissioners found twenty-seven-thousand acres were enclosed in Northamptonshire. Fifteen hundred people lost their homes as 350 farms were destroyed over eighteen villages. The world Cliven Bundy conjures simply did not exist. Edward Montagu of Boughton, who put down the rebellion at Newton, was also sheriff of Northamptonshire, twice. A landowner and representative of royal authority, he was not serving or accountable to the county peasantry.

Drawing and quartering, the punishment anti-enclosure leaders faced, wasn't officially abolished in Great Britain until 1870. The only recorded use of this punishment in what is now the United States was on Joshua Tefft, an English colonist. In 1676 in Rhode Island, Tefft was so executed for fighting alongside the Narragansett Tribe against the colonists.

The noble families that privatized the British commons still own much of the land. Some of their surnames are well-known outside of the county, including the Spencers, the family of the late Princess Diana. Another, the Montagus, who put down the Newton Rebellion under order of the king, include among their descendants the Duke of Buccleuch, who with twenty-five thousand acres, remains one of Britain's largest private landowners.

In twenty-first-century America, our modern-day Captain Pouch has met with greater success than his English forebears. Instead of moldy cheese, Bundy and his followers carried copies of the United States Constitution in their shirt pockets to protect them. Never mind that Bundy's interpretation of the property clause in the Constitution, the basis of his claims that the federal government has "no jurisdiction or authority" over his self-claimed grazing rights, is unsupported by constitutional scholars. The property clause outlined in Article 4, Section 3, Clause 2, states that "the Congress shall have Power to dispose of and make all needful Rules and Regulations respecting the Territory or other Property belonging to the United States; and nothing in this Constitution shall be so construed as to Prejudice any Claims of the United States, or of any particular State."

The federal government's right to own land under federal application of the property clause has been repeatedly supported in legal cases going back to 1840. "In an unbroken line of cases, the Supreme Court has upheld federal management of public federal lands under the property clause," Michael Blumm, a law professor at Oregon's Lewis & Clark College who specializes in public lands, told *High Country News*.

Equally unsupported is Bundy's fanciful recounting of the historical and legal role of sheriffs at the county administrative level, which appears to be created whole cloth from a romantic notion of English common law in ye ole England.

Nineteenth-century Mormon leaders like Brigham Young held no such romantic illusions about the brutal conditions most English people endured. In fact, it was the impoverishment of the majority of Queen Victoria's subjects that made recruitment efforts for new believers, called Saints, so successful. It also helped entice them to emigrate first to Nauvoo, Illinois, and later to Utah, billed to factory workers in manufacturing centers like Manchester and Liverpool as the Promised Land. By 1870, 35 percent of the population in Utah Territory was foreign-born, and by statehood in 1896, more than fifty thousand had immigrated to the Beehive State from the British Isles. By 1890, immigrants (many also from Scandinavia) and their children made up two-thirds of the state's population.

The accounts of the lives of converts recorded in branch records kept by Victorian Mormon missionaries in Manchester vividly recall the suffering faced by the working poor in industrial cities, from which most Latter-day Saint converts were drawn. Many joined the church hoping for a better life. Even with members pooling their resources,

Mormon converts perished in even the largest LDS branch in England. In Manchester, members like Sarah Duckworth died in workhouses from hunger or illness before they could emigrate.

"In some cases, the branch was unable to give any aid," Jan G. Harris notes in her article "Mormons in Victorian Manchester" published in *BYU Studies Quarterly*. "The 1844 Manchester branch historical record preserves a pathetic plea from a member for help due to 'extreme poverty.' The leadership told him that the church could not help because of the 'extreme poverty' of the branch. However, in response to a report that some Saints were perishing from lack of food, the branch council later that year passed a resolution to have a collection on Sunday for the needy."

Tragically, even if they were able to make the arduous journey from the British Isles to Salt Lake City, many died en route. There are reports that some immigrants, natives of a small island nation, were unable to conceive of the distances involved even after reaching New York City. Their desire to do so illustrates how bleak their situation was in their own country that they were willing to take that chance.

In the United Kingdom, the monopolization of land has not changed substantively even into the twenty-first century. As recently as 2019, a mere twenty-five thousand landowners own half of England. While most British households own their own homes, this real estate accounts for only 5 percent of the land in England and Wales.

Astonishingly, fully one-third of the land in the country is still owned by the same landed gentry that came over from Normandy with William the Conqueror in 1066. Much continues to be passed down within these ancient families, the majority of which still practice primogeniture, passing it whole to the oldest male heir. Since it is inherited and not sold, land held by these families is not required under British law to be registered with the land office for generations. On paper, the total acreage owned by noble families is down 20 percent from a hundred years ago. However, it's unclear how much land title landed families have hidden by transferring their holdings to opaque corporations, a category that accounts for 18 percent of land ownership.

Yet, all these figures are based partly on speculation since only two surveys of land ownership have been conducted in British history. The first was the Domesday Book in 1086, ordered by William the Conqueror to inventory his new possessions. He counted everything down to the last swine and duck.

His descendant Queen Victoria did the second in the 1873 Return of Owners of Land, often called the Modern Domesday. This accounting arose out of demands by the ordinary people, encouraged by the press, to know who owned the land and to bring about an end to their monopoly of the land. Even today, due to this sporadic accounting (and the issue of primogeniture and lax land registration rules), in a real sense, the British government does not know who owns all of its lands.

John Steinbeck's observation that "great families became and remained great because they owned things" remains a truism to this day in America's homeland, Great Britain.

All this shows there is some real basis for the fears of what landlessness means as articulated by Bundy family members, but it is a stretch to say these fears are historically informed in any factual way. Perhaps they are, to a degree, in the same sense as the intergenerational trauma Native Americans passed down due to genocide and colonization.

But, to a more significant degree, the narrative the Bundy family invokes in their fight against what they see as an oppressive federal government is the language of colonial rights to the spoils of invasion. They are using the language of oppression of their ancestors to lay more extraordinary claims to those privileges, an expression of their identities as colonists.

This is why their efforts, initially dismissed as kooky and ridiculous by many, have met with so much success. For decades, Americans have been told we live in a post-colonial, post-imperial, and post-white-supremacist world. A world where "racism is solved when…" It was assumed that rhetoric that laid claim to colonial spoils had been sufficiently delegitimized and marginalized as to be unthinkable but by the very few and very racist fringes of our society. But the immediate and armed support provided to the Bundys' standoffs with the government and their victories in court, particularly with juries, deserve serious study—especially as their actions garner support from the highest levels of government, and especially after the election of President Trump, who taps into a similar American zeitgeist.

A belief system emerged from the trauma derived from both the ancient feudal system and the later industrialization that occurred in the Bundys' homeland. Counterbalance this with the power-sharing English colonists gained through participation in the successful occupation of Indigenous lands. Together, these elements inform the Bundy family's actions and rhetoric, and merely dismissing their conclusions (erroneous and extralegal as they may be) is a mistake. Engagement with these ideas is necessary in order to understand how the Bundys maintain a belief in legally baseless claims with such conviction.

History shows us that stories, coupled with power, can make dreams reality. After all, William the Conqueror started with a story that England was his, and, backed by a powerful cavalry and luck, it became fact. Captain Pouch was not so aligned with power, and his story didn't carry the day. The Bundys' story aligns with power, mainly colonial power structures, giving them victories.

Comparing this to my own Dakota family's understanding of that same historical period and informed by our interpretation of events, I found parallel processes at work to transmit familial cultural-historical accounts. Families' stories (whether Dakota or Mormon) reflect and transmit not only the unique nature and particular cultures of each people but also the philosophical underpinnings of the intergenerational struggle to survive—both materially and politically.

It is no surprise then that these struggles are tied to land—or the lack of it. But the rules and relationship to the land that evolved in England may not work here in the landscapes of the several hundred Native nations. As John Steinbeck noted in *East of Eden*: "The early settlers took up land they didn't need and couldn't use; they took up worthless land just to own it. And all the proportions changed. A man who might have been well-to-do on ten acres in Europe was rat-poor on two thousand in California."

This is the lesson that the Bundys do not want to learn or to know; they are putting off that reckoning by demanding more from the federal government, and this tactic is working. As colonizers, they have claims their English peasant ancestors did not. Now, when they arm themselves against a colonial government built on a system not of feudal patronage, but of corporate profiteering and white supremacy, they have value.

When they raise their guns and put federal employees in their sights, they are not holding them captive, according to a jury of their peers. Bundy and his followers know the government cannot afford another Waco or Ruby Ridge, two events they referenced frequently. They gain concessions from the colonial state by holding themselves hostage. That is the real meaning of their victories—just as revealing of the nature of the colonial administration of the occupation of Native lands, which are what public lands are, as the military response at Standing Rock.

Burns Paiute members told the press during the takeover of Malheur that if they had done it they'd be dead, because Native people are now the ones holding unenforceable common law title to the land against the new Norman rulers.

After three centuries on this continent, it appears the Bundys have truly refashioned the answer to the plaque on their wall reminding the family to "remember what the name Bundy means."

To be fair, there are Bundys who trace their name to le Bonde, a Norman family that came to England with William the Conqueror. But the family tree assembled by Cliven Bundy's relatives only traces the name back a few generations before the family, then Quakers, immigrated to North Carolina in the seventeenth century. The last home the ancestors of these scofflaw would-be ranchers knew in England was in Amesbury, near Stonehenge. Perhaps it is the ancient Bundy homeland, the one they knew for thousands of years as a People before they became Bundys. They didn't need to know what the name Bundy meant, because they knew a deeper one, a relationship to the land, their mother, based on kinship, not the mechanics of domination as colonizers.

CHAPTER FOUR

Two Paths to Sovereignty: The Great Sioux Nation and the American Colonies

It is vitally important that the Indian people pick the intellectual arena as the one in which to wage war. Past events have shown that the Indian people have always been fooled about the intentions of the white man. Always we have discussed irrelevant issues while he has taken the land. Never have we taken the time to examine the premises upon which he operates so that we could manipulate him as he has us.

—Vine Deloria Jr., *Custer Died for Your Sins: An Indian Manifesto*, 1969

County commissioners is the closest government to the people… Granting limited power to the US government created the Constitution of the United States of America, gained independence, and won the Revolutionary War. And this was the original colonies'…divinely inspired form of government. This is how it should be set up, and so we're trying to pull it back to this.

—Shawna Cox, Bundy spokesperson, explaining *The Nay Book* to a crowd in front of the Las Vegas Courthouse during the Bundy trial, 2017

If you were to ask Americans what Native American treaties are, most would probably describe them as the terms of surrender to the United States by the tribes that signed them. Implicit in this perception is the notion that tribes, or, more correctly, Indigenous nations that preexisted the United States, ceased to exist as political sovereigns even before the ink was dried on their signatures.

This perception, commonly held by hundreds of millions of Americans when they consider "Indians" at all, is incorrect. This understanding of treaties, or lack of it, facilitates the project of genocide. For the most part, Americans, informed only by vague propaganda promoted by the victors, do not come to this reading of history out of spite or malignancy. These twenty-first-century beneficiaries of the nineteenth-century "Indian Wars" lack the information to appreciate how this framing of the treaty process with Native nations is part of a narrative of the genocide of Indigenous peoples. The information provided, that is, the way the story is told, leads colonists to set conclusions and assumptions.

It is not surprising that when these same Americans are implored by well-meaning Native activists and allies to "honor the treaties," they hardly know what that means. After all, the definition they have been given does not lend itself to any discernible action other than accepting the political disappearance of Native nations. If tribes are legally dead, what is there for even the most sympathetic American to do besides feel bad? For a large segment of the American population, this demand to honor treaties, read as a demand to feel guilt about being American, leads, predictably, to backlash. They ask: Shouldn't

Indians move on with their lives, leave reservations, and get jobs else-where in the United States like everyone else? Why is the Indian prob-lem still the white man's burden? Why won't it just go away? Without the framing of sovereignty, nothing Native people ask for makes any sense to most Americans.

At the Vienna Convention on the Law of Treaties in 1969, a treaty was defined as "an international agreement concluded between States in written form and governed by international law, whether embodied in a single instrument or in two or more related instruments and what-ever its particular designation."

This convention is often called the "treaty of treaties," yet it was signed but not ratified by the United States. Although, according to the US State Department, the United States "considers many of the pro-visions of the Vienna Convention on the Law of Treaties to constitute customary international law."

I wonder which provisions the State Department would consider customary law, since the United States' handling of treaties with Native nations violates many of them. Does the US handling of the treaty pro-cess with tribes meet "the principles of free consent and good faith and the pacta sunt servanda rule"?

Was this the case at Standing Rock when the tribe demanded consultation as agreed upon in the Fort Laramie Treaties of 1851 and 1868?

Pacta sunt servanda is Latin for "agreements must be kept" and is held to be a fundamental principle of civil and international law. But of course, in his 1870 address to the Cooper Union in New York City, Oglala Lakota Chief Red Cloud, Maȟpíya Lúta, describes a very dif-ferent approach by US representatives.

> In 1868, men came out and brought papers. We are ignorant
> and do not read papers, and they did not tell us right what
> was in these papers. We wanted them to take away their forts,

leave our country, would not make war, and give our traders something. They said we had bound ourselves to trade on the Missouri, and we said, no, we did not want that. The interpreters deceived us. When I went to Washington, I saw the Great Father. The Great Father showed me what the treaties were; he showed me all these points and showed me that the interpreters had deceived me and did not let me know what the right side of the treaty was. All I want is right and justice... I represent the Sioux Nation; they will be governed by what I say and what I represent.

The false dealing described by Red Cloud is painfully familiar even to Americans who do not understand tribes as sovereign nations. However, it stands in contrast to the accepted legal standards of tribal treaty interpretation upheld by US courts today. Standing Rock Sioux historian Vine Deloria Jr. and co-author Clifford M. Lytle enumerate these canons of federal Indian law in *American Indians, American Justice*: "Ambiguities in treaties are to be constructed in favor of the Indian claimants. Indian treaties are to be interpreted as the Indians would have understood them. Indian treaties are to be liberally construed in favor of the Indians and Treaties reserve to Indians all rights that have not been granted away (reserved rights doctrine)."

In short, treaties are international agreements entered into only by sovereign nations. The United States does not make treaties with its citizens or random groups of people. Ratifying treaties with the Great Sioux Nation meant the United States recognized the sovereignty of the Great Sioux Nation. Also, under international law, nations cannot treaty away their sovereignty. Signing a treaty does not extinguish sovereignty; it's an act of sovereignty.

Supporters of the Standing Rock Sioux Tribe, asserting these treaty rights and standing on established international law, faced mass arrest and violence. The violence water protectors faced included several hours of water cannons sprayed at them at night in freezing North Dakota weather streamed live via social media for all the world to see.

Granted, the treaty is a law the United States has been actively breaking for 165 years, despite being, according to the Constitution, "the supreme law of the land." These unconstitutional acts were conducted for several months using all the tactics deployed in the theater of war, and not "settled by peaceful means" as prescribed by the Vienna Convention on the Law of Treaties.

It's hard to fathom how a de facto militarized reprisal conducted by the local sheriff's department of Morton County, in close collaboration with private security hired by the Dakota Access Pipeline builder Energy Transfer Partners, conforms to the principles of justice and international law—or of the Constitution. Under the commerce clause in Article 1 of the Constitution, only Congress is empowered to "regulate Commerce with foreign Nations, and among the several States, and with Indian Tribes." This clause has been interpreted as reserving all dealing with tribes to the federal government, to the exclusion of state interference. Certainly, a county like Morton County does not possess the same political standing as a sovereign nation, even an Indigenous one.

Corporate use of state-sanctioned violence has a long history in this country. The utilization of the state in service of corporate interests goes back to the founding of the first colony at Jamestown by the Virginia Company of Adventurers, a joint-stock company given governmental powers by the Crown.

The county's militarized partnership in defense of Energy Transfer Partner's right to build the pipeline without tribal consultation was not limited to Morton County. Morton County sheriff's department police proudly thanked, on Facebook, police departments from twenty-four counties, and sixteen cities in ten different states who came to protect the privately-owned infrastructure project that would deliver oil for export in the Gulf.

TigerSwan, the private security force hired by the pipeline builder, included former military personnel who had served overseas. They brought to the high plains of North Dakota tactics learned in Iraq and Afghanistan. Although the Obama administration did little for most of the conflict, the National Guard participated, maintaining a road-block for all traffic entering the Standing Rock Sioux Reservation. The twenty-four-hour checkpoint amounted to a de facto economic block-ade of the tribal nation and cost the tribe's casino millions of dollars in lost revenue.

In Oregon just months earlier, law enforcement had allowed the Bundys and their followers to come and go as they pleased, even while engaged in an armed standoff at a federal facility.

The role of the county sheriff in Morton County and during Bundy takeovers in Nevada and Oregon, plus Cliven Bundy's unusual notion of the county sheriff's role in political affairs, helps illuminate not only the judgement of the individuals involved but what the stakes are. At Standing Rock, the county sheriff led a military-style response against the tribe and water protectors, and while the sheriffs of Harney County in Oregon and Clark County in Nevada showed remarkable restraint, they dismissed the Bundys' appeals to use their alleged supreme power to uphold county residents' preeminent rights to public lands.

"He [Sheriff Gillespie] is the man that has constitutional jurisdiction and authority," Cliven Bundy declared at a Moapa Valley community meeting during his standoff with the Bureau of Land Management in 2014. "He has policing power here in Clark County Nevada, and he has arresting power, so we elected him, and we pay him, what do we pay him to do? Don't we pay him to protect our life, liberty, and property?"

Bundy went on to declare his love of the people, the land, freedom and liberty, and "the sovereign state of Nevada." He told the crowd, "Nobody can tell me the United States owns this land." He then reiterated his claim he would pay grazing fees to Clark County but not to the federal government.

Cliven Bundy and his parents had paid their grazing fees to the BLM from 1954 to 1993 for permits to graze their cattle on six hundred thousand acres of federal land called the Bunkerville Allotment.

In 1993, Bundy stopped paying his fees, declaring he did not recognize the federal government's authority over the public land he grazed. Under Bundy's interpretation of the Constitution, Article 1, Section 8, Clause 17 restricts the US from owning property outside of Washington, DC.

He did attempt to pay his fees once, though, after 1993. In 2017, the *Las Vegas Sun* obtained documents showing that in March 1994 Cliven Bundy sent a check for $1,961.47 to Clark County, which brought his grazing fees up to date. By 2014, when the BLM faced off against Bundy and his supporters in Bunkerville, the Nevada rancher owed the federal government nearly one million dollars in missed payments and added fines.

On the grazing form he sent with the check in 1994, Cliven wrote in a blocky script: "I have read and understood the terms and conditions of Attachment A. I fully disagree and reserve the right to protest, appeal, and file a takings in compliance with executive order 12630."

President Ronald Reagan issued Executive Order 12630 in 1988. Reagan sympathized with the ranchers and landowners opposed to environmental protection of public lands who led a movement called the Sagebrush Rebellion that began in the 1970s. In this order, Reagan invoked the Fifth Amendment's compensation clause to prevent federal agencies from taking actions on behalf of the environment that would burden private property owners. Cliven Bundy's one-time attorney Karen Budd-Falen advocated extending this executive order's protection of property rights to include public lands grazing permits. Budd-Falen is from a ranching family in Wyoming and became the solicitor general of the Bureau of Land Management under Trump.

Budd-Falen made her career representing publicly subsidized livestock operators seeking to wrest control of public lands from the federal government. A frequent opponent of environmental groups, she represents ranchers challenging federal grazing restrictions and fights to prevent documentation of ecological damage caused by livestock grazing.

In 2007, she used a federal racketeering law intended to combat mafia groups to sue BLM employees for implementing longstanding laws. If the future BLM solicitor general had succeeded, all government employees could be taken to court for merely doing their jobs. As expected, she and her client, a Wyoming livestock operator, lost before the US Supreme Court.

This fight against the federal agency she now legally represents is a family affair. Budd-Falen's husband has been her law partner for decades, and her father-in-law, John Falen, has headed the Public Lands Council, a lobbying group for ranchers who graze livestock on our public lands. Her appointment sent a clear message as to the direction the Trump administration desired to take with the Interior Department.

In November 2017, outside the federal courthouse in Las Vegas, Shawna Cox, who calls herself the Bundys' personal secretary, read aloud from *The Nay Book*, essentially a scrapbook of quotes from the Constitution, the Book of Mormon, and other sources that was assembled by Cliven Bundy's friend and fellow rancher Keith Allen Nay. Declaring that the county sheriff is their protector of life, liberty, and property before a cluster of supporters of the Bundy family, on trial inside the courthouse, Cox reaffirmed to the crowd Cliven's unique (and some would say self-serving) interpretation of the Constitution, notably, his reading of the property clause in which the federal government has "no jurisdiction or authority" over his self-proclaimed right to graze his cows on public lands. On Facebook, an even larger audience watched as she live-streamed her reading.

The property clause states that Congress has the power to "dispose of and make all needful Rules and Regulations respecting the Territory or other Property belonging to the United States." The Bundys are adherents to an interpretation of this clause, also favored by the sovereign citizen movement, that believes this limits federal land ownership to just Washington, DC, and military forts. Cliven, Ammon, and

Ryan, on trial for the 2014 standoff at the Bundy ranch near Bunker-ville, Nevada, expounded on this reading of the Constitution at length in defense of their actions.

Often, coverage of the Bundys and their followers centers on guns and right-wing extremists. It veers away from discussion of the potent mix of Mormons and a political framework that espouses sovereignty that is the crossover point between the two.

The Nay Book's central thesis is anchored by a reading of the prop-erty clause in the Constitution that claims the federal government only has a right to own the ten square miles around Washington, DC. This reading is flatly dismissed by legal scholars and judges. The Bundy patriarch has lost case after case on this point for decades.

And yet, even without legal standing, both Ammon and Ryan Bundy won their cases in Oregon by indirectly utilizing it. What saved them was their belief in an alternate interpretation of events based on *The Nay Book*'s religious understanding of the Constitution and the county supremacy doctrine. These legal doctrines had been popular-ized in the 1980s and 1990s by their father's former attorney Karen Budd-Falen. Since this worldview informed their actions, it could not be proven they intended to interfere with the work of federal workers using terror.

The law[4] they were charged under had been written during the Civil War, when civilians were attacking federal officials focused on intent—and intent is tough to prove. Most of the jurors (all of whom were white) could not bring themselves to assign that intent to the Bundy brothers.

4. § 372. Conspiracy to impede or injure officer
If two or more persons in any State, Territory, Possession, or District conspire to prevent, by force, intimidation, or threat, any person from accepting or holding any office, trust, or place of confidence under the United States, or from discharging any duties thereof, or to induce by like means any officer of the United States to leave the place, where his duties as an officer are required to be performed, or to injure him in his person or property on account of his lawful discharge of the duties of his office, or while engaged in the lawful discharge thereof, or to injure his property so as to molest, interrupt, hinder, or impede him in the discharge of his official duties, each of such persons shall be fined under this title or imprisoned not more than six years, or both.

This firmly embraced alternate worldview was also sufficient to protect some of their followers, including Kenneth W. Medenbach, a sixty-three-year-old Oregon man described by the Southern Poverty Law Center as having "sovereign-citizen leanings." During the occupation of Malheur, Medenbach covered the wildlife refuge's sign with a new sign that read "Harney County Resource Center." He said he did this to "let the local community know they're going to be getting their land back soon." Since Medenbach sincerely believed this rebadging of the refuge to be a more accurate legal reading of ownership of the building based on his interpretation of the US Constitution, this altered any reading of his intent and actions (like using federal property).

Medenbach was charged in what appeared to be a clear case of theft, or at least joyriding. He had been shopping at a grocery store in Burns while driving a US Fish and Wildlife pickup truck. Once again, his crime was difficult to prove because Medenbach believed the vehicle belonged to the Harney County Resource Center. He had covered the USFW logo with a Harney County Resource Center one. Since he was on "Harney County" business, shopping for the occupation, he was, according to his construction of the universe, not intentionally stealing the truck.

"The federal government has no authority to own land in the states," Medenbach claims. And he not only shares the Bundys' interpretation of the Constitution regarding limited federal ownership of land, but their religious convictions as well: "I've been called by a higher power to do what I'm doing."

For decades Medenbach has challenged federal control of public lands by building cabins without permits on BLM and US Forest Service land in Oregon. A judge in one case noted that he had lost all of his motions under "adverse possession" since 1988. In response, Kenneth declared the judge's ruling against him was only his "opinion" and that judges "don't have the power to interpret the Constitution."

<><>

Despite the poor Constitutional scholarship, the Bundys' legal fantasy met with greater success in court than the invocation of treaties by the Standing Rock Sioux Tribe and ratified by the US Senate. This speaks to a sort of white privilege US citizens enjoy that Indigenous nations do not.

In stark contrast, Lakota and Dakota tribes found no legal relief in their desperate attempts to stop the pipeline. They lost injunctions and could not get treaty violations heard by Judge Boasberg, who presided over most of the cases brought by the tribal governments to federal court. He refused to hear arguments based on treaty rights despite a previous Supreme Court ruling finding the United States in violation of the 1868 Fort Laramie Treaty. In 1980, the US Supreme court in an 8-1 majority upheld a United States Court of Claims ruling (*The United States v. Sioux Nation of Indians*) that awarded the Sioux Nation $106 million, the most substantial sum ever given to an Indigenous nation for illegally seized territory. Tribal attorneys Marvin Sonosky and Arthur Lazarus sued under the Fifth Amendment for due process and illegal takings. Ironically, that's the Bundys' favorite amendment. However, the Lakota tribes refused the settlement. They wanted the land. In 2011, the unclaimed settlement was said to be worth more than a billion dollars.

Beyond insupportable interpretations of the Constitution, Bundy followers also fervently espouse the county supremacy doctrine, which asserts the supremacy of the sheriff within the county over every other elected official in the nation, even the president of the United States. It's another doctrine that has been declared by courts and legal scholars to have no basis in law whatsoever. It is a useful ideological Trojan horse that allows the Bundys and their allies to claim more rights, and not just to public lands—that's a beachhead. With the armed protest against the federal government, and consciously referencing the disastrous FBI handling of Waco and Ruby Ridge, the Bundys had hit upon a strategy that amounted to holding themselves hostage as a gambit to gain concessions from the government.

The Bundys' armed standoffs with federal agencies, animated by a faulty reading of the Constitution, were embraced by conservative and Libertarian elected leaders across the country. Initially, in the 2014 Bunkerville confrontation with the BLM, Cliven received support from US Sens. Dean Heller and Rand Paul, both Republican. That support melted away when the elder Bundy was caught on video musing to a reporter, "I've often wondered, are they better off as slaves, picking cotton and having a family life and doing things, or are they better off under government subsidy? They didn't get no more freedom. They got less freedom." Yet, even in 2016, unabashed support from outspoken Republican state legislators remained, with some, like Washington State representative Matt Shea and Nevada assemblywoman Michele Fiore, traveling to the remote Malheur Wildlife Refuge.

The county supremacy doctrine also holds an appeal to some in law enforcement, including hundreds of county sheriffs—with Harney County sheriff David Ward a surprising example. Even after Ward's wife fled their home when her tires were slashed during the occupation of Malheur, Ward's cousin testified that the sheriff was still "80 percent in agreement with the Bundys." The cousin suspected Bundy supporters had slashed the tires. Ward's philosophical accord with the occupation suggests either he regarded the anti-public-lands argument as so compelling that even the violence directed at his family was reasonable—or he could separate the calm demeanor of Ammon Bundy from the actions of his followers. In a video of his meeting with Ammon, the two men can be seen on the road outside the refuge, both ruddy-faced and blond, burly in build, giving each other a stern and curt handshake. Each man dressed for his official role: the sheriff in his green uniform and the cowboy in his easily recognizable regalia of a cowboy hat, jeans, and boots. Both exhibited a studied demeanor, like actors portraying these roles in classic western films. Contrast this to the immediate arrest and strip-search of then-Standing Rock Sioux tribal chairman Dave Archambault II by the Morton County sheriff. In North Dakota on land illegally occupied in violation of the treaty, the local sheriff saw no reason to engage with the chief executive of a Native nation as an equal or as someone trying to do the right thing for his people. Instead, a leader nonviolently protesting against the Dakota Access Pipeline in August 2016 was treated as a criminal. To the sheriff, the American Indian in Hollywood westerns is always an existential threat to the very existence of the social order that the sheriff, with the help of the cowboy leader, is seeking to create and heroically protect.

The sheriff's role is an old one going back to feudal times in England, when actual counts ruled counties, and the sheriff was a tax collector appointed by that count or earl. Despite what Cliven Bundy and others believe, it is not a position elected by the people. It was so unpopular that in the sixteenth century, when selecting sheriffs, Queen Elizabeth I had to mark the nominee's name with a hole through the hidebound parchment to make sure the assignment was not erased and foisted on someone else on the list of names.

Today, the sheriff is an elected position, and no background in law enforcement is necessary to run for the job. The Constitutional Sheriffs and Peace Officers Association claims over four hundred dues-paying members. On its face, their membership in an organization that espouses county supremacy can only be seen as evidence that a startling number of sheriffs from across the country hold a shared belief: they alone should decide which laws to enforce.

Just two years earlier, on a sunny June day in 2014, President Obama came with much fanfare to the Standing Rock Reservation. He attended a powwow held in Cannon Ball, the same community that would become the frontline in the fight against the pipeline. The crowd included Chairman Dave Archambault II and his sister Jodi Gillette, who served in the White House as Obama's very first special assistant for Native American affairs.

In his speech that day, he promised to be "a president who honors our sacred trust, and who respects your sovereignty, and upholds treaty obligations, and who works with you in a spirit of true partnership, in mutual respect, to give our children the future that they deserve.

"And I think we can follow the lead of Standing Rock's most famous resident, Chief Sitting Bull." Speaking to thousands of tribal citizens gathered under the arbors that surrounded the community's powwow grounds, the president quoted the Hunkpapa leader. "He said, 'Let's put our minds together to see what we can build for our children.'"

The tribe opposed the pipeline because it endangered the drinking water of its children. Yet, during much of the fight, the leader of the free world was silent and did not publicly condemn the military response in terms many Native supporters had expected.

Obama, a former law professor unlike any other US president that preceded him, was both sympathetic to the plight of Indigenous people and acquainted with federal Indian law. He acknowledged, "You deserve to be safe in your communities and treated equally under the law."

Tribal members thrilled at the president's words that day as he and first lady Michelle Obama hugged their kids and took selfies with them later. The violence community members would endure at the hands of state and county authorities was still another traumatic event in the tribe's relations with the US in an unimaginable future. That day, it seemed impossible to believe that Chairman Archambault and other members of his family would suffer arrest and state violence during Obama's administration.

During an interview with NowThis News on November 1, Obama said that his administration would seek "to accommodate sacred lands of Native Americans," and possibly reroute the pipeline. However, when the reporter questioned the violence being used against protestors, Obama gave a "both sides answer" saying, "There is an obligation for protesters to be peaceful, and there's an obligation for authorities to show restraint." Worse, he said, "We're going to let it play out for several more weeks." This thrilled supporters of the pipeline like North Dakota rightwing blogger Rob Port, who noted this was all the time the president had left in office, and signaled Obama was "punting on the issue."

<<>>

Two years after Obama's promises to the Lakota people, at an event overseen by his former staffer Jodi Archambault Gillette, the FBI, under his watch, hired an informant who engaged in a relationship with a Lakota woman. In short, Obama's government had conducted what amounted to state-sponsored sexual assault of a Native woman. A Lakota *winyan* (woman) targeted because she was an activist fighting for treaty rights to protect her relatives' access to clean drinking water.

It was a turn of events no one who basked in the joy of his 2014 visit to Standing Rock could have predicted. In photos of that day, tribal members of all ages look happy and confident of a new, brighter future. As they danced in full regalia for the Obamas and placed on his shoulders a star quilt and on her shoulders a shawl, none saw it coming.

"The history of the United States and tribal nations is filled with broken promises," Obama wrote in an op-ed published in *Indian Country Today* before his visit. "But I believe that during my administration, we've turned a corner together." And he promised, "We're writing a new chapter in our history—one in which agreements are upheld, tribal sovereignty is respected."

No president of the United States came into office with so much goodwill towards Native people. Certainly, none had ever written down those sentiments and placed them in a national Native newspaper. How did all these good intentions, policies, and tribal summits come to naught?

In July of 2016, I first heard of the Army Corps of Engineers' approval of the DAPL easement under the Missouri River from Yankton elder Faith Spotted Eagle. She told me the Yankton Sioux Tribe held a strategy meeting at our tribal casino to discuss how to unify nationwide opposition to the pipeline.

"The travesty about that, of course, is that it is attacking the first medicine, which is our water," she told me, "and the second thing is it is such a hypocritical move to [name the pipeline] Dakota. Dakota is our word, it's our name, it's our spirit, and it's who we are. And they have the nerve to call a pipeline Dakota Access?"

In August, I wrote the first of a series of articles about the anti-pipeline camp at Standing Rock featuring tribal member LaDonna Allard and the Sacred Stone Camp. It was Labor Day weekend when I was camping with my family that the first reports came in of several water protectors, including a pregnant Lakota woman and her child, who were attacked and bitten by dogs hired by Energy Transfer Partners. The dog attacks were the first intimation of the level of violence this corporation, owned by CEO Kelcy Warren, was willing to undertake to get the project done.

Those scenes, recorded live by *Democracy Now!*'s Amy Goodman, recalled the violent canine attacks on Black civil rights protestors in Selma, Alabama, in the 1950s.

At stake was a sacred site identified in a court filing just the day before by the Standing Rock Sioux Tribe's former historian, Tim Mentz Sr. The tribe was seeking an injunction to prevent further desecration of eighty-two features and twenty-seven graves within the construction corridor. In defiance, on a Saturday morning, Energy Transfer Partners moved heavy construction equipment several miles to the site identified and began to methodically destroy any cultural or sacred evidence, scraping an area 150 feet wide for two miles.

"It's a coupe stick of the Strong Heart Society (Chante Tinza Wapaha)," Mentz explained in a video shared by the tribe. He described the feature to the court as unique, the only one of its kind in North Dakota.

Later, it was discovered the dog security units were not licensed at all, not in Ohio, where the outfit was based, nor in North Dakota. The company paid only a nominal fine for the destruction of the burial and sacred ceremonial sites. None of those bitten (including a child) were compensated and none received their day in court. Unlike at Selma, no political price was paid for the dog attacks and wanton destruction of archaeological sites. In the media and Congress, it hardly registered at all. When the Bismarck AP correspondent filed his story, he led with the injuries to the dogs. Later, the legal defense hired by the Water Protectors Legal Defense Fund would fail to meet a deadline to file charges on behalf of the victims.

Obama said nothing that Labor Day weekend, and four days later, *Native News* reported "Major Disappointment: Obama Clueless about Standing Rock." C-SPAN had carried a video of a Malaysian college student asking Obama at a town hall in Luang Prabang, Laos, about the Dakota Access Pipeline. It was apparent from Obama's answer he knew nothing about it.

"I can't give you the particulars on this particular case," he told the young woman after giving a brief overview of his ambitious policy to recognize tribal sovereignty. "I'd have to go back to my staff and say how are we doing on this one?"

His answer raised the possibility that all the letters sent to the White House by the Standing Rock Sioux Tribe and their supporters were not reaching him. Even attempts by the president's former staffer Standing Rock Sioux tribal member Jodi Gillette did not appear to have had the desired effect of at least letting him know what was happening. It called into question whether his tribal outreach had been just a lot of smoke and mirrors. How real could it be if even high-profile tribal members like Gillette and her tribal chairman brother could not reach him while their community was being assaulted by a corporation? Where was he? What was real? Distressing questions to have to ask in the face of the very real violence meted out by the corporation and the county.

In late October, law enforcement conducted brutal arrests of some 140 demonstrators. Pictures and video were shared on social media of police dragging Native people out of sweat lodges, slicing open tipis and dragging women out, and violent beatdowns. Even if water protectors attempted to leave peacefully as police instructed, they were maced and pushed by batons. While trying to bring a ten-year-old boy to safety, Lauren Howland, a twenty-one-year-old member of the International Indigenous Youth Council, was shoved forcefully by an armed officer.

"My hand got in the way of it, and it was almost fractured," she said in a video she streamed live from outside the Morton County jail in Mandan, North Dakota, "We were peaceful, we were unarmed, we had our tobacco in our hand, we were praying, and they rounded us up like sheep and took us out one by one."

The Morton County sheriff's department shared photos on Facebook of the 142 water protectors arrested. Some had been hooded and left sitting in the mud with their hands bound by plastic ties. "Hooding" has been classified as cruel, inhuman, and degrading treatment or punishment (CIDT) and the UN Committee Against Torture has found "hooding under special conditions" to constitute torture. In 2016, after photos depicting the horrific treatment of prisoners in the US-run Abu Ghraib prison in Baghdad were published, the US Army manual was updated to ban torture, including hooding, of prisoners.

"I understand that the Lakota word for children, *wakanyeja*, comes from the word *wakan*, sacred. That's what young people are, they're sacred," President Obama had said in Cannon Ball in 2014. "And every day that I have the honor of serving as your president, I will do everything I can to make sure that you see that our country has a place for everyone, including every single young person here... That is my commitment to you, to every single young person here."

Then came Thanksgiving week, which saw water protectors drenched with water cannons for several hours while trapped on a bridge in the subfreezing weather of a North Dakota winter night. They also incurred severe injuries by being shot with "less-than-lethal" weaponry at close range.

The *New York Times* editorial board published an indictment of the violent tactics. Thousands watched helplessly live on Facebook as dozens of water protectors were trapped for several hours on the bridge, unable to go backwards as they were sprayed with water in freezing temperatures.

Watching all of this was Wesley Clark Jr., son of General Wesley Clark, former supreme allied commander of NATO and candidate for the 2004 Democratic nomination for US president. He had been in contact with Phyllis Young, a Standing Rock elder, since the dog attacks in August. Following the raid on the Treaty Camp, he put out a call for veterans to join him to "self-deploy" to Standing Rock and defend the water protectors from assault and intimidation. Days before the Army Corps of Engineers issued a December 5 deadline to close the camp, some four thousand American veterans of all backgrounds arrived at the Océti Sakówin camp. They were unarmed, unlike the Bundy supporters. Still, they were determined to fulfill their military vows to protect the people and declared their willingness to put their very bodies between the water protectors and law enforcement. Before they marched in the thousands to the DAPL drill pad on the Missouri River, the Obama administration, through the Army Corps of Engineers, finally took decisive action. On the afternoon of December 4, 2016, they canceled the easement to drill under the river north of the reservation. They claimed they had not received direct orders from the president but had read his previous statements that this would be the preferred course of action.

After the announcement and apparent victory, veterans led by Wesley Clark Jr. knelt before traditional Lakota and Dakota elders of the Océti Sakówin, including Leonard Crow Dog, the Lakota American Indian Movement spiritual leader at the Wounded Knee siege in 1973. They offered an apology for the atrocities committed by the US armed forces against Native people and nations.

"Many of us, me particularly, are from the units that have hurt you over the many years," Clark said, wearing a dark blue Cavalry uniform and hat decorated with gold braid. He had once served in the 2-7 Cavalry unit that Lt. Colonel George Custer had led against the Lakota at the Battle of Greasy Grass (Little Big Horn). "We came. We fought you. We took your land. We signed treaties that we broke. We stole minerals from your sacred hills. We blasted the faces of our presidents onto your sacred mountain. Then we took still more land and then we took your children and ... we tried to eliminate your language that God gave you, and the Creator gave you. We didn't respect you, we polluted your earth, we've hurt you in so many ways, but we've come to say that we are sorry. We are at your service, and we beg for your forgiveness."

The apology and the kneeling veterans were met with great emotion, and some tears, by the gathered onlookers and tribal members. Held indoors in the tribe's Prairie Knights Casino due to a blizzard, the forgiveness ceremony between the two people, two ideas of nationhood—colonial and Lakȟótiyapi—felt like a new beginning.

On January 19, 2016, Ryan Payne, a Malheur occupier and founder of Operation Mutual Aid, a militia coalition based in Montana, read the preamble of the Declaration of Independence at a community meeting held at the refuge. "We hold these truths to be self-evident, that all men are created equal, that they are endowed by their Creator with certain unalienable Rights, that among these are Life, Liberty and the pursuit of Happiness."

"Well, where did this come from?" Payne, a principal planner of the occupation, asked rhetorically before proceeding to draw a direct ideological line between the armed standoff of Malheur and the Founding Fathers' revolution. "But there was a process here, and reasonable men did pursue a path to redress grievances against the government, and they were ignored all the way. Any government becomes destructive to these ends; it is the right of the people to alter or to abolish it."

Political instruction in the philosophical beliefs that brought anti-government activists together in armed rebellion against the feds was common both at the refuge and during Cliven Bundy's standoff in Bunkerville, Nevada, two years earlier.

Also common during both events were tiny pocketbook Constitutions. Payne, the militia leader, read from one. Called Skousen Constitutions, they are published by the right-wing organization the

National Center for Constitutional Studies (NCCS) in Malta, Idaho. The center was founded by Mormon elder and FBI man W. Cleon Skousen. Skousen was also one of the founders of the John Birch Society, a far-right group that emerged in 1958 attacking communism and espousing limited government. The Southern Poverty Law Center classifies the Birch Society with "patriot" anti-government groups, which include militias that actively engage in military-style training.

These little books were everywhere at the refuge, tucked into everyone's front pockets, and pressed upon journalists covering the takeover. One reporter was given about ten copies while covering the occupation. Ammon Bundy wore one in his prison jumpsuit pocket while testifying at his trial in Portland, Oregon, in 2016.

"It's something I've always shared with everybody, and I carry it with me all the time," said Cliven Bundy, who claimed he got his copies from a wealthy friend who buys them by the millions and gives them away. "That's where I get most of my information from. What we're trying to do is teach the true principles of the proper form of government."

Since 2004, over fifteen million copies have been sold and distributed. The booklet features George Washington on the cover, not one of the usual eighteenth-century portraits we are used to seeing, but one of him standing looking directly at the viewer. His face is blandly drawn, as though all the puffiness and uneasy countenance painters of his day imbued his face with are airbrushed off.

The pamphlets were being sold in bulk for thirty-five cents each. They go for one dollar on Amazon. Due to the low price, they became popular with schools from Florida to Arizona. School districts are required to celebrate Constitution Day due to a law passed by the late senator Robert Byrd, a former cyclops in the Ku Klux Klan. Schools teach about the Constitution on that day, and many districts began purchasing this tiny version to hand out to students. The religious framing in the NCCS version raised concerns about the separation of church and state across the country. Skousen was determined to impress upon the minds of young Americans the idea that the Constitution was a sacred, divinely inspired document. And he wasn't alone.

Another of Skousen's books, *The 5000 Year Leap*, was promoted extensively by Glenn Beck, the American conservative political commentator, on his radio and TV shows. Beck touted it as a "divinely inspired" interpretation of early American history, and following his endorsement, the book was a big seller at Tea Party events. It continues to be taught across the country, particularly at conservative schools like Heritage Charter School in Arizona. However, chapters like "Concerning God's Revealed Law Distinguishing Right from Wrong," generated pushback. In 2016, Heritage, a chain of publicly-funded charter schools, was sued by Americans United for Separation of Church and State for "teaching religious beliefs in a public charter school" in violation of the First Amendment.

Beck's promotion of these fringe political ideas was key to the philosophical education of millions across the country. His show effectively created a ready audience for the Bundys to recruit for their occupations. Indeed, many of the central tenets held in common by Bundy supporters can be traced directly to Beck's 912 Project.

"The 912 Project is designed to bring us all back to the place we were on September 12, 2001," Beck told his viewers. "That same feeling—that commitment to country—is what we are hoping to foster with this idea."

On September 13, 2009, more than 1,500 people gathered on the Utah capitol lawn to support the 912 Project. Despite claims that it was a nonpartisan effort, speakers included Republican congressman Jason Chaffetz, and Gayle Ruzicka, president of the Utah Eagle Forum. Speeches were critical of the Obama administration and the Democratic control of Congress.

"This is one of the most American things you can do," Chaffetz told the crowd while standing in front of a white bus emblazoned with the slogan "American Liberty Tour."

Beck outlined to participants the nine principles and twelve values that he believed to be key to conservatives regaining control of the federal government. These included pronouncements of America's goodness and the centrality of God and family, the importance of abiding by the law, and self-improvement mantras, but also included some sentiments that undoubtedly would have appealed to Bundy and his followers:

- My spouse and I are the ultimate authority, not the government;
- I have a right to life, liberty, and pursuit of happiness, but there is no guarantee of equal results;
- I work hard for what I have, and I will share it with who I want to. Government cannot force me to be charitable;
- It is not un-American for me to disagree with authority or to share my personal opinion;
- The government works for me. I do not answer to them, they answer to M.E.

Although Beck condemned Cliven's Battle of Bunkerville standoff, Jerry DeLemus, leader of what he billed as "the largest Glenn Beck-inspired 912 group in New Hampshire," arrived in Bunkerville in 2014 and immediately took command of the militia camp.

In an interview with Stewart Rhodes, founder of the far-right, anti-government, militaristic group Oath Keepers, DeLemus pleaded for Beck to travel to Bunkerville and support the Bundys.

"What we will do is we will stand, and we will fight if the government tries to oppress the Bundys or tries to attack us." DeLemus, a balding sixty-year-old US Marine veteran who favors fatigues and a baseball cap, cited his military oath as his reason to take this stand. "I took an oath to the Constitution as you did, and they don't de-oath us when we get out. And when we're fighting somebody to protect our Constitution within or without of our country."

Despite DeLemus's predictions of an imminent fiery clash with law enforcement, no violent stand was necessary. The government backed down and returned Bundy's cattle. The feds, and an administration led by the first Black president, were faced with the specter of a shootout, another Waco, against an armed white volunteer militia in fatigues and on horseback in cowboy hats, a compelling iconographic mashup of heroes from both Hollywood western and war movies.

In 2016 DeLemus, now cochair of Veterans for Trump in New Hampshire, showed up at the Malheur Wildlife Refuge in Oregon. In an interview with Reuters, he trumpeted the Bundy family's "great success" in their fight against the federal government, which he described as "thug-like" and "terroristic." His new idol, Trump, was initially more cautious, saying, "You cannot let people take over federal property."

But unlike the Bundys, the militia aficionado did not fare as well in court. In 2017, he was arrested even as his wife, Susan DeLemus, a birther and Republican New Hampshire state representative, made international news headlines for declaring the Pope the anti-Christ. She took offense at Pope Francis's criticism of Trump's plan to "build the wall" on the Mexican border. The couple had a knack for the media spotlight, independent of the Bundys. Earlier, a rally Jerry organized also made international news when Trump failed to correct a man who called President Obama a Muslim.

Despite traveling thousands of miles cross-country with weapons and declaring he was willing to "take a bullet" to protect the Bundys, DeLemus claimed he would never have shot at law enforcement.

"It wasn't the cows," he told the judge. "I didn't want that family injured. God will know in the end." He then quoted a passage from the Bible saying there is no greater love than to lay down one's life for one's friends.

Calling him a "bully vigilante," Chief US District Judge Gloria Navarro sentenced him to seven years in prison for his role in the 2014 Bunkerville standoff. He subsequently appealed to President Trump for a pardon.

<><>

Today, the outcome of all this right-wing fundamentalism with a constitutional veneer is that hundreds of Bundy cattle are still roaming more than half a million acres of public lands in the Mohave Desert, the driest desert in America. Reports are that they are starving and not properly cared for, which amounts to not only animal abuse but poor ranching skills. Some of the cattle have been hit standing on roads, endangering themselves and innocent people.

One court document describes the state of the Bundys' ranching expertise:

> Rather than manage and control his cattle, [Bundy] lets them run wild on the public lands with little, if any, human interaction until such time when he traps them and hauls them off to be sold or slaughtered for his own consumption. He does not vaccinate or treat his cattle for disease; does not employ cowboys to control and herd them; does not manage or control breeding; has no knowledge of where all the cattle are located at any given time; rarely brands them before he captures them; and has to bait them into traps in order to gather them...Bereft of human interaction, his cattle that manage to survive are wild, mean, and ornery.

Meanwhile, Cliven Bundy continues to profit off of the feral cattle he lets loose on federal lands. Between 2011 and 2015, he sold nearly 1,300 cows, and while in jail for two years, he sold about another 400.

"They have paid some of the bills, so I've been blessed," he told a reporter.

Cliven's "ornery" cows have also been found inside the Gold Butte National Monument created by President Obama in 2016. In 2020, the monument was opened to mining by President Trump.

Two paths to sovereignty and two paths taken on behalf of one's nation. Overall, Bundy supporters came out relatively unscathed.

Despite Trump's lack of support during the occupation of Malheur, he pardoned the Hammonds in July 2018. The ranchers Dwight and Steven Hammond flew home in style on the private jet of Lucas Oil founder and CEO Forrest Lucas. Lucas, a donor to Vice President Mike Pence, gave at least fifty thousand dollars to Pence while he was running for governor of Indiana. The oil millionaire was for a time under consideration by Trump to run the Department of the Interior, which oversees the Bureau of Land Management. This agency manages not only public lands but also Native American reservations held in trust by the federal government.

For the Standing Rock Sioux Tribe and their allies, their victory in December 2016, when the Army Corps of Engineers canceled the permit for the Dakota Access Pipeline to cross the Missouri River, was short-lived. One of the first executive memorandums Trump signed when he got into office in January 2017 was an order directing the Army Corps of Engineers to expedite easement and right-of-way approval of the Dakota Access Pipeline. He also signed a memorandum inviting TransCanada to resubmit an application for building the Keystone XL. Trump had turned back the clock on all the hard-won victories of Lakota and Dakota activists going back to 2015 when they were able to convince then-president Barack Obama to veto the proposed Keystone XL Pipeline.

Meanwhile, Energy Transfer LP (the company has dropped "Partners" from its name) completed the Dakota Access Pipeline. Five hundred thousand barrels of crude oil a day flow under the Missouri just north of the community of Cannon Ball on the Standing Rock Sioux Reservation.

"I talk about DAPL like I talk about my son," the company's CEO, Kelcy Warren, told the press. "I'm so proud of that project."

North Dakota regulators remain unmoved by the concerns of Lakota/Dakota activists, leaders, and the thousands who came to stand with them at Standing Rock. In February 2020, the Public Service Commission approved an Energy Transfer request to double the pipeline's capacity to 1.1 million barrels of crude oil per day.

"To some, this may be just another pipeline in just another place. But to us, it's not just a pipeline, it's a threat," writes Mike Faith, chairman of the Standing Rock Sioux Tribe, in response to the likely increase in oil flowing just upstream from his nation. "And it's not just a place. It's our home—the only one we have. Every day the pipeline operates represents a threat to our way of life. We are still here. We are not giving up this fight."

CHAPTER FIVE

Standing Rock, Treaties, and the Violent Nature of the Occupation of Unceded Lands

The work of Hor'e Win (She Makes a Mark) was in danger of being interrupted and a time of choice was among the nations. A red and blue day.

—Jacqueline Keeler, "The Black Hills and Stone Boy: A New Interpretation"

On Saturday, September 3, 2016, Labor Day weekend in North Dakota, near the Standing Rock Sioux Reservation, private security forces hired by Energy Transfer Partners loosed attack dogs upon a crowd of Native Americans and their allies. The demonstrators—water protectors, as they preferred to be called—which included children, were nonviolently trying to stop the desecration of graves and archaeologically significant sites by the builders of the Dakota Access Pipeline. Six people were bitten, including a child and a pregnant woman. Thirty were maced. No one was charged, and culturally significant sites to the Lakota/Dakota people were likely destroyed in order to prevent a legal challenge to the construction of the pipeline.

The tribe's former historic preservation officer, Tim Mentz Sr., had filed a sworn declaration with the court on Friday, the day before, describing the site as containing "one of the most significant archaeological finds in North Dakota in many years."

According to that declaration, Dave Meyer, a white man who owned land within the construction corridor of the pipeline, had expressed concern to the tribe about "potential destruction of culturally important sites." The buffalo rancher then allowed Mentz and his team onto his ranch to look for cultural artifacts. Mentz, who wears his white hair in braids and now runs an independent archaeological consulting firm in Bismarck, examined an area about 1.75 miles from the spot where Dakota Access was supposed to cross Lake Oahe. When he visited on August 28, the pipeline route had been staked and mowed, but no construction equipment was in sight.

We immediately observed a number of stone features in the pipeline route plainly visible from the edge of the corridor. I am very confident that this site, located within the center of the corridor, includes burials because the site contained rock cairns, which are commonly used to mark burials. Two cairns were plainly visible, and a possible third one existed above the cut area. I then noticed to the east twenty meters of this area a prairie dog town and multiple stone rings visible at that distance... The stone rings were also directly in the cleared pipeline corridor.

The destruction of these important cultural sites and the violent measures taken by the pipeline builder to stop nonviolent demonstrators came just a month after Dave Archambault II, the chairman of the tribe, Dana Yellow Fat, a tribal councilman, and four other tribal members were arrested and strip-searched. Typically, heads of state enjoy diplomatic immunity and rarely endure such indignities at the hands of local foreign governments, but not in Morton County, North Dakota. Morton County, like two other counties in the southwestern corner of the state, exists in direct violation of the Fort Laramie Treaty of 1868. Pursuant to the treaty, which is both international law and, as stated in the Constitution, the supreme law of the land in the United States, the county is part of the Great Sioux Nation, of which the Standing Rock Sioux Tribe is a part.

Alarmed by this bold show of brutality by the company, I drove down from a camping trip on Labor Day to the nearest town to get Wi-Fi service to file my story. My editor, who was based in Central America, immediately made the connection between the dogs being used by Energy Transfer Partners to intimidate and assault water protectors and the dogs used by Columbus's soldiers on the Caribs and Tainos, the Indigenous people of the Caribbean. The picture he chose to illustrate my op-ed was a sixteenth-century etching of such an atrocity, and he titled my response "The Vicious Dogs of Manifest Destiny Resurface in North Dakota."

In 2014, the Obamas visited the very site of the encampment, Cannon Ball, North Dakota, and Barack Obama promised the Standing Rock Sioux Tribe he would be a president who "respects your sovereignty, and upholds treaty obligations, and who works with you in a spirit of true partnership, in mutual respect, to give our children the future that they deserve."

Despite hundreds of calls upon the president to honor these promises via social media and even tribal council resolutions, it appeared to have taken video and photos of private security dogs with peaceful protesters' blood in their mouths to finally spur the administration toward some kind of action.

A few days after the dog attacks, the Obama administration issued a statement supporting the tribe's request for a temporary restraining order against Dakota Access Pipeline construction, noting concerns about the oil company "engaging with or antagonizing" the NoDAPL resistors warranted a restraining order. This was the first comment on the situation given by the administration, despite the protest going on since April. No personal statement from President Barack Obama accompanied the announcement of the order. The president's silence in the light of this criminal and violent use of dogs on people by a corporation seeking favor from his administration to complete its pipeline seemed not only strange, but inexplicable in light of his campaign promises of hope and change.

Obama's silence left Lakota/Dakota people and their leaders uneasy, wondering what it meant when state or state-backed corporate modern conquistadors used dogs and violence to suppress the peacefully expressed will of the People peacefully expressed. For many, the brutality of Energy Trust Partner's hired security forces, with law enforcement's tacit support and favorable coverage by the mainstream media, is a sign that this pipeline is yet another example of the forced occupation of Océti Sakówin lands.

"Dakota is our name. It means allies, friends," Faith Spotted Eagle had told me in July when the Army Corps of Engineers approved the easement for pipeline. An Ihanktonwan (Yankton Dakota) grandmother and founder of the Brave Heart Society from my dad's reservation, she was one of the Dakota and Lakota elders who were a constant presence at the camp and together represented all seven bands of the Océti Sakówin.

"How can they use it for their pipeline?" she had wondered a couple of months before the company brought dogs to quell opposition. "They are not being allies to us or to our Mother Earth."

The pipeline builder's malicious use of dogs on the People, the allies, the true Dakota, simply served to underscore the impunity corporate power enjoys even in an allegedly post-colonial world. After all, Native people did not enter the fight against the pipeline with any illusions regarding the nature and extent of the rights of a CEO like Kelcy Warren, empowered by US laws and the state, to use our homelands as he saw fit, with little to no regard for our well-being. This opening salvo made that reality clear enough.

The use of violence in the service of American domination has a bloody and well-remembered history among our people of the Great Plains and the Great Lakes. In 1863, the Dakota rose up as their treaty provisions were denied and their children were starving in what is often called the Minnesota Sioux Uprising. They were quickly put down, and four thousand fled to join their relatives among the Dakota, Lakota, and Nakota bands in the Dakotas and in Canada. The day after Christmas, thirty-eight Dakota men were ordered hung by President Lincoln in the largest mass hanging in US history in Mankato, Minnesota. Two more Dakota leaders were later captured and also hung.

This latest assault on our people by an oil company took place almost exactly 153 years to the day since the Whitestone Massacre, which occurred on September 3, 1863, not far from the present-day protest at Cannon Ball, North Dakota.

LaDonna Brave Bull Allard, founder of the Sacred Stone Camp, wrote about what her great-great-grandmother, Mary Big Moccasin, a

Santee survivor of that violent attack (Big Moccasin's father was one of the thirty-eight hung at Mankato) remembered about that day:

> The attack came the day after the big hunt when spirits were high. The sun was setting, and everyone was sharing an evening meal when [Colonel] Sully's soldiers surrounded the camp on Whitestone Hill. In the chaos that ensued, people tied their children to their horses and dogs and fled. Mary was nine years old. As she ran, she was shot in the hip and went down. She laid there until morning when a soldier found her. As he loaded her into a wagon, she heard her relatives moaning and crying on the battlefield. She was taken to a prisoner of war camp.

This history of violence begs the question, what was Manifest Destiny? What was the United States of America built on? The image the term calls to mind for many Americans is the 1872 painting "American Progress" by John Gast of a blond female figure in Roman garb leading American pioneers into the West and bringing progress in the form of technological innovations like the telegraph, trains, and ships while buffalo and Plains tribes flee before her. To many Americans, until fairly recently, this image symbolized the civilizing of the savage and poorly utilized continent, and the advancement of humanity materially, spiritually, and socially. This image also illustrates that the price of this progress would be genocide and the entitlement required to believe that everything here, everything belonging to the nations of people that already were here, even their very lives, were free for the taking. The question facing more recent immigrants and each new generation born into this present state of affairs is: Will they continue to partake in this barbarism?

I compare the inhumanity implied in this system to the term Energy Transfer Partners dared to appropriate from us for their pipeline, Dakota. Consider Dakota, meaning allies or friends, versus Dakota Access, which clearly means access to everything that belongs to everyone in the pathway of the pipeline. Dakota Access is a latter-day declaration of Manifest Destiny, a Dallas oil executive's expression of the impunity with which he can pursue profit.

In Lakota, *ikce wicasa*, variously translated as a free, humble, and common man, is held up as the epitome of what a man can be. The goal of our sacred ceremonies like the sundance is not power, but to be humble and to sacrifice so the people will not have to suffer as much. It may seem odd that a people known around the world for the exploits of Sitting Bull and Crazy Horse would think of themselves in those terms—and regard being a "common man" as the highest achievement that could be expressed in anyone's lifetime. For our ancestors, to be humble was to be truly free. To be allied with each other to preserve lives, to nurture their relationship with each other and the earth, was what it meant to be human.

I can't help but compare ikce wicasa to the term *pioneer*, derived from the French term for peons, peasants who were considered expendable and sent ahead of the regular army. Pioneers, now portrayed in heroic terms, were similarly treated by powerful interests like the railroad, which dumped white families off in North Dakota with nothing but a box to live in. They were left alongside railroad lines to act as a buffer between the railroad and the tribes. Ironically, it was our people who often came to their aid when they were left to starve, exposed to the elements, by the nineteenth-century versos of oil executive: the railroad tycoon.

There was a term in our language my Lala, Phil Lane Sr., once told me, which he said meant "that which looks human, but is not." When I look at a photo taken of Kelcy Warren, builder of the four-billion-dollar pipeline, watching a NoDAPL protest outside his Texas corporate offices and smirking, the day before he ordered dogs to bite Native Americans and even children and pregnant women, I can't help but wish I remembered what that word was.

Because that is what he is.

<></>

"This was all premeditated," former Standing Rock tribal chairman Dave Archambault II told Amy Goodman, host of *Democracy Now!* "They knew something was going to happen when they leapfrogged over fifteen miles of undisturbed land to destroy our sacred sites. They knew that something was going to happen, so they were prepared. They hired a company that had guard dogs, and then they came in, and then they waited."

When the Rev. Jesse Jackson came to Standing Rock a month later, he told the press, "This is the ripest case of environmental racism I've seen in a long time. Bismarck residents don't want their water threatened, so why is it okay for North Dakota to react with guns and tanks when Native Americans ask for the same right?"

For Reverend Jackson, the photos and videos taken that day of the use of dogs on nonviolent water protectors recalled for him similar assaults on protests he took part in as a young man during the sit-ins and marches of the civil rights era.

The pipeline builder had a stubbornly different take in a press release they issued that portrayed the company's hired security, including dogs, as the real victims.

We are greatly saddened and extremely bothered to confirm that unwarranted violence occurred on private property under easement to Dakota Access Pipeline, resulting in injury to multiple members of our security personnel and several dogs. It is unfortunate that what has been portrayed as a peaceful protest by the opponents of the pipeline has now turned to violence and intimidation by a group of criminals and activists. Assailants broke through a fence and attacked our workers. We are working with law enforcement to ensure that all offenders are arrested and prosecuted to the fullest extent of the law.

This corporate spin had the desired effect on some of the media coverage of the dog attacks. The Associated Press led with a quote from Morton County spokeswoman Donnell Preskey, who claimed, "Four private security guards and two guard dogs were injured… One of the security officers was taken to a Bismarck hospital for undisclosed injuries. The two guard dogs were taken to a Bismarck veterinary clinic."

Ashley Nicole Welch, an unlicensed dog handler from Ohio, became infamous as photos of her were shared widely on social media. Video of the attacks showed that she goaded her dog and was responsible for most of the bites. Some Facebook posts even alleged it was her dog that bit a child's face. Welch's aggression is apparent in the footage captured by *Democracy Now!*, the only major media on the scene when it happened.

"Ma'am, your dog just bit this protestor," an alarmed Amy Goodman, host of *Democracy Now!*, is seen telling Welch. "Are you telling the dogs to bite the protestors? The dog has blood in its nose and its mouth."

The ponytailed young woman ignores the question. Later, she can be seen in front of the rest of the security team goading her dog to attack the crowd.

In the week following the dog attack, before heading to North Dakota, I corresponded with the father of the young Lakota woman who had been bitten in the breast by Welch's dog. Despite the woman, Ta'Sina Sapa Win, being willing to come forward, I can say that, in 2016, yet another colonial invader of Indigenous lands got away with assaulting Native women, elders, and children. The Water Protector Legal Collective, which handled her case, failed to file a lawsuit before the statute of limitations expired.

None of the dog handlers, including Welch, from Frost Kennels, based in Hartville, Ohio, have been charged—even after the North Dakota Private Investigation and Security Board found the kennel was not licensed to provide private security in North Dakota (or in Ohio). This offense is a misdemeanor under North Dakota state law.

In an interview with the *Cleveland Scene*, Bob Frost, the twenty-nine-year-old owner of Frost Kennels, denied any of his dogs bit a child and called water protectors "morons" for bringing children, saying, "Soldiers don't take their kids to Afghanistan."

"As far as the pipeline goes, I'm not for it or against it," he claimed, "but when I'm contracted to stand in a fenced-in area, patrol an area and protect equipment, using dogs as a visual deterrent, that's what I'm going to do."

He told critics to "kiss my ass," and claimed his wife was half Native American. He wouldn't answer requests for proof, but regardless, it would not have made the use of dogs any less brutal or callous.

Three years later, in a Facebook post, Ta'Sina recalled how the dog was commanded three times to lunge at her. It seemed confused by the order the first two times, and then on the third command, it bit her right breast. "Covered in blood," she wrote, "I didn't feel a thing. People say adrenaline; I say, ancestors." Despite the brutality she faced, she never received her day in court to hold the dog handler responsible. Yet she concludes, "I'll never forget September 3, 2016. It was a day that felt like a victory."

Despite the public witnessing via social media the vicious assaults on water protectors, and a small amount of media attention (not all of it sympathetic, particularly local coverage), the company, with police support, did not change its approach. Instead, it continued with alarming regularity, showing this was not a one-off event, but the plan.

On October 23, 2016, Unicorn Riot reported the establishment of a new camp in the proposed pipeline route by the Océti Sakówin was to "take back unceded territory affirmed in the 1851 Treaty of Ft. Laramie." The new camp, called the 1851 Treaty Camp, was partly on the highway and water protectors closed the road by erecting blockades.

Four days later, law enforcement escalated the violence and brutally cleared the camp. In riot gear, over three hundred police officers from five states, on eight ATVs, five armored vehicles, two helicopters, and numerous military-grade Humvees showed up north of the newly formed frontline camp just east of Highway 1806. Both blockades established to enable that occupation were also cleared.

"Pepper spray, percussion grenades, and shotguns were fired into the crowd with less-than-lethal ammunition," Bold Nebraska, an anti-pipeline organization from Nebraska, reported in a press release. "A sound cannon was also used. At least one person was tased, and the barbed hook lodged in his face, just below his eye. Another was hit in the face by a rubber bullet."

A tipi erected in the road was recklessly dismantled by law enforcement, despite initial assurances they would be marking the tipi with a yellow ribbon and requesting that its owners remove it. A circle of elders, including Ponca elder Casey Camp, were praying, some carrying sacred pipes, which were taken from them. Standing peacefully, they were pepper sprayed and arrested. Horses ridden by young Dakota men from the Crow Creek Sioux Reservation in South Dakota were also shot at with rubber bullets by police who chased them in ATVs.

Taking screenshots from a video shared on Facebook, I felt like I was watching a modern reenactment of the old US military raids on Lakota people from the 1860s. As I froze frame after frame, the images that emerged were disturbing documentation of the lack of respect the white American county governments from five states had for our culture. I saw Native people being dragged from a sweat lodge built in the pathway of the pipeline, and police officers in riot gear ripping open a tipi to drag out a Native woman. These images recalled for me descriptions of the 1863 Whitestone Massacre, in which the US Calvary killed or wounded three hundred peaceful Lakota/Dakota, including women and children. Young people, notably members of the International Indigenous Youth Council who began the fight against the pipeline on Standing Rock, were maced multiple times, and one, Danny Grassrope, twenty-four, from the Lower Brule Sioux Reservation in South Dakota, was beaten down by police, who wrenched the organization's sacred staff from his hands before arresting him.

"While we were praying, the cops came and told us we couldn't be there," Grassrope told a reporter. "We were just standing there and then this police officer came and opened up with some pepper spray... I don't understand why it was a riot, the police were in riot gear, we were just praying."

The Standing Rock Sioux Tribe requested the Department of Justice investigate law enforcement abuses, including unlawful arrests, and criticized the militarization of law enforcement at the site. The tribe blamed the police for causing "escalated violence at the campsite" against "peaceful protesters protecting sacred places and water from the Dakota Access Pipeline."

"I am seeking a Justice Department investigation because I am concerned about the safety of the people," Tribal Chairman Dave Archambault II said in a statement.

Morton County chairman Cody Schulz defended the law enforcement's professionalism and claimed the county respected the First Amendment rights of pipeline opponents, saying, "The protesters' rights are just as important as those of the citizens of Morton County. But they are not more important."

A DAPL security guard named Kyle Thompson sped through the crowds towards camp in a company truck. Fearing this would harm women and children there, water protectors set up a blockade and caused him to spin out on the riverbank. He emerged from his vehicle carrying an AR-15 and threatened to shoot anyone who stood in the way of the pipeline. Members of the camp were able to diffuse the situation and talk him down. Thompson, a veteran and a tribal citizen of the Three Affiliated Tribes, was taken into custody by the Bureau of Indian Affairs police.

The 142 arrested were temporarily housed in kennel-like enclosures and, in what was seen by water protectors as a chilling echo of the tattooing Jewish prisoners endured in Nazi concentration camps, had identification numbers written on their arms. When the items, including the canunpa, the sacred pipes taken from praying elders, were returned to the main camp at Standing Rock, they were in plastic bags with numbers on them that matched the numbers written on the prisoners.

Arvol Looking Horse, a traditional Lakota elder who lives on the nearby Cheyenne River Sioux Reservation, was very visible as one of the tallest men at camp. Looking Horse is the keeper of the White Buffalo Calf Pipe Bundle reputed to be the same one given to the Lakota/ Dakota people by the White Buffalo Calf Woman. Though not a political leader, he holds a central position among the Seven Council Fires as the caretaker of a living medicine that is the definitive proof of our people's spiritual kinship to the land.

Looking Horse prayed over the defiled pipes and sacred items before they were returned to friends and family of the arrested owners.

In the midst of this, the elders were challenged by leaders of the Red Warrior Camp, a camp within the larger camp, led by well-known Ojibway leader Winona LaDuke. Early on, the Red Warrior Camp took on the more radical role in the camp and actively communicated with the media. The two Red Warrior Camp women, according to first-person accounts, came forward and demanded to know why they had to take orders from the Lakota elders at camp. The traditional leadership representing the Océti Sakówin had been chiding them to not commit violence. They told the Red Warrior Camp members that they had been told in ceremony to conduct themselves in a prayerful way. The day of the raid on the 1851 Treaty Camp, there was reportedly arguing on the front lines as Red Warriors became tired of the elders praying, which led to police laughing at the lack of unity.

Now, dissatisfied with the elder's explanations about why prayer was their preferred strategy, Red Warrior Camp members did what they had reportedly also done on the front lines: turned up the music in their vehicles to drown out the sound of the elders' prayers.

The violence had found its way into camp.

In a letter to Obama, Looking Horse implored him to keep his word to honor the treaties and to address violations against the Lakota people. He described how the elders had been "pleading for sanity" without weapons, were met by an "army of lethal weapons," and had been arrested.

"Once we stand with our sacred filled C'anupa, we make a commitment to the Creator that we cannot break," he explained to the president. "We stand under the Freedom of Religion Act of 1978 with our Pipe of Peace and the Treaty of 1851."

He ended the letter with a statement from the Traditional Elders Council at the camp: "We are a part of Creation; thus, if we break the Laws of Creation, we destroy ourselves."

On October 28, while hundreds of water protectors were assaulted with "less-than-lethal" weaponry and many arrested at Standing Rock, a very different scene played out at the US District Court in Portland, Oregon. Brothers Ryan and Ammon Bundy and five of their followers were all acquitted of federal conspiracy and weapons charges for their forty-one-day armed takeover of Malheur, which US Fish and Wildlife calculated had damages exceeding four million dollars.

"We came to Oregon…seeking justice, and we found it today," one of the defendants, Neil Wampler, crowed to reporters, calling it a "stunning victory for rural America."

Shawna Cox, a defendant and Bundy family secretary through both the Bunkerville and Malheur standoffs, thanked the jury for not listening to the prosecution's "nonsense" and concluded, "God said we weren't guilty. We weren't guilty of anything."

Cox had every right to be thankful; the most serious charge—conspiracy to impede federal officers through intimidation, threats, or force—carried a maximum penalty of six years in prison. However, the Depression-era law they were charged under requires proof of intent, which proved difficult for the prosecution to provide.

The Bundys and their followers subscribe to an interpretation of the Constitution that says the federal government has no authority over them, thus threatening or obstructing the work of federal employees was not the intent of the takeover. Some legal experts saw Ammon Bundy's ten hours of testimony as the factor that may have won over jurors. Soft-spoken and insisting on wearing his prison garb, a small booklet containing the Constitution in his front shirt pocket, he sat on the stand for more than three days. In that time he was allowed free rein to lay out his views on the Constitution, the federal government, and his duty to protect his rights.

"I think it's really hard to see this as anything other than jury nullification," Lewis & Clark law professor Tung Yin opined.

Jury nullification occurs when jurors believe a defendant is guilty, but choose to acquit anyway because they believe the law is unjust or has been misapplied, or that the punishment for breaking the law would be too harsh. Jury nullification was the stated goal of the Bundys and their primary legal strategy. Cliven Bundy called repeatedly for nullification by the jurors in his sons' trials.

Ethan D. Knight, an assistant United States attorney, argued that the case was simple: Ammon Bundy had been selective in deciding which laws applied to him and had led an armed seizure of property that did not belong to him.

In court, the jury was provided with an abundance of evidence plainly showing that the occupiers declared they would fire upon federal agents if they attempted to enter the facility and that they were indeed wielding firearms. Prosecutors, through witnesses and in their final arguments, asserted that it was a threat of force and violence, driven by Mr. Bundy's call for people nationwide to come to the refuge with their guns. While court observers felt the jury understood the evidence presented, the jurors were unable to bring themselves to bring forth a guilty verdict.

Ammon Bundy argued the takeover was unplanned and informed by religious direction from God, and by his interpretation of the Constitution. In this alternate legal reality, the federal government is restrained from owning more than a ten-mile-square area of land and other land to build forts, etc. Also, the sheriff is the ultimate authority, even above the president of the United States.

Yet, the 1851 Fort Laramie Treaty Camp was founded on the idea that the signatory tribes have a right to the land in question under the boundaries agreed upon under the 1851 Fort Laramie Treaty by the

Great Sioux Nation and ratified by the US Congress; and this could not win in court.

On October 27, amid all of the violence, the arrest of Red Fawn Fallis, a thirty-nine-year-old Lakota woman from the Pine Ridge Reservation in South Dakota, stood out.

In a video posted to YouTube, Fallis, a medic at the camp, can be seen arriving on an ATV where a line of police in riot gear are faced off with water protectors. A petite woman wearing a backpack, she gets off her vehicle and approaches the line of large (mostly white) men. The wall of men parts and a deputy tackles her. Later, the deputy says he heard her shouting "water is life." Then, the men break formation for a moment, and she is grabbed and pulled behind by several officers. The line of armored law enforcement reforms and the crowd cannot see her as five men pile on top of her. They pin her arm behind her back, and with their knees hold her legs down. All of this takes less than a minute. Police later allege that while being held down in this manner with one arm pinned behind her back, she managed to fire three shots from a revolver underneath her stomach into the ground. The discharge of bullets did not result in any injuries.

The shocking images of Fallis's arrest garnered millions of dollars in donations, not to her personally, but to a crowdsourced legal fundraiser for all water protectors at Standing Rock run by a group from Minnesota calling itself Freshet. Police arrested 142 people—more than on any other day in the eleven-month-long Standing Rock struggle. Seven, all Native Americans, were arrested with federal charges.

More than a year later, leaks were reported that indicated that the gun in question belonged to a paid FBI informant who was in a romantic relationship with Fallis. The informant was Heath Harmon, forty-six, from the Fort Berthold reservation just north of Standing Rock. His tribe benefits enormously from fracked oil as a third of the vast Bakken oil field is on his reservation. He infiltrated the Red Warrior camp in August 2016 and was with Fallis for much of the day before her arrest.

After interviewing legal scholars and activists, it became clear to me that Red Fawn's relationship was more than just an FBI informant's convenient cover to infiltrate the camp, but was also evidence of a government law enforcement agency conducting spying activities that included sponsoring sexual assault of Native women at Standing Rock as a strategy of suppression.

I say "women" because I suspect this strategy was utilized by more than one informant in the camp. Government complicity is suggested not only by Harmon entering into a sexual relationship with Fallis under false pretenses, but by the dramatic manner of her arrest. The way she was set upon by law enforcement suggests his government minders utilized this intimacy to set her up for a confrontation with the police, while wearing his jacket and carrying his gun (unknowingly, she claimed) in the backpack he had given her shortly before her arrest. This deception rises to the level of sexual assault because Red Fawn, an activist with a family history of movement work, has said she would never have agreed to a relationship with the informant had she known the truth, and on that basis the relationship was not consensual.

Sexual assault conducted in service of government surveillance of activists is not limited to the United States. When interviewing Fallis's legal team, I brought up cases I had researched in other countries, and asked if they might be referenced when challenging her charges in court. However, the legal team was unable to successfully apply this line of questioning in her defense. Perhaps in the future, greater awareness of this tactic—an outrageous and harmful invasion of Native women's lives and bodies—could help other movement women who are targeted by law enforcement.

The documents on Fallis's case were allegedly leaked by a law enforcement employee; speculation pointed to someone working in Morton County in an office position. The belief that the source was working for the police led many journalists and activists who were offered access to the material to decline the overture. They were concerned it was yet another setup.

The leak included a copy of a transcript of an interview the Bureau of Alcohol, Tobacco, Firearms, and Explosives and the North Dakota Bureau of Criminal Investigation conducted with Harmon in which he tells them he was an informant working for the FBI and that the gun Fallis allegedly fired during her arrest, a .38 revolver, belonged to him.

According to a motion to compel discovery filed by her defense attorneys, Harmon "seduced Ms. Fallis and initiated an intimate, albeit duplicitous relationship with her. He spent the majority of the 48-hour period prior to Ms. Fallis's arrest with her and had access to her and her belongings... He used their romantic relationship to rely upon her as an unwitting source of information for informant activities."

Close family members of Fallis, her aunt and her uncle Dave Archambault Sr. (parents of the then-chairman of the Standing Rock Sioux Tribe), affirmed her legal team's version of events, telling me the FBI plant literally "jacketed" her by putting his jacket with the gun in it on her right before her arrest and planting items in her backpack. They had met Heath at the camp and the couple would use their home to shower. The Archambaults, elders who were a constant presence at camp, told me they had liked Heath and thought he was good to their niece, unaware of his true purpose. Dave Sr., his long gray hair in a ponytail, is a tall and imposing man, a well-respected educator who has served as head of both the American Indian College Fund and Sitting Bull College at Fort Yates on Standing Rock.

Harmon can be seen in leaked police drone footage leaving on Fallis's abandoned ATV just twenty seconds after his purported girlfriend's arrest. He drives to the end of the line of demonstrators and can be seen speaking to a Dakota water protector whom I also spoke to. This water protector asked me not to be identified, but told me Harmon did not mention Fallis's violent arrest. In his leaked interview with Alcohol, Tobacco, and Firearms, Harmon claims he immediately returned to camp to collect all of Fallis's possessions and return them to her family on Standing Rock. Harmon did see it worthwhile to mention his girlfriend was tackled by several large men in front of him. Fallis's aunt and uncle confirmed that he had done this. Immediately after their niece was arrested, they told me, after gathering her things from the trailer the couple shared at camp, Harmon arrived at their house and left her stuff with them. It was behavior they regarded at the time as strange, and, by the time I spoke to them, damaging.

After giving false and contradictory testimony to law enforcement regarding the gun, Harmon continued the pretense of being Fallis's boyfriend even after she was arrested. In leaked audio of their phone calls, Fallis can be heard tearfully confiding, unknowingly to a paid infiltrator, her fears and desire not to serve time for something she did not do.

To hear her voice and trust in this man illustrates the level of violation and state-sponsored abuse of an individual's right to emotional and physical intimacy. A vibrant woman, Red Fawn Fallis was described by members of the International Indigenous Youth Council as an inspiring and selfless activist.

Five days before she was arrested, IIYC members described to media how Fallis, the medic, rode her ATV in and out of an area where police were violently putting down a prayer walk. She went back innumerable times, transporting elders, children, and other people who were hurt to safety.

"Anyone at the camp that needs help, she's always been the one to stand up," said Mia Stevens, a twenty-two-year-old member of the youth council. "She wouldn't do nothing like that. Where is the proof?"

Harmon reportedly had been recruited by his brother, a Bureau of Indian Affairs police officer in North Dakota, to work for the FBI as "an observer" of the protest and monitor both camps, Očéti Sakówin and Sacred Stone, at Standing Rock for evidence of "bomb-making materials, stuff like that."

Harmon said further that the FBI wished for him to confirm the presence of specific "AIM members" at camp, a reference to the American Indian Movement, and claimed he was the one who reported to police the existence of a vehicle carrying lockdown devices used by protesters to conduct nonviolent actions to disrupt pipeline construction.

Red Fawn Fallis, daughter of the late Troy Lynn Yellow Wood (a cousin raised as a sister of Betty, Dave Archambault II's mother), had been born into the American Indian Movement in Denver, Colorado. Her mother had helped start the Colorado chapter of AIM in the 1970s, and it was from her home in 1975 that fellow Native activist Anna Mae Aquash, a Mi'kmaq woman from Nova Scotia, was kidnapped. Aquash's body was later found in the Badlands on the Pine Ridge Reservation in South Dakota. In 2003, two AIM members, Arlo Looking Cloud and John Graham, were charged for her murder by a Canadian court. Yellow Wood's testimony in the case proved instrumental in obtaining their conviction in 2006.

Initially, the FBI was blamed for Aquash's murder, especially after gruesome details of their investigation revealed they had cut off her hands to obtain fingerprints. Even after the trial concluded, many AIM members questioned the conviction and traced the atmosphere of distrust that clouded the movement to a covert intelligence program the agency ran at the time called COINTELPRO. The goal of this program was to use infiltration to disrupt political social justice groups that emerged in the 1960s and '70s like the American Indian Movement and the Black Panthers.

"I had a spy who was being paid by the government to spy on me," an activist identified only as Jacqui told the London press, "to the extent that he watched me give birth, so he saw every intimate part of me."

In 2012, Jacqui was deeply traumatized after discovering a top-secret, decades-long infiltration program that had targeted her. The Special Demonstration Squad of the London Metropolitan Police had spied upon progressive groups for decades, with some officers engaging in undercover long-term sexual relationships, and, as in

Jacqui's case, even fathering children. She described the experience to the media as being "raped by the state." She settled her case for £425,000 (about $560,000), and the practice was outlawed in Britain. It is unclear when this sort of intelligence operation will be disavowed by American law enforcement.

The London police targeting women activists based on their political beliefs is clearly a form of gendered violence; the targeting of Native American women is also intimately tied to the history of the United States. Particularly since it gained its present land base through total wars waged against Indigenous nations, including noncombatants like women and children and elders, and the resulting colonial society marginalizes Native women and leaves them vulnerable to violence.

A widely quoted 2010 Department of Justice report found Native women experienced rape and murder at rates nearly two and half times that of other American women. In some counties, the murder rate is nine times as high. Criminal database statistics find that 70 percent of Native women's reported attackers are men not of their race—most are white men. Men of their own race primarily assault American women. More data is needed to address the vulnerable picture this paints of Native women in America.

At the hearing, Red Dawn Foster, a Lakota/Diné candidate for the South Dakota state senate and a hunka sister (adopted in the traditional Lakota way) of Red Fawn Fallis, recounted to the judge Fallis's history of abusive relationships that made her susceptible to manipulation by someone like Harmon.

US District of North Dakota chief judge Daniel Hovland permitted Fallis to wear civilian clothing at the nearly six-hour hearing. She appeared shackled and was wearing a traditional ribbon dress.

It was partly Hovland's refusal to allow for further discovery into Harmon's role in the defendant's arrest (and the role of pipeline owner Energy Transfer Partners' security contractors like TigerSwan, whom he determined were not part of the prosecution) that forced the defense to agree to a non-cooperating plea deal in late January. Under the deal, the most serious charge against Fallis, of firing a weapon at law enforcement, was dropped. That charge could have put her in prison for thirty years. The judge also refused to allow any defense based on treaties that were violated by the building of the pipeline.

After her sentencing was postponed in June, friends, family, attorneys, and supporters of Fallis gathered for prayer in a Bismarck hotel meeting room. Her hunka uncle, University of Colorado professor Glenn Morris, spoke to those gathered, telling them that he had spoken to his niece that morning. She had been in custody for more than twenty months.

"She told me," he said, "'I'm a wild Oglala. I was born free, I will live free, and I will die free. And I know what day this is.'"

That day was the 142nd anniversary of what the Lakota call Victory Day, the Battle of Greasy Grass, or, as the Americans call it, the Battle of the Little Big Horn. In 1874, Custer led one thousand men in search of gold into the Black Hills in violation of the Fort Laramie Treaty. Since then, mines on Lakota land have produced, according to some estimates, nearly 10 percent of the world's gold. In 2016, the transportation of heavy crude from the Bakken through unceded Lakota treaty lands, which potentially endangered Lakota communities and millions of Americans downriver, precipitated the Dakota Access Pipeline protests at Standing Rock.

For Red Fawn Fallis and several other Standing Rock water protectors still facing felony charges, the battle between the Lakota, their allies, and the American government has never really ended.

Glenn Morris and Fallis's legal counsel, Bruce Ellison, requested I hold off publishing any reporting on her case until after her sentencing. They feared any coverage would anger the judge and increase the length of her prison sentence.

On Wednesday, July 11, Fallis was found guilty of one count of civil disorder and one count of possession of a firearm and ammunition by a felon. The most high-profile water protector charged with a felony at Standing Rock was sentenced to fifty-seven months in federal prison with eighteen months for time served. Her legal team did not appeal.

<<>>

A week after the arrests at the 1851 Treaty Camp, on November 3, water protectors gathered to pray at a site along the river where they claimed the remains of the Standing Rock Sioux tribal members who once owned Cannonball Ranch and older Lakota and Mandan burials were threatened.

The ranch, recently purchased by Energy Transfer Partners, the owners of the Dakota Access Pipeline, enjoyed the protection of a phalanx of black-garbed law enforcement that lined the top of the bluff overlooking the Missouri. Nonviolent demonstrators were met with a hail of rubber bullets. As they approached the shore and stood in the water, huge blasts of pepper spray were administered by police standing on the shore. The images of water protectors being cared for by medics, white foam streaming from their eyes, down their faces, into the water, were disturbing and unforgettable.

Journalist Erin Schrode of CNN was shot on camera with a rubber bullet, and despite the video of her shooting, the police denied it happened. The assault lasted for hours as tens of thousands from around the world watched it all live on social media.

This was followed up a few weeks later, just days before Thanksgiving, with live-streamed videos of police deploying water cannons and tear gas for five hours on protesters in below-freezing weather. One hundred sixty-seven protesters were injured.

Finally, on November 21, after the assault, the *New York Times* addressed the brutality at Standing Rock in an opinion piece written by the editorial board, saying, "When injustice aligns with cruelty, and heavy weaponry is involved, the results can be shameful and bloody. Witness what happened on Sunday in North Dakota, when law enforcement officers escalated their tactics against unarmed American Indians and allies who have waged months of protests against the Dakota Access oil pipeline."

<<>>

The Océti Sakówin camp had started out as merely the overflow camp for Sacred Stone, but quickly eclipsed the original camp simply because it had more room to grow. The larger camp was located on a wide meadow next to the shoreline and photos of the thousands of tipis and tents and other structures are of Océti Sakówin, not Sacred Stone. The Army Corps had assumed ownership of this area when a dam was built that created Lake Oahe. The dam also flooded the original village of Cannon Ball, which was rebuilt on the bluff where Sacred Stone was located. The tribe negotiated with the corps to allow the camp in exchange for agreeing to return the land to its previous state and taking out an insurance policy. The tribe also paid for garbage pickup from the camp and provided chemical toilets.

The governor of North Dakota applied more pressure, ordering an emergency evacuation, and Morton County's Sheriff Kirchmeier, not to be left out, threatened anyone providing any kind of material support to the camp with thousand-dollar fines.

Despite this, veterans came by the thousands, responding to Wesley Clark Jr.'s call to "assemble as a peaceful, unarmed militia." News reports cited figures ranging from two thousand to four thousand veterans arriving in time for the eviction and swelling the Océti Sakówin camp to between ten and fifteen thousand, according to some estimations.

The afternoon of December 4, as the camp welcomed in veteran after veteran, the Army Corps of Engineers announced the revocation of the permit for the Dakota Access Pipeline to cross the Missouri. The agency was going to consider other routes, actually complete an environmental impact statement, and, finally, enter into meaningful consultation with the Lakota and Dakota Tribes. The standoff had worked; the Lakota/Dakota people had won. The Obama administration would finally truly do what the president had said that long ago day in 2014: honor the treaties. What had begun as a grim standoff in the snow became a celebration with dancing, singing, and fireworks.

I wrote on Medium about what I saw that first week of December—the week US veterans gathered, and Obama announced the revocation of the approval of the easement crossing for the pipeline. The following is an excerpt from that article, which is titled "On the Icy Edge of Trump's Empire: Standing Rock and Hoth."

It's Cannon Ball, North Dakota, but with the temperature hovering around -25 degrees Fahrenheit with windchill factored in, it feels like the planet Hoth in The Empire Strikes Back. *The whiteness of the landscape and the intense cold brings such comparisons to mind. The NoDAPL camp, which numbered ten thousand in early December before the first blizzard, is a testament to the support the Standing Rock Sioux Tribe enjoys in its fight against the $3.7 billion Dakota Access Pipeline that they say threatens their lands, water, and people.*

In a warm felt-lined yurt, the Dakota headsman from Lower Brule, Lewis Grassrope (Wicahpi Ksapa Peji Wikan), told me that he and about two hundred others will remain, as they say, until "the Horn comes down," and their elders tell them to leave. The Horn is a traditional encampment of tipis in the shape of a horn representing the Seven Council Fires and pointed at the enemy in defiance. There, the fire still burns.

"Well, when this movement first started, it started on prayer, and you know through ceremony," Grassrope explains. "The wakening of our spirits...to knowing that we need to rethink our societies and rethink the way that we look at life and restore the old values that our ancestors carried, so we actually become true human beings (Ikce Wicasa)."

When I saw The Empire Strikes Back *as a kid and saw Han cutting up the tauntaun to shelter Luke in the warm carcass, I thought of the Dakota stories I heard as a child where a person would take shelter from the deathly cold of a Great Plains winter in the carcass of a buffalo. Our stories differed, however, in that the buffalo would come back to life with the man or woman still stuck inside. As a child, I would pester my dad with questions like, how could they breathe?*

Today, as an adult, my perspective has changed, and I long to be gently swinging to the buffalo's gait, to be part of such a powerful creature that is the center of Lakota/Dakota culture.

The camp feels like that center, the center of the buffalo, and I understand when Grassrope says, "Most of us don't want to leave after we're done because of the feeling and the kinship and everything that was gained here."

My son, who accompanied me to the camp, actually asks to wait a while before seeing Rogue One, *the next Star Wars installment. I agree, and we wait. We wait to return to camp in the spring as the United States of America inaugurates Donald Trump as their forty-fifth president. We'll return to see if the miracle will happen as it did in the old stories. We want to see if our Oyate (nation), our people, and the buffalo that holds them still lives.*

In the end, I see the place on the plains north of the Cannonball River, and even the Missouri itself, where all that violence was endured on behalf of my father's people by so many from all walks of life, as a birthplace. Not to underplay the trauma that so many still carry to this day, but because I believe that prayer can be carried. I believe in the power of that relationship to that land that made us Dakhóta.

CHAPTER SIX

CAN THE LAND MAKE US ONE PEOPLE?

For years, all of these takings have happened, and it has been at our expense, so that the nation can benefit.

—Dave Archambault II, Standing Rock Sioux Tribal
Chairman

Our greatest concern is that the federal government Wacos the people right down that hill.

—Joseph Santoro, Oath Keeper

The estimated ten to fifteen thousand water protectors who traveled to NoDAPL camps to support the people of Standing Rock's right to clean drinking water constituted by far the largest gathering of Indigenous people and their supporters seen in the United States in modern times.

But what does it mean, politically and personally, for non-citizens of an Indigenous nation to invoke treaty rights on behalf of a Native nation? The role of volunteers and NGO workers—or even their Native staff who may be from tribes that are not signees—invoking treaties remains unquestioned. At Standing Rock, what were the consequences of this in practice? Does this form of advocacy, conducted with little or no coordination with the tribes whose treaties with the US are being invoked, amount to dictating international policy for Native nations? Little has been written about how this sort of allyship was viewed by Standing Rock Sioux tribal members and leaders. Or, in the broader context, by treaty representatives of all the Seven Council Fires of the Océti Sakówin, not to mention other tribes (like the Cheyenne), who were also signees of the Fort Laramie treaties. This aspect of support for Standing Rock in 2016 needs to be studied to improve best practices and outcomes for future collaborative actions on behalf of tribes, particularly those based on treaty law.

Contrast this paternalistic role in dictating strategy played by certain allied NGOs at Standing Rock with the role the right-wing, self-identified militia played in Oregon. The Three Percenters from Idaho and other militia arrived at the Malheur Wildlife Refuge, answering the call of Ammon Bundy for "patriots all over the country" to come and stand with him. Bundy made a public appeal to his supporters to help him "free up" federal land, explicitly saying, "We need you to bring your guns." While many militia leaders acted as bodyguards and were a presence on the refuge during the occupation, Bundy remained clearly in charge of the tactical direction of the takeover. While the armed insurgent group the Three Percenters aired their disagreement with the takeover strategy in press releases and media interviews, they still chose to position themselves as a physical and potentially deadly buffer between the Bundys and law enforcement. Their actions supported Bundy's approach and did not take away from his leadership.

The two standoffs differ in obvious ways: unarmed vs. armed, Indigenous vs. colonial, protection of resources vs. unlimited access, and treaty rights vs. constitutional, but they are similar in certain ways. Each is a conflict with the federal government's authority (Army Corps of Engineers vs. Bureau of Land Management/Fish and Wildlife Service) and each had critical support from auxiliary groups.

At Malheur, the chief accomplice in the occupation was the militia. Ammon Bundy, responding to a reporter asking about why they didn't stage an unarmed protest, said, "Because they probably would just came in and stopped it from happening before it ever even started and that's why we have our Second Amendment rights."

On the other hand, at Standing Rock, in an early statement in August 2016 from then-tribal-chairman Dave Archambault II, the camp's pacifist nature was clear from the beginning: "This peaceful demonstration is a cry to stop the desecration of land and water." The protest drew support from many nonprofit organizations.

These strategic partners illustrate the intrinsically different socio-philosophical underpinnings and moral authority drawn upon by each of these events. The differing historical origins of the county supremacy movement and the Océti Sakówin were apparent as early as 2014, when comparing Cliven Bundy's standoff with the BLM in Bunkerville, Nevada, to the Indigenous-led pipeline protest against TransCanada's Keystone XL Pipeline.

<\<>>

The standoffs of the Bundys contrast markedly with Native-led anti-pipeline protests not just in the use of arms but also in the level of partnership with other ethnic/racial groups. This collaboration was evident in the organizing of the Keystone XL Pipeline fight that preceded Standing Rock. Like the Battle of Bunkerville, the KXL fight served as both a forerunner to events in 2016 and a training ground for future leaders.

In 2013, Native American and white landowners in South Dakota and Nebraska joined together to form the Cowboy Indian Alliance to fight the pipeline. Many of the leading players in the NoKXL protest went on to play even more high-profile roles in 2016 in the fight to stop the Dakota Access Pipeline. The unity forged by the Cowboy Indian Alliance is, in many ways, a truer manifestation of the ideals of the collective and pluralistic national identity the United States motto, e pluribus unum—Latin for "out of many, one"—extolls. This motto refers to Roman statesman Cicero's *De Officiis*, in which he paraphrases Pythagoras, writing, "When each person loves the other as much as himself, it makes one out of many (unus fiat ex pluribus).

But the motto can also be seen in a speech given by Canassatego, leader of the Onondaga Nation and spokesman for the Haudenosaunee (Iroquois) Confederation, in 1744 in Lancaster, Pennsylvania, to negotiate what became known as the Lancaster Treaty. The *sachem* (chief) addressed the envoys from Maryland, Pennsylvania, and Virginia, saying, "We heartily recommend union and a good agreement between you, our brethren. Our wise forefathers established union and amity between the Five Nations; this has made us formidable; this has given us great weight and authority with our neighboring nations. We are a powerful confederacy, and by your observing the same methods our wise forefathers have taken, you will acquire fresh strength and power."

The transcripts of the Onondaga leader's speeches at this meeting were sent to Benjamin Franklin by his friend, a trusted interpreter of the Iroquois leader, to be published. Franklin published thirteen treaty accounts over twenty-six years and in the 1750s, served as an Indian commissioner for Pennsylvania, his first diplomatic assignment. These were bestsellers in the decades before the Revolution. As such, the speeches in them inspired the Founding Father's generation and provided them with a vision of a new political framework they would employ to challenge the British Crown's supremacy. Canassatego's words can be seen as exerting a decisive role in the United States' origin story. Franklin noted this debt to the Haudenosaunee, although in not such complimentary terms. "The First American" adopted a sarcastic tone while writing to his printing partner James Parker in 1751, arguing for a union of the English colonies: "It would be a strange thing if Six Nations of ignorant savages should be capable of forming a scheme for such a union, and be able to execute it in such a manner as that it has subsisted ages and appears indissoluble; and yet that a like union should be impracticable for ten or a dozen English colonies." In 1988, the contribution of the Iroquois Confederacy to the development of the Constitution was formally recognized by the 100th Congress in a concurrent resolution. Canassatego, described as a tall, well-made man with a kindly smile, was assassinated in 1750 by pro-French forces. "Savages we call them," Franklin wrote in 1784 in France after he had successfully shepherded the creation of the new nation inspired by the Onondaga leader's words, "because their manners differ from ours, which we think the Perfection of Civility; they think the same of theirs."

It is in this spirit of respect and in a rare recognition of mutually held ties to the land, even 230 years after Franklin wrote those words, that the Cowboy Indian Alliance sponsored peaceful tipi encampments along the Keystone XL Pipeline route in 2014. This tactic was coordinated for the alliance by Joye Braun of the Cheyenne River Sioux Tribe. In 2016, Braun would be invited by grassroots Standing Rock Sioux tribal activists to start the first NoDAPL camp on their reservation near Cannon Ball, North Dakota.

<<>>

The tipis in the pathway of the proposed pipeline were more than just picturesque reminders of a long-ago culture. The circular encampments called *tiyóspaye* (a circle of tipis), were a political statement: our social structure, represented by the circle, is still valid and alive to challenge the extractive, one-way relationship represented by the black snake of the oil pipeline. My great-great-aunt Ella Deloria described the tiyóspaye as representing how "all Dakota people were held together in a great relationship that was theoretically all-inclusive and coextensive within the Dakota domain." She noted that these bonds that tie us together through kinship are essential to what makes us Dakota (allies) and that without it, we would cease to exist as a People or, as they say in Dakota, *oyate*. It was this cultural context that NoKXL organizers in the anti-pipeline fight from 2013 to 2016 were able to connect in a meaningful way to the early twenty-first-century political and economic struggle, and which later brought the pipeline fight to national and international prominence at Standing Rock.

Similarly, Cliven Bundy's claims to unlimited access to public rangeland relied heavily on what the Bundy paterfamilias termed his "ancestral rights."

"I've lived my lifetime here. My forefathers have been up and down the Virgin Valley here ever since 1877," Bundy intoned to a local television station reporter from his small ranch home in Bunkerville, Nevada. "All these rights that I claim have been created through preemptive rights and beneficial use of the forage and the water and the access and range improvements."

Yet Bundy's vaunted "preemptive rights" are themselves preempted by the Paiute, who have preexisting claims not only to the public lands he grazes his cows on but also to the 160 acres he owns and grew melons on. The Bundy homestead was once part of their reservation under treaty. The melon farm, Gold Butte, and other BLM lands Bundy ranges his cattle on were their homeland for thousands of years before a Bundy or his cows appeared in this hemisphere. Ideally, in a just world, the defiant rancher would pay taxes or grazing fees to the Paiute Nations, not to Clark County (as he asserts) or the federal government. Indeed, the Shoshone Tribe has a claim. The Shoshone treaty with the United States allowed only passage through their territory by Oregon Trail pioneers. But to Cliven and his sons, these tribal nations' land claims have no bearing on their fight to privatize those same lands. Both Cliven Bundy and his son Ryan have been outspoken in their opposition to the designation of the Gold Butte National Monument, a site sacred to the Paiute people, which includes public lands the Bundy cattle range. They attempt to mask the fact that their land claims are based on the extinguishment of Indigenous land rights by claiming they want Native people also to be free of the "federal yoke."

Cliven Bundy does, however, recognize one government as the "sovereign" entity empowered to charge him range fees: Clark County, Nevada. In the 1970s and 1980s, Bundy and fellow ranchers like his neighbor Keith Nay were galvanized by the Sagebrush Rebellion. It got its name because it appealed to ranchers and miners in the sagebrush steppe of western states. Supporters of this insurgency demanded state and local control over these lands with the possibility of privatization schemes that would transfer millions of acres of publicly held lands to their ownership. This movement evolved in the 1990s to the county supremacy doctrine, which holds the county sheriff to be the county's highest authority. Under this ideology, which has no basis in law, anti-public-lands activists do not recognize the federal government's jurisdiction. Hence their battles with the Bureau of Land Management that administers rangelands and mining claims, the US Forest Service that manages forests, and the US Fish and Wildlife Service that manages wildlife refuges like Malheur.

This interpretation of land-use rights was employed again two years later in 2016, when Ammon Bundy proclaimed his goal to return public land in Harney County, Oregon, to white ranchers, miners, and lumberjacks. A Bundy on the national media, once again asserting a legal interpretation of ownership of the land that excluded Native nations, immediately caught my attention. It took me a minute to find the Burns Paiute Tribe's webpage and read the tribal history, which, shockingly, described the forced removal of the tribe in the dead of winter almost precisely 137 years earlier. Using this framing, I began to write about the occupation of Malheur from the perspective of the actual owners: the Paiute people.

This manifest disregard for Indigenous land rights pales in comparison to the overt racism Ammon Bundy's father displayed in 2014. After an interview showed him wondering if "Negroes" were "better off as slaves" hit the national news, Cliven Bundy quickly went from right-wing folk hero to persona non grata. Fox News commentators, Republican senators, and even Libertarian Rand Paul, who had championed his cause a few days earlier, quickly beat a full retreat, with Sean Hannity denouncing Bundy's remarks as "beyond repugnant" and "despicable."

Indeed they were. Still, militia leaders and right-wing Christian and Mormon "patriots" who flooded in droves to the Bundys' cause denied their movement was racist. Yet, for most Americans, the video of Bundy chatting arrogantly with a TV news reporter and proposing that millions of Black Americans and their children would be happier in perpetual servitude laid bare how out of touch and racist Cliven's worldview was. The spectacle of a white man, owing the federal government one million dollars in unpaid grazing fees, pontificating on the need for Black people to get off "the government subsidy" was grotesque to the extreme. As was Bundy calling Americans whose ancestors had been freed from bondage "less free" when they possess the constitutional rights he so proudly pontificated on from the pocket-sized Constitution he kept in his shirt pocket.

Adding to Bundy's sordid spectacle on the national stage, it turned out the welfare rancher's "ancestral rights" to graze his cattle without paying taxes for the past twenty years were easily disproved. His forefathers had not "been up and down the Virgin Valley here ever since 1877." A simple search by a local television station of Clark County property records revealed his parents had purchased the ranch in 1948. There was also no record supporting his maternal relatives, the

Jensens, had ever owned it. Bundy's parents had not begun grazing cattle on it until 1954—eight years after the founding of the Bureau of Land Management, which he claimed his rights had superseded by several decades. When the news of this discovery broke, the Moapa band of Paiute Indians poured salt on the wound by sharing with the media a map demonstrating that the Bundy's land was promised to them in a treaty with the US government.

As a Native American, I find Bundy's unsupported claims of ancestral rights a calculated overreach. There are many ways to get what you want, and this outrageous claim is a form of bluff that moves your interests forward. It's been depicted in western films and not unheard of in the history of western land grabs and resource wars. The tribes, by law, retain all remaining preemptive rights in Nevada. These do not belong to late arrivals like the Bundy family but to the sovereign nations that have called the Great Basin—the Sagebrush steppe—their home for thousands of years.

This inability to take the ancestral rights of American Indian nations seriously is not limited to Bundy and his supporters. This blind spot is shared even in liberal bastions like the Pacific Northwest. In Oregon, farmers in the Klamath River Basin were outraged in 2002 when a judge ruled in favor of the Klamath Tribe's senior water rights. This ruling meant, in effect, the tribe could turn off the water during drought years. In 2013, after a drought emergency was declared, Tom Mallams, vice chairman of the Klamath County Board of Commissioners, warned, "They shut water off here, there could be some violence." A local rancher claimed reduction in his water rights would force him to cut his beef operation from 1,050 to 350 cattle.

Even as many Americans continue to deny the existence of Native nations' rights to land and resources—or are threatened by them—gun rights advocates are eager to co-opt our history to promote their ends. Second Amendment defenders regularly use the tragic photo from 1891 of frozen Lakota victims of the Wounded Knee Massacre being buried in a mass grave in tone-deaf efforts to protect their gun rights. They reframe the genocide their government engaged in to obtain their land with the tagline "Wounded Knee was among the first federally backed gun confiscation attempts in United States history. It ended in the senseless murder of 297 people." Another meme features a photo of a Native leader emblazoned with the words, "I'm all for total gun control and trusting the government to protect you. After all, it worked great for us" around his face.

Disregard, if you can, the incredible callousness of using such tragedies to limit sales of automatic weapons and prevent waiting periods for gun purchase—all of which have been shown to save lives. My great-great-uncle was a witness to Wounded Knee, and my grandmother claimed he died of a broken heart from it. Instead, note the genuine and meaningful difference between these two fights for the land. One, a battle for the sovereignty of Native nation-states reduced by genocide and held in poverty by an economic extractive enterprise disguised as a state. And the other, what Bundy and his supporters term a fight for their liberty. Which involves, in its specifics, making up the rules and getting what they want.

One reason why Native Americans do not figure readily into the worldview the Bundys espouse is not due solely to self-interest, but a glimmer of the truth. For as dishonest and disingenuous their push is for a legal framework that permits their land grab, it is also politically perceptive, as are all great cons. This is more than a well-held bluff. It is more akin to a computer virus that, once inserted, can rewrite the code that defines America in favor of the Bundys and their allies. And the truth they have discerned or intuited is that Native Americans are more than just an ethnic group or another type of American citizen. Until the 1924 Indian Citizenship Act, most were not only not citizens of the United States but were still, in essence, citizens of their own nations persisting under occupation. Once granted citizenship, Native Americans' right to vote was not guaranteed until the Voting Rights Act of 1965. Therefore, for most of US history, the only real citizenship Native people could claim was with their respective Native nations.

<\<>\>

I don't lay it at the Bundys' feet to comprehend tribal sovereignty, of course. I doubt that they understand that when tribes speak of being nations, they are not being poetic or nostalgic. No Bundy making his stand on the primacy of county supremacy could accept that states, much less counties, have no jurisdiction over our lands. Tribes are in the process of rolling back Public Law 280. PL280 is a 1953 law that gave six states (California, Minnesota, Nebraska, Oregon, Wisconsin, and Alaska) criminal and civil jurisdiction over tribal lands within their respective boundaries. Also, tribes seek international recognition of their retained sovereign status following invasion and occupation by the federal government. In this vein, the Iroquois issue passports for international travel. Although Canada refuses to accept them, and in 2010, the United Kingdom refused to allow the Iroquois Nationals field lacrosse team to use the passports to travel to the UK for the 2010 World Lacrosse Championship. (Modern lacrosse is based on the Iroquois version of an Indigenous game of stickball, which they call the Creator's Game.) I also doubt the Bundys understand the concept of honoring treaties; they would likely drop any pretense if a tribe's treaty rights conflicted with their interests—as they have long done with the Paiute tribes in Nevada.

I return to the peaceful Cowboy Indian Alliance in South Dakota and Nebraska as a counter to the armed and primarily white stand-off at the Bundy ranch. This coalition of Native American and white landowners created a giant crop art in a Nebraska cornfield that read "Heartland #NoKXL." *Canté* is the Lakota/Dakota word for heart, and it makes sense to me that such an unforeseen collaboration would be in the heart of Maka, our mother. That it would be my Yankton Dakota Sioux relatives and white farmers and ranchers from South Dakota and Nebraska who would be leading the fight is surprising—yet still a logical consequence of what a relationship to the land, to our mother, would nourish.

Dakota elder Faith Spotted Eagle played an active role in helping to shepherd that alliance into being. When I was home on the Yankton

Sioux Reservation in South Dakota in 2013, I found her busy at the Fort Randall tribal casino conferencing with Bold Nebraska, a progressive political advocacy group. There I met Jane Kleeb, the founder of Bold Nebraska, and sat in on some of their discussions as they formed the Cowboy Indian Alliance. I saw what it took to unite their efforts to protect their respective ways of life imperiled by the pipeline. I later wrote about their 2014 Earth Day event, where they presented their message to Washington, DC. That group of white farmers and ranchers and Dakota, Lakota, and Ponca people, once and still mostly embattled with one another in a fight for resources on the Great Plains, held a tipi encampment on the Washington Mall. All week those beautiful tipis faced the Washington Monument and were a sight to see. There stood the tiyóspaye, glorious in the long rectangular green grass surrounded by Federalist Greek Revival temples, a testament to America's vision of itself. In DC, the coalition presented a specially painted tipi to the National Museum of the American Indian as a gift to President Obama, to remind him of his obligations to protect the water and the land. All of this happened just two months before the president went to Cannon Ball, North Dakota, and promised the people of Standing Rock he would honor the treaties and regard their children as his own. He was not in the country to receive the tipi or the Cowboy Indian Alliance. If he had been, would Standing Rock have happened?

If this is the vision of the relationship and shared consequences the Cowboy Indian Alliance brought to the mall of national self-conception, what does the Bundys' Christian-based, armed militia bring? We have the assurances of the Bundys: they are not racist. They tell us their liberty will not impinge on any of ours. Is this true?

For a glimpse of a Bundy America, I turn to an elected official in the Pacific Northwest. Although much of the examination of the Bundy's ideological basis has focused on the family's Mormonism, the militia movement the family attracts is firmly based in the Pacific Northwest—and the Christian ideology associated with it is not limited to

LDS theology. While there is some crossover with the theology of Latter-day Saints, it would be inaccurate to see this solely as a Mormon endeavor, because the majority of the armed militia draws support from the broader right-wing Christian movement.

Let me introduce you to (now former) Washington State representative Matt Shea, a Republican representing the fourth legislative district of Spokane County until January 2021. He chose not to run again after it was revealed in 2018 that the FBI investigated Shea for distributing a "four-page manifesto" titled "Biblical Basis for War." The document included strategies a "Holy Army" could use upon a successful takeover of the country, including killing all non-believing men. The conservative legislator admitted the leaked document was written by him but claimed they were notes he had taken from the Bible for a sermon on "just war." Of course, this raised the question of why an elected official would preach such a lecture and also lifted the veil on an extreme sect that had festered for decades in the northeastern corner of Washington State with little notice.

Shea is a Bundy supporter who traveled to Bunkerville, Nevada, in 2014 and to Oregon in 2016 to support the Bundy-led takeover of Malheur. Each time, he was joined by several far-right state legislators, sheriffs, and other elected officials.

After Shea's "just war" fiasco came to light, Ammon Bundy claimed not to recall seeing him at Bunkerville but didn't doubt he was there. In early 2020, Bundy came around and gave the embattled legislator his wholehearted support in a YouTube video after the Republican legislators in Olympia, Washington, the state capital, blackballed Shea from committee assignments and even denied him office space.

Bundy has also spoken at events with Shea, including those associated with the Marble Community Fellowship.

In 2014 I wrote what I thought was a precise analysis on the superior nature of the tribes' claims to the land. On January 2, 2016, I was forced to reckon again with the Bundys reiterating the same "ancestral" pretensions to the land, this time in the state where I lived. And they once again attracted the media, twenty-four-hour tickers on CNN, MSNBC, and Fox News proclaiming Ammon and Ryan Bundy's soundbites on their father's theories of their "ancestral rights" to exploit as they pleased more Paiute homeland.

This time, I wrote more than one piece, turning out article after article focusing on providing what I saw was missing in the mainstream coverage: the perspective of the Burns Paiute Tribe. It was their ancestral lands and former reservation the Bundys were now occupying in the name of white ranchers Dwight and Steven Hammond. Ammon had come to stand for the Hammonds, father and son cattlemen convicted of arson and poaching on public lands. That week they were turning themselves in to be resentenced under mandatory minimum sentencing laws. Republicans had pushed these laws through in the Reagan years, and they led to the mass incarceration of generations of Black men and women. Dwight Hammond, like Cliven Bundy in Nevada, leases public land to run his beef operation and has repeated run-ins with federal authority.

When Ammon Bundy ensconced himself in the Malheur Wildlife Refuge headquarters, he made it clear his objective was to take it from an "overreaching" federal government and return it to its "original owners." The refuge encompasses 180,000 acres of wetlands surrounding the Malheur, Mud, and Harney Lakes and the Donner und Blitzen River. These owners were, of course, not the Burns Paiute Tribe, which he freely admitted to knowing nothing about before the takeover.

When the former truck maintenance shop owner arrived in this vast, remote, and sparsely populated county, he had done some research, noting it had gone from being the most prosperous counties in Oregon to one of the poorest as the sawmill was closed down—due, he surmised, to burdensome environmental regulations.

As in Bunkerville, Nevada, where the Bundy family has run cattle since the 1950s, it is the Burns Paiute Tribe and other Northern Paiute bands who are the "original owners," possessing the most substantial legal claim to the territory. The Burns Paiute claim is particularly applicable to the wildlife refuge, which was part of the Malheur Indian Reservation. This 1.78-million-acre reservation was later opened to white settlement after the Paiute and another tribe, the Bannock, facing starvation, rose up against settler depredations. And after they lost the war, in January 1879, five hundred Paiutes were force-marched, shackled in twos, knee-deep in snow some three hundred miles northward to the Yakama Nation in Washington State.

Unlike at Standing Rock, the Northern Paiute's treaty with the United States negotiated in 1868 was never ratified by Congress and made their disappearance from their homeland a more straightforward process. White ranchers like the Millers who owned Cannonball Ranch, where the Dakota Access Pipeline crossed, had to deal with a visible and significant Lakota presence adjacent to their ranch, but in Harney County that was not the case. Although the tribe had made a comeback in the twentieth and early twenty-first century, they still numbered less than four hundred, and much of the land they had recovered and put into trust was in adjacent counties. Their interests could only be felt through negotiation with federal agencies tasked to oversee remaining public lands in the county.

By its very definition, the treaty process entails the US government's recognition of the preexisting sovereignty of the tribes over the lands they wished to acquire title. So, even though the treaty was not ratified, there was a recognition of Paiute autonomy. Otherwise, why send representatives to negotiate a treaty with tribal leaders in a remote part of Oregon Territory? The independence and self-determination of the Paiute people are limited primarily by force by the most powerful country in the world, the United States. And that force is still seen by tribal members as a viable threat. "What if I did that with my Native brothers and sisters, and we went and occupied something," said tribal council member Jarvis Kennedy. "Do you think we'd be let running around free, going in and out of it? No, we'd be locked down."

<<>>

In 1969, when the federal government finally compensated the Burns Paiute for the land taken, tribal members were paid at 1890 prices: twenty-eight to forty-five cents per acre. Sweet deal if you can get it—and you can, if you make the rules. In this regard, the Bundys are attempting to emulate the federal government and capitalize on the ongoing occupation of Native homelands, which constitutes much of what is called public lands today.

By 2016, when Ammon Bundy arrived, the tribe had regained federal recognition, and their enrollment was at 420 members. For comparison, the Paiute population before the US Army declared war on them in the late 1860s was 2,000. Some 160 years later, the Watadika (as they call themselves) still have not recovered their numbers. They no longer have a 1.8-million-acre reservation, but the one-time landless tribe now owns over 12,000 acres, and 1,000 acres held in trust by the federal government.

Many Americans like Bundy remain utterly unaware of the existence and sovereignty of tribes, even on lands they live on, sometimes for generations. This ignorance is the result of a longstanding policy, practiced by both the federal and colonial governments, of clouding the true nature of Native nations' land claims. I see the shock on my non-Native American audiences' faces when, two-thirds through my lecture, they come to understand tribes' land claims are based on real and senior political sovereignty. It is understood, even under US Indian federal law, tribes have a status higher than states—and higher than that of county government. On this point, the Bundys' county supremacy ideology is in irreconcilable conflict with Indigenous sovereignty. The very basis upon which they claim their right to take up arms and use their property (land) and defy federal administration of public lands disappears. Even at the state level, it could be argued that most states had no preexisting autonomy as independent nations. The exceptions would be the original thirteen colonies and Texas, which respectively won their independence from Britain and Spain. Previous to statehood, most states were territories waiting to meet the goalposts set by the Northwest Ordinance and even be divided up, as occurred with the Oregon and Nevada territories. The only sovereign entities within the boundaries each state now claims were Native nations.

This leads us to back to the question posed by the Cowboy Indian Alliance: Can the land make us one people? Even as the legal rationale concerning land rights conflict or, in the case of the Doctrine of Discovery, utterly blot out another senior party's rights, can these fundamental parameters to our historical relationships be made more just? To answer this, we should take a look at how the land was shared or not shared, both during the occupation and historically.

On January 19, 2016, my editors at *Indian Country Today* slapped the title "Oregon Militia Nuts Hold Paiute History, Artifacts Hostage" on my article. I'm not sure that's the title I would have chosen, but it was accurate. During the Malheur takeover, the Bundys' followers dug up the bones of Paiute ancestors as well as desecrated unmarked sacred sites. The occupiers had found a bulldozer and were using it to build defenses and latrines, disturbing archaeological sites on the refuge. The refuge contains over four thousand artifacts at undisclosed locations to protect them from looting. While rifling through paperwork in the refuge building, the militants found maps detailing where the graves and other culturally significant sites were located.

"That whole area is an artifact area," Jarvis Kennedy explained. "If you just walk across there, you'll see chips on the ground where someone made an arrowhead. It's everywhere."

In February 2016, US attorney Billy Williams released a report in district court, which provided a thorough description of the Malheur Wildlife Refuge's condition after the forty-one-day armed standoff. Disturbingly, Williams writes, "Occupiers appear to have excavated two large trenches and an improvised road on or adjacent to grounds containing sensitive artifacts. At least one of these trenches contains human feces."

When asked what he thought of the latrines, Kennedy said, "Just see this...this is their mindset—not really caring about anything. For them to do that in that area is so disgusting."

This traumatic incident was a particularly difficult thing for me to cover from the perspective of the tribe. The defilement of a place that holds so much of a tribe's history is something tribes face every day, but to see it happen with such extraordinary ignorance in real time with the whole world watching was something else.

In response, the Burns Paiute tribal council formally declared Malheur Lake and its shoreline under their protection in a resolution titled "Sacred Places and Traditional Cultural Properties." The council cited the tribe's own Aboriginal Lands Protection Policy, which covers "the Tribe's aboriginal territory beyond current Trust lands." Chair Charlotte Roderique vividly and movingly described to me the importance those sacred places held for her and the plants and wildlife that made their home around the lake, some of which are facing extinction.

"We are the Wadatika people," the chairwoman told me. "The plants we are named after grow on the banks of the Harney and Malheur Lakes. If they put cattle in there, they will destroy these plants."

Roderique went further to describe how, as a little girl, her family and other tribal members would take her along the river in the marshes of the refuge. In this riparian area set aside in 1908 by President Theodore Roosevelt "as a preserve and breeding ground for native birds," the children learned to make tule baskets. The 187,757 acres the refuge encompasses is a significant stop on the Pacific Flyway and provides breeding habitat for up to 66 percent of the birds migrating on this flyway.

It was also here that she was told by elders to always leave enough eggs to continue the species. "We restrict our hunting and gathering accordingly to ensure there is a future. We don't have the attitude that the Bundys have."

CHAPTER SEVEN

CENTER OF THE BUFFALO

At camp, you existed in a technological black hole—no social media access except on "Facebook Hill" and sometimes not even any cell service, even at the casino. But here I stood outside the white clapboard low-slung building in Little Eagle, South Dakota, on the Standing Rock Sioux Reservation. It's the home of the local tribal community station, KLND 89.5. On one side was a banner that gave the call numbers of the radio station with the tagline, "The lodge of good voices." I was there to interview and be interviewed by Virgil Taken Alive, an elder and popular DJ known as the Lakota Soulman. He had wanted to interview me on air about the Bears Ears National Monument and the book I had edited called *Edge of Morning*. I've noticed that when I am among my father's people, it sometimes seems that they want to know more about my mother's people and vice versa when I am on the Navajo Nation—they want to know all about my father's people. I guess they feel my connection to both made each tribe accessible to one another: one the proud people of the Plains and the buffalo, and the other shepherds who worked with silver and turquoise and wove rugs.

He greeted me in the control room, and we began the interview. I read the introduction of my book over the airways because it included references to the work of my great-great-aunt Ella Deloria, who had grown up in Wakpala, about thirty miles due east from the radio station. Virgil and his friend Alex Looking Elk had begun working on bringing a station to the reservation in 1990, and in 1997 they went on air, initially serving the Standing Rock and Cheyenne River Sioux Reservations. In the era of live-streaming over the internet, the tiny station now reaches the world. In 2018, after twenty years of broadcasting, and nine months after he interviewed me, Lakota Soulman hosted his last show and retired from the airwaves. Lakota listeners wished him well in his retirement and said they'd miss listening to him in the morning on their way to work or drinking their first cup of coffee.

After my interview, in the staff lunch room over bologna sandwiches, it was my turn to interview Taken Alive about how the camp came to be. He began by describing a meeting held on February 12, 2016, in McLaughlin, South Dakota, in the southern part of the reservation where he lives. It is called in Lakota mathó akíčita or Makáȟleča, Bear Soldier. His nephew Jonathan Edwards, a former paramedic, organized these first meetings, held in the southern part of the reservation, the South Dakota side. It wasn't until about the third meeting that the community of Cannon Ball in North Dakota was approached. The NoDAPL organizers sought permission from the district to set up a camp in their community to oppose the Dakota Access Pipeline. LaDonna Brave Bull Allard, the founder of the Sacred Stone Camp, attended this meeting and volunteered her land. Joye Braun, an anti-KXL Pipeline activist from the Cheyenne River Sioux Tribe, was also present at the meeting and had proposed the camp. She was quickly invited to help the grassroots activists at Standing Rock establish the camp. She advised starting immediately, on April 1, 2016.

"Really powerful in that camp, the prayer that was offered to stop this pipeline. The prayer power was tangible in those early days," Taken Alive reminisced, his voice warm, recalling that time at Sacred Stone Camp. He spoke frankly and directly, sharing the difficulties he faced later on while working with leaders of the Red Warrior Camp and the Indigenous Environmental Network (IEN):

> Then came those GoFundMe people. I was naive to it, to what was then occurring with IEN, Red Warrior Camp, and what they would be doing within that camp and outside that camp. When I started speaking at that camp, about prayer

and peace and no arrests. They didn't let me know what was going on and the things that were going with nonviolent direct action. So this Red Warrior Camp led by Deb White Plume was initially the main ones that were talking violence, and Chairman Archambault, my nephew, came to my camp. "We're going to remove the Red Warrior Camp. I need your help." I have ten or eleven nephews who were constantly at my camp. So he went to the public address at the front of the camp. This was in August. Go over and get Oglala Tokala boys and any young men who are going to be in support of the chairman. They must have gathered close to fifty. They went across—150 feet from where I was. I told the young men to not say a word, let the chairman talk. Deb and Vic Camp swayed the chairman to not do this and used his Oglala background. My hunka boy said it wasn't an AIM camp or an IRA camp. I kept thinking that. I'm not AIM. I'm a Hunkpapa Lakota. You want to go back decades I can go back generations. I came on pretty strong and started to get warnings. I was told, "Guys after you. They don't like the rhetoric."

After that, he felt local Lakota leadership that had been leading the fight against DAPL was sidelined. Even before he told me this story, I heard rumblings of issues with Red Warrior Camp. In the early fall of 2016, as the Standing Rock encampment began to attract the attention of at least the Native and environmental community via social media, many of the media releases and messaging were coming from the Red Warrior Camp. In interviews in August, Chairman Archambault was identifying Red Warrior as being in charge of nonviolent training. Océti Sakówin, the massive overflow camp, had already been established on the Missouri's western shore. But by early September, I received disturbing reports of harassment of the other water protectors in the camp conducted by RWC. An elder, a grandmother, told me on background that the grandmothers had gotten together to write a letter demanding Red Warrior leave the Océti Sakówin camp.

<><>

LaDonna Brave Bull Allard, the founder of the Sacred Stone Camp who told a DAPL worker, "I'm the closest landowner. Remember my face," was adept at turning a phrase. She compellingly tied pressing environmental concerns to her connection to the land and the history of her people. Later, some of the details of her claims, particularly to land ownership, were questioned. The property she declared at meetings was her property was under fractionated ownership—very common for Lakota and Dakota people due to outdated probate laws that apply to Indian lands held in trust by the federal government. For example, when my dad died, my mom and I were confronted with four pages detailing his property. He had fractionated ownership of land on several Lakota and Dakota reservations from Rosebud to Nebraska. This system grew out of the 1887 General Allotment Act when communally held tribal lands were divided among tribal members. Initially, full fee-simple title was to be given to Native landowners after twenty-five years, but for many, that period was extended. Combined with minimal probate laws, this meant heirs did not inherit acres but fractionated interest in the land held in trust. Development of the property became unwieldy as fractions grew smaller and so many had to agree upon any possible action.

My dad was interested in returning to the Yankton Sioux Reservation for his retirement. One day, while visiting my grandmother in Lake Andes, South Dakota, on the reservation, he opened the local paper and saw on the front page a photo of his great-aunt Sophie's adopted son, Richard. The headline proclaimed a local man had come into a vast inheritance of land when a relative died. My dad saw this and decided to visit Richard at the nursing home to see if he could purchase this land. Richard had been in and out of prison in Springfield, mostly for bad check writing and fraud. Originally from Rosebud, he had been a handsome young man, but had a violent streak. My dad remembered when Richard hit his girlfriend in my grandmother's home, and his older brother Bill drove him out of the house and gave him a beating for striking a woman. But he was a beautiful young man, and the women couldn't stay away. It didn't take my dad long to realize, while visiting the elderly man, that it was all another scheme of his. He had inherited a fractionate portion from a relative. This is what I came to surmise LaDonna Allard was telling the unsuspecting white reporters and followers she had accumulated.

Allard had similarly inherited a tiny percentage, one-fifteenth (6 percent), of the property her father's family had once owned. She had several siblings who had inherited equal portions, and several step-siblings as well. The stepsiblings had already sold their shares back to the tribe. Fractionated ownership can stifle land use and development on the reservation. Parcels with more than six to ten owners must obtain consent from 80 percent of the owners to use the land for non-agricultural purposes, like leasing to tenants for housing. In this case, the tribe, owning about two-thirds (or 66 percent) of the 317 acres of "LaDonna's land," would have to consent, along with two of her siblings, who still had shares. Since the 1990s, tribes have instituted buyback programs to reduce fractionation, free the reservation of these constraints, and make land more available to help the entire tribe by allowing greater economic development or, conversely, conservation. When tribal leaders pointed out she didn't own the property in the way she was implying, Allard told her white donors she'd use the millions they gave her to repurchase the land sold to the tribe by her relatives. She failed to tell her supporters that the Standing Rock Sioux Tribe's constitution requires a majority of adult tribal members to vote to approve the sale and that it would be difficult, if not unlikely, to obtain such approval. Allard did later use her millions to buy real estate on the reservation but in other locations.

The overflow camp, Océti Sakówin, was created when Allard refused to allow a busload of supporters from the Cheyenne River Sioux Tribe to camp. Sacred Stone, on top of a bluff overlooking the Missouri and Cannonball Rivers and the floodplain below, was too narrow. The Standing Rock Sioux Tribe negotiated with the Army Corps of Engineers to use the flood plain. They had to agree to take out an insurance policy and supply drinking water and chemical toilets, but they struck a deal, and the bus from Cheyenne River made its way back through the community of Cannon Ball and back to the state highway and the new camp.

Later, when Océti Sakówin swelled in size to the thousands, beautiful photos of the hundreds of tipis filling the meadow below Sacred Stone Camp became the image of the movement itself. As Océti grew, so did the donations accruing to the Sacred Stone online fundraiser. I asked Allard why she didn't edit the description of her GoFundMe campaign to explain that her camp was not the camp people saw in the news coverage and live streams. At this point, she had raised millions of dollars, but the tribe was not so savvy and late to the crowd-sourced fundraiser game, so all the money flowed to her. She refused to change the wording on her page and said that Chairman Archambault and the tribal council had created the Océti Sakówin camp to obscure that hers was the original camp. Native friends who tried to gain entry to that camp were turned away by Allard's white guards and told to go to the "Indian camp," meaning Océti. By then, her camp was mostly composed of white people. Sometimes, the white women of Sacred Stone would bring some of their camp's largesse to share with the more numerous "Indian camp," resulting in scenes reminiscent of the early reservation period, with white nineteenth-century women visiting impoverished Lakota tipi encampments.

Allard's brother lived near the entrance, but he was repeatedly denied entry to his home by her guards. Tribal members told me that he went without propane that winter until Cannon Ball community members helped him obtain the funds to refill his tank. Once, while on crutches, he called the BIA tribal police when he was denied entry to his home. Myron Dewey, a Paiute from Nevada and founder of Digital Smoke Signals, streamed the confrontation live on Facebook. Dewey did not mention Allard's brother's distress in his coverage. Instead, he told his audience the BIA police were trying to force their way into Sacred Stone without any authority to do so. He showed a white

Sacred Stoner being maced by the police. Many tribal members I spoke to felt betrayed by his depiction of events. Coverage like this, uncritical of Allard and lacking context, helped turn public opinion and potential donors against the tribe.

Explaining the unique challenges to Native land ownership on the reservation proved, at times, an insurmountable problem. An embedded reporter at Standing Rock, Jordan Chariton, from the digital news network the Young Turks, did a series of live-streamed interviews with Allard. He took her claims to sole ownership of the land where Sacred Stone Camp was established at face value. Utilizing ordinary real estate law in the United States as a frame of reference, Chariton excoriated the Standing Rock Sioux Tribe for not believing her. He credulously reported Allard's claim that the paperwork the tribe presented had been falsified by the federal government to defraud Allard of her property. A mutual friend of Chariton and myself, another embedded journalist, asked me to explain to Chariton what fractionated land is. When I spoke to Chariton, a journalist who has broken important stories about the Flint water crisis, over the phone, he listened intently. However, the next time I caught his broadcast via Facebook, he continued to describe Allard's ownership solely in the terms she had presented to him.

"Yankton is hosting a strategy meeting on Thursday at the Fort Randall Casino," Yankton Sioux tribal elder Faith Spotted Eagle told me in July of 2016. The Lakota and Dakota Tribes were meeting to figure out how to unify in the face of "this latest thing that we have been dreading"—the Army Corps of Engineers had issued a nationwide permit for the Dakota Access Pipeline.

Throughout the spring, the Yankton Sioux Tribe had tried to meet with the US Army Corps of Engineers, sending two written requests in March and April and numerous phone calls. Finally, the tribe hand-delivered a written request to the Omaha district commander, Col. John W. Henderson, at an event and received a response. In May, the Army Corps of Engineers agreed to a consultation with the Yankton Sioux Tribe about the newly proposed Bakken pipeline, offensively termed the Dakota Access Pipeline. The tribe wished to discuss the need for a full environmental impact statement as stipulated by the Environmental Policy Act and recommended by the Department of the Interior and the Advisory Council on Historic Preservation.

Colonel Henderson arrived half an hour late to what was scheduled to be a two-hour meeting at the tribe's Fort Randall Casino. Tribal leaders made it clear that ninety minutes was not adequate to constitute a meaningful government-to-government consultation. The Yanktons are a non-Indian Reorganization Act tribe; thus, they are still governed by their traditional general council, which mandates a several-step process to consultation. Present at the meeting that day were elected members of the Business and Claims Committee, including Chairman Robert Flying Hawk, and other Lakota/Dakota representatives of the Océti Sakówin, including Rosebud, Standing Rock, and Cheyenne River. Also in attendance were Iowans who oppose DAPL, and Dakota Rural Action of South Dakota.

The meeting ended abruptly after an elderly Yankton woman confided in the colonel that his attending tribal meetings wearing full combat clothes distressed her. His uniform recalled, she said, the history of violence between the US Army and the Dakota people and was traumatizing. Hearing this, Colonel Henderson reportedly slammed his notebook shut, said he had not come to this meeting to have his uniform insulted, and quickly exited the meeting. Consequently, the Yankton Sioux tribal leadership felt Henderson's abandoning a legally mandated consultation process with the tribe was a violation of federal law. At the very least, it meant no consultation had taken place, and the tribe classified the meeting as a pre-consultation affair. Tim Mentz Sr., a Standing Rock tribal elder and former historic preservation officer, noted that because consultation broke down, little of the pipeline was surveyed with tribal involvement, and much archaeological information was missed—in some cases, even destroyed.

In February of that year in Standing Rock, as Jonathan Edwards and others began organizing on the reservation in McLaughlin, South Dakota, the meetings and Facebook posts bore fruit. A grassroots-based collective called Chante Tin'sa Kinanzi Po (People, Stand with a Strong Heart) emerged. This community-based activism arose even as Standing Rock Sioux tribal council resolutions failed to stop the pipeline or gain meaningful consultation after years of back and forth.

As the impotence of their government's efforts became clear to young people on Standing Rock, they realized they would have to step forward, even during the harsh winter of early 2016, to stop the pipeline construction. The youth honed their message, focusing on the threat the pipeline posed to Standing Rock's primary drinking water source, Mni Sose, where it crossed the Missouri River. A movement grounded in direct action and guided by ceremony was born.

Bobbi Jean Three Legs, a twenty-two-year-old mother from the community of Wakpala on the South Dakota side of the Standing Rock Sioux Reservation, saw on Facebook in March of that year a photo of Jonathan Edwards and several others standing in the middle of a street in McLaughlin holding signs saying things like "No Access for Dakota Access." She was also contacted by a relative who told her more about DAPL, what it would mean for Standing Rock and the tribe's future. Thinking of her daughter and the youth basketball players that she coached, she listened as her relative told her, "We need to do something; we need to do something." The result was "Run for Your Life," Standing Rock's first public NoDAPL prayer action, a run to the Army Corps of Engineers office in Omaha, Nebraska. Three Legs recalled in an interview seeing three horses galloping across a field to the fence line to jog alongside the runners as they reached McLaughlin, Standing Rock's Bear Soldier District. She heard a sudden loud crash of thunder at the same time. "I knew the ancestors were with us. I knew we could do it," she said.

Lakota youth from other Océti Sakówin reservations joined the run as members of the One Mind Youth Movement. The grassroots group also made their presence known to representatives of the Army Corps of Engineers at listening sessions on the Standing Rock Reservation. It was at this time, during these early events, that the well-known chant "Water is life, Mní Wičóni" first made its appearance. Every community event opposing DAPL began with prayer and was guided by ceremony. The eagle staffs of traditional headsmen and spiritual leaders led the actions.

In late July, around the time the consultation process had broken down with the USACE and the tribal leadership, the youth set off for Washington, DC, two thousand miles away. They brought with them more than ten thousand signatures and found the camp swelling in size. When the youth runners returned to Standing Rock in late August, a standoff had begun along ND Highway 1806. On one side: dozens of armed state and county law enforcement officers guarding the pipeline survey crews. And on the other: supporters first in the hundreds, then in the thousands. LaDonna Allard's Sacred Stone could not accommodate them; north of the Cannonball River on treaty land claimed by the Army Corps of Engineers, Océti Sakówin was established. The camp, filling with tipis and young and old, soon caught the attention of Hollywood, and Shailene Woodley and Mark Ruffalo were tweeting out #nodapl, #mniwiconi, and #waterislife. Suddenly #StandingRock was trending.

During the summer, when the USACE had found DAPL's 2012 nationwide permit sufficient to allow construction of the pipeline at ten different sites under the corps' jurisdiction in South Dakota, the tribe's historic preservation officer was given only five days' notification. Tribal leadership was astonished by the approval, as formal consultation, required by federal law, had not yet commenced.

Worse yet, President Obama, despite a strong social media presence and an engaged and informed policy of tribal consultation, appeared to be completely unaware of the brewing standoff near Cannon Ball. Initially, tribal and grassroots leaders had the impression they had the ear of the president after the fanfare of his visit in 2014. He had made promises of support that were clear and undeniable. When questioned by a college student in Laos about the situation in North Dakota, Obama admitted he didn't know about the protests.

His ignorance was jarring following the dog attacks on water protectors, which had occurred just days before. The brutal and bloody use of dogs on water protectors captured by Amy Goodman of *Democracy Now!* was drawing comparisons on social media to the use of dogs on Black civil rights protestors in Birmingham, Alabama, in 1963. In contrast to Obama, President Kennedy, viewed by civil rights leaders as noncommittal before Birmingham, announced he would send comprehensive civil rights legislation to Congress following it, saying, "The heart of the question is whether all Americans are to be afforded equal rights and opportunities." At the heart of the standoff at Standing Rock was equal access to clean drinking water and a long history of encroachment upon the sovereignty of the Great Sioux Nation by which Lakota and Dakota people's rights and opportunities are guaranteed. Sovereignty Obama had committed his administration to honor.

Standing Rock Sioux tribal chairman Dave Archambault II was asked if he had yet heard from Obama regarding the tribe's concerns. He expressed the hope the president's staff would finally give their boss the letters his tribe had been sending. Old hands, retired tribal leaders I spoke to, viewed this as a sad yet typical demonstration of the lack of access tribal leaders have to virtually every level of federal and even state and county governments. This lack of access was particularly astonishing because the chairman's sister Jodi Archambault-Gillette had been the special assistant to the president for Native American Affairs. It was she who had arranged the dazzling 2014 visit.

More puzzling was how or why the task of informing the president about the dire straits the tribe faced was done by a Malaysian college student halfway around the world in Southeast Asia. The only way to reach the leader of the free world was indirectly, through informing the public on platforms like Twitter. The old assumed ways of doing the business of achieving change had altered. Social media was the playing field of power now.

And it was on social media, not television as was the case with the civil rights movement, that the most vivid and disturbing scenes of the struggle against the pipeline played out.

"The tribe has just practiced eminent domain," Myron Dewey intoned to his audience on his Facebook Live feed, "and is taking back their traditional land. The treaties have been broken, and now they have been reestablished by the tribe."

Dewey, a Paiute from Nevada, had set up shop at Sacred Stone Camp to cover the standoff on his Digital Smoke Signals platform. A stout, middle-aged figure, he walked his viewers through what was billed as the "1851 Fort Laramie Treaty Camp." There were tipis and even a sweat lodge with a ceremony in progress. The new smaller camp was established on October 24 directly in the path of the pipeline on land recently purchased by Dakota Access just east of Highway 1806.

Astonished by this bold move by the Standing Rock Sioux Tribe, I contacted Dallas Goldtooth of the Indigenous Environmental Network to ask him when the tribe had done this. I had not seen a press release from the tribe regarding an invocation of eminent domain over unceded treaty land. Goldtooth got back to me half an hour later; his organization had received verbal confirmation of tribal support for the Treaty Camp, and the tribal council would be voting on it at their next meeting on Tuesday, November 1. Before the council could meet, the camp was forcibly cleared on Friday, October 28, in a military-style police raid.

Following the friction between the praying elders and the Red Warriors who turned up their car radios to drown out the prayers, the police raid was vicious, with scenes evoking US Army assaults on Lakota/ Dakota villages in the 1850s and 1860s. Native women were cut out of tipis by heavily armored law enforcement, and sweat lodge participants yanked from their prayers, thrown to the ground, and zip-tied. It was at this Treaty Camp standoff that Red Fawn Fallis was grabbed and brutally tackled to the ground by several armed law enforcement and arrested.

The day after the raid, I was interviewed by BBC World about the violent clearing of the camp. "Today, the Océti Sakówin has enacted eminent domain on DAPL lands, claiming 1851 treaty rights," I read to the radio host from the Indigenous Environmental Network press release. "This is unceded land. Highway 1806, as of this point, is blockaded. We will be occupying this land and staying here until this pipeline is permanently stopped." But as I read it over the air, I noticed the quote was attributed to Mekasi Camp, a Ponca man employed by the nonprofit Bold Nebraska. The Ponca Nation is not a signatory of the treaty, nor is it a member of the Océti Sakówin. I quailed inside as I scanned the press release and was left puzzling over whether Camp possessed any standing to invoke the treaty. He was basically a foreign national. Could a Belgian invoke a treaty on behalf of the French government? Could even a French citizen do so? I wasn't sure.

By the following Tuesday, when the resolution to support the Treaty Camp finally came to a vote before the tribal council, the tribal attorney advised against it. If they pressed the right to eminent domain in the courts, they could lose. This would set a negative precedent leading to the loss of retained rights in the treaty. Heeding legal counsel, the tribe tabled the resolution. The Cheyenne River Sioux Tribe, however, led by the irrepressible and bold Chairman Harold Frazier, did support the camp. But when the Yankton Sioux Tribe was finally approached, they decided not to support the camp. Several more tribes are signees of the treaty, and I do not know if they were approached. For me, this incident was the first glimpse of how little coordination was happening between certain NGOs and the tribes they were there to support. The fact the Indigenous Environmental Network and Bold

Nebraska only sought approval after they had invoked the treaty on behalf of the tribe meant no consultation had taken place. Ironically, consultation is what the tribe had sought from the federal government. Furthermore, the very public and disrespectful actions of Red Warriors toward elders were contrary to Lakota/Dakota cultural mores that honors elders. How can anyone be warriors for an Indigenous people and yet not respect them?

Once again recalling the police violence against Black civil rights protestors in Birmingham, Alabama, in 1963, the world finally woke up to what was happening at Standing Rock. On November 20, live-streamed videos of water protectors being sprayed with high-powered water hoses were shared on Facebook. The Morton County sheriff's department turned what were initially described as water cannons (later, water hoses) on protesters trapped on Backwater Bridge for more than five hours in subfreezing temperatures. According to first-person and news accounts, the officers fired rubber bullets, pepper spray, concussion grenades, and tear gas at close range on the crowd. More than 160 people were reported injured.

The most shocking photos were of the young medic Sophia Wilansky, pale in the backseat of a car with her arm torn apart, revealing the bone, by a concussion grenade. Due to the roadblock maintained by the National Guard, she could not be transported by ambulance to Bismarck to receive medical care. Because she wasn't a tribal citizen, she couldn't receive care at the Indian health clinic and so relied solely on medical attention offered by the volunteer medics at camp. Also among those seriously injured by close-range use of less-than-lethal devices was Vanessa Dundon, a Navajo from Phoenix, Arizona, who was struck in the eye by pepper spray at close range and was in danger of losing her sight.

Sophia Wilansky's father, New York attorney Wayne Wilansky, gave poignant interviews concerning his daughter. Finally, more than eight months into the standoff, the national paper of record, the *New*

York Times, published an unequivocal condemnation of state violence at Standing Rock.

The confrontation occurred as Americans prepared to gather with their families for Thanksgiving. A holiday dressed up in the story of the English colonists (pilgrims) and the Wampanoag (Indians) coming together peacefully and in friendship to a harvest feast. It is a feast of thanksgiving for the English colony's survival, mostly due to the kindness of Squanto, a Wampanoag man who had been enslaved by Europeans and finally found his way across an ocean to find his village gone. Everyone whom he loved, dead from a viral scourge brought on the ships that had stolen him. He tried to honor their memory by helping these starving English. Yet, at Backwater Bridge, on a state highway linking the Standing Rock Sioux Reservation and Bismarck, North Dakota, the lie of the benign nature of colonial occupation was laid bare. That night, burned-out trucks and a police barricade made the bridge impassable. Water protectors were trapped, unable to retreat from the freezing water, rubber bullets, pepper spray, and concussion grenades. The tribe and camp leaders pointed out the roadblock was a needless threat to public safety—forcing emergency vehicles to detour about twenty miles and endangering lives. All of this done to protect a pipeline construction site that jeopardized the water and future of the Lakota/Dakota people. It seemed like the virus that had taken Squanto's village had never left. It was wherever the colonists wanted to be.

The election of Trump that same month was accompanied by an aggressive agenda of policies to dismantle hard-fought wins tribes had achieved in the last years of the Obama administration. According to a 2015 financial disclosure form, the president-elect had invested between five hundred thousand and one million dollars in Energy Transfer Partners, builders of the Dakota Access Pipeline, and an additional five hundred thousand dollars in Phillips 66, which would be a 25 percent owner of the pipeline upon completion.

Some suspected that Trump, as a failed former casino-operator, still harbored a grudge against tribes. He testified before Congress in 1993 against tribal gaming operations, telling lawmakers that organized crime "is rampant—I don't mean a little bit—is rampant on Indian reservations." Infamously, he also claimed that leaders of the Mashantucket Pequot Tribal Nation, a federally recognized tribe in Connecticut, did not look like Indians to him. The tribe's casino, Foxwoods, proved to be significant competition to Trump's casinos, which were emerging from bankruptcy in the early 1990s. Regardless of his reasons, the form of capitalism celebrated in his book *The Art of the Deal*, and played out on his reality TV show with his catchphrase "You're fired!" was ruthless and venal. The performative nature of Trump's capitalism was bound to favor a kleptocratic petrostate over Native nations.

The 2016 presidential election results represented not only a threat to environmental issues and public land advocates generally, but also proved to be a stunning loss for tribes. Trump immediately signaled his intentions to dismantle tribal wins. In the first month of his presidency, he signed an executive order granting the permit for the Dakota Access Pipeline and the restarting of the Keystone XL Pipeline. Trump's press secretary, Sean Spicer, claimed the White House was constantly in touch with both the Standing Rock Sioux Tribe and the governor of North Dakota. Chairman Dave Archambault II forcefully denied this, calling the claim "absolutely false." He said they received no notification about the easement and that "it was an insult to me and to the tribe."

Still, tribes could not forget that despite the overtly friendly leadership of the previous administration and Trump's obsession with rolling back his predecessor's policies, it was under Obama's watch that brutal state violence was unleashed on NoDAPL protests at Standing Rock. As president of the United States, he did little to stop it or publicly address it. He did not order the National Guard to protect the water protectors. Instead, troops maintained a checkpoint on the main highway onto the reservation. Despite Obama's assurances that a nation-to-nation policy would guide his administration's relationship with tribes, he did little to stop the violence waged on the tribe when it tried to invoke treaty rights of consultation. This was met not only by law enforcement, but corporate security, hired by Energy Transfer Partners, that Obama's administration failed to check. Was this hands-off approach taken to protect the senate seat of the Democratic senator from North Dakota, Heidi Heitkamp? If it was, it failed. She lost to Rep. Kevin Cramer, a rabid pipeline supporter. The Native American vote in 2011 had granted Senator Heitkamp a narrow win by some two thousand votes. State legislative efforts to suppress the Native vote by requiring identification with street addresses, something many reservation residents do not possess, led to a scramble to use the 911 emergency addressing systems and update tribal IDs. Despite these efforts, North Dakota sent Senator Cramer to DC.

Demands to consultation are one of the mildest ways to invoke the terms of the Fort Laramie Treaty. So why were unarmed Indigenous demonstrators so threatening? Without even the bare minimum of consultation, the suppression of the sovereignty of the Great Sioux Nation is nearly total. State and county governments, established by the federal government to administrate the colonization effort of the United States at the local level, are made more secure and emboldened in their jurisdiction over Native nations.

Or are they? The heavily militarized response by the United States and its state and county governments raises the question: To what extent is the United States still a colony? When tribal citizens and their respective governments demand any form of recognition, they reanimate inconvenient claims to the land that predate the United States. And without our land, America is not a country, but an idea, a colonial endeavor as transnational as corporations like TransCanada or Energy Transfer Partners.

Every time I return to Lake Andes, the town where my dad grew up, on the Yankton Sioux Reservation in South Dakota, another building is gone. South Dakota is like that. My dad used to tell me that people would move not only their belongings but their entire house. As a child he'd see houses being transported on the roads. Trees on the prairie are scarce. The early pioneers built their infamous sod houses using the thick prairie grass, which had built up over thousands of years a dense and rich soil for crops. But it took just decades for them to use it up. By the 1930s the dust storms hit much of the breadbasket, which white farmers had industriously made the prairie into. Like a swarm of grasshoppers, the dust storms fell upon our homeland, killing us, killing millions of our relatives, the buffalo, and turning the richness of the soil airborne.

Back in the day, Lake Andes had been a white town on the reservation, but now it was becoming an Indian town. One by one, buildings disappeared off Main Street. But one remained, and this was my destination. Just a few blocks from my grandmother's house is the Brave Heart Lodge, founded by Ihanktonwan elder Faith Spotted Eagle. A small single-story brick building, it has been made over inside into a comfy meeting place with a kitchen, with a garden in the lot adjacent to it. In March 2017, 325 miles away from the NoDAPL camps, Faith Spotted Eagle held what amounted to a debriefing on Standing Rock. The camps had been closed for a month. The meeting was attended by many Lakota and Dakota leaders, including Chief Arvol Looking Horse, keeper of the sacred pipe given to the Lakota people by the White Buffalo Calf Woman, Oglala elder Regina Brave, who took the final "treaty stand" at Océti Sakówin, and Waniya Locke, one of the original grassroots NoDAPL leaders from Standing Rock. We were like orphans after the storm. The memory of the camp at its height and greatest promise was still there like a dream, even after months of dissension, infighting, removal, and reversal (Trump's executive order fast-tracking completion of both DAPL and KXL).

As I entered the building, another Yankton and distant cousin was giving a presentation on the layout and running of a traditional encampment. While waiting in line for food cooked on site, I struck up a conversation with Regina Brave. A veteran of both the US Navy and the 1973 Wounded Knee occupation, the seventy-six-year-old from the Pine Ridge Reservation had been one of the last to leave camp and was forcibly removed by law enforcement. Beginning in the 1980s, she had also fought for the Yankton Sioux's original treaty territory. At the Océti Sakówin camp, she had written with black marker on a plastic tub: "Article VI – Treaties are the Supreme Law of the land (US Constitution). Treaty Territory. You are in violation! State has no jurisdiction." The frail, elderly woman had been arrested just weeks before with forty-seven others, but she was still confident and energetic. The police had not broken her. As I spoke to her she immediately launched into her outrage at the burning of the tipis that last day when the camp was cleared. I probed her for her take, as the descendant of a treaty signer, on the right of NGOs or members of tribes that are not party to our treaties negotiating on behalf of the Océti Sakówin. She agreed they had no standing to do so.

In early February, after it became clear the tribe would carry out the district's resolution to clear LaDonna Allard's Sacred Stone Camp, I began to investigate why. It seemed strange the tribe would close the only remaining camp, since the larger Océti Sakówin camp was facing an "evacuation" by the federal government on February 22. The original NoDAPL camp appeared to be the perfect fallback location after that date because it was located on the reservation and not subject to the jurisdiction of the county or state. Indeed, tens of thousands of dollars were raised by the Indigenous Environmental Network to winterize the camp.

Interviewing residents of Cannon Ball, I heard claims that white Sacred Stone campers were menacing the community. Tribal members described the camp as a "white colony" that refused oversight by the tribal government. However, even as local Cannon Ball residents forcefully disagreed with Chase Iron Eyes and LaDonna Allard's refusal to clear their respective camps (Last Child and Sacred Stone), they respected Grandma Regina's treaty stand. They said she was quiet, dignified, and, as the great-granddaughter of a treaty signer, Ohitika, who negotiated the 1868 Treaty of Fort Laramie on behalf of the Oglala Lakota leader Red Cloud, she had the right to invoke the treaty and to do it this way.

Observing the discussion online between Sacred Stone Camp leaders and media who were close to Allard, it became apparent that these (mostly non-Native) spokespeople had not developed a relationship with Cannon Ball's community in the ten months since the camp's establishment. I found this extraordinary, since white Sacred Stone residents had to drive daily through the Cannon Ball community to reach the entrance to Allard's camp. During the first four months of the camp's existence, the local community had been supportive. Locals described bringing coffee and other supplies daily to the camp. As that relationship deteriorated, some pointed to Allard's leadership, and the grassroots support instead flowed to the massive Océti Sakówin camp. A funeral was invaded by a white "Sacred Stoner" (as campers were sometimes called), which led to the resolution to close Sacred Stone. Cannon Ball residents cited this as the final straw. There were complaints that the white campers were leaving the community center a mess, and the youth had to clean it every evening to be able to use it for basketball games. White campers could be seen parked in the community center parking lot. Lakota residents felt they were being monitored by them because the outsiders were fearful of being kicked out. They viewed the white visitors as "white colonists" and Sacred Stone as a white colony. Some even suspected Allard of signing rental agreements with these colonists. Fueled by such suspicion, tensions between the two groups were high. And they erupted during a wake. It is customary in Lakota and Dakota reservation communities to hold a four-day wake where the body is displayed and the community can pay their respects. Community centers often serve as locations for these communal events. While Lakota people were entering the community center, a white man barged in screaming and cussing. The moment everyone recounted was when he pushed an elder who was trying to calm everyone down.

Complicating the picture even more, Cannon Ball district chairman Robert Fool Bear was accused by Sacred Stone supporters of engineering the vote. Repeatedly voted into office as district chairman for over a decade by an extensive network of family support, he had been indicted in April 2016 for sexual abuse of a minor. Despite this, he remained in office, and Fool Bear could be seen on CNN characterizing opponents of the Dakota Access Pipeline as "dangerous," saying he wanted them to leave the community. In April 2017, two months after the camps were cleared, he was convicted on three counts of sexual abuse of a child and one count of incest. Fool Bear was later sentenced to thirty years in prison. Not to relieve him of responsibilities for his crimes, but his case demonstrates how our struggle is not just external—Morton County, the federal government, scary black ops groups like TigerSwan—it is also dealing with internal division, much of which is exacerbated by intergenerational trauma created by US policies. Boarding schools and Catholic churches were places where our people were molested as children and taught to hate themselves. Our language and the kinship system, the engine that drove and defined our culture, were broken. How do we come together when that poison pill has been laid within our own families?

Yet, standing on the bridge where the protesters had set trucks alight, Robert Fool Bear's brother Archie Fool Bear, a former chairman of the Standing Rock Tribe, said: "The fight is not going to be over, it's never going to be over."

Even as I recoil in horror at his family's protection of a sexual predator, I agree the fight continues, but I hope we shall win, and a lasting accord and respect will emerge between our people and the Americans.

The eviction looming, I asked Sacred Stone residents and supporters if LaDonna Allard could help them broker a deal with the community to rescind the expulsion order. However, the self-proclaimed landowner was not only a controversial figure but legally could not vote in the district elections, because her residence was in Fort Yates. The tribal council's resolution in support of Sacred Stone was for a small temporary camp. They envisioned it growing to as many as fifty supporters. Tribal members I spoke to compared this to a makeshift campsite set up during hunting season. The BIA police and tribal officials were criticized by Allard's community's online supporters when they entered the camp to examine the new latrines. These were supposed to be environmentally friendly, but community leaders allege that tribal officials found ordinary outhouses constructed over the Cannon Ball community's drinking water.

Swan American Horse, a resident of the Sacred Stone Camp, presented a petition with sixty-six signatures (not all from district voters), asking for another district vote on the January resolution to close the camps. The petition asked for a special district meeting, but district chairman Robert Fool Bear delayed the meeting due to two deaths in the community. In addition, the ten-point resolution for the closure of the camps and opposing the creation of a winter camp near Cannon Ball was approved by the tribal council and backed by five out of eight districts on the reservation. It was unclear what effect a district vote would even have. The tribal council could not overrule the district without a constitutional reason for doing so.

And what about the utter breakdown of communication between Sacred Stone Camp and the community of Cannon Ball? The failure of camp leaders, guests, and organizers to effectively organize and consult with the community? These conflicts illustrate both the potential and challenges of allyship and social media-based information dissemination.

One of the thrilling aspects of the rise of social media is its ability to spread the iconic images of the protest and live-stream clashes at Standing Rock, even as mainstream media virtually ignored these things. The other aspect is crowdsourced fundraising or the GoFundMe activists. This also had a downside for Standing Rock, and that was the lack of accountability.

In February 2017, the local Standing Rock newspaper the *Teton Times* published its heavily researched exposé "Legitimizing Plunder at Standing Rock." It was the first in-depth look at some of the largest crowdsourced fundraisers that took the lion's share of donations in the name of the NoDAPL effort. Non-Native journalist Georgianne Nienaber shares a byline with the paper's publisher, Avis Little Eagle, a Standing Rock Sioux member and former editor-in-chief of *Indian Country Today*. Little Eagle is currently a tribal council member, although she was not serving in 2016-17.

This article was received in a hostile manner by some of the non-profit employees featured in it. Nienaber alleges she received harassment online and death threats from the staff of Honor the Earth and Freshet. The Indigenous Environmental Network was able to regain the trust of the tribe by presenting financial records. The role of allies, both from other tribes and NGOs and their employees speaking for tribes and communities without proper accountability, raises important questions that need to be addressed for future actions in Indian country to be as effective as they should be. This is especially so for a tribe as impoverished as Standing Rock, with a per capita income of $13,474, which is less than half of the US per capita.

The article notes that "tribal budgets, as well as the annual tribal audits, are available upon the request of tribal members at the tribal finance office. This is most often not the case with crowdsourced funding." The Standing Rock Sioux Tribe took in, at the time of the reporting, six million dollars. That amount was to be used to pay for the legal costs of the tribe's lawsuit against the Army Corps of Engineers and DAPL, and for "waste management at the camps, and budget shortfalls incurred because of the closure of Highway 1806 and local boycotts of the casinos." The tribe's annual income from Prairie Knights Casino dipped precariously from fourteen million dollars in 2015 to near eight million dollars in 2016, and even lower in 2017. It has not, in 2020, recovered to its 2015 income level.

The article opens with a vivid description of the difficulty of facing poverty on the reservation, where freezing to death during the winter is a real possibility. I was first called upon to investigate a GoFundMe run by Chase Iron Eyes called "Heating the Rez" in 2014. After the death of three Standing Rock Sioux tribal members due to lack of propane to heat their homes made national news in the winter of 2013, Iron Eyes raised sixty thousand dollars via GoFundMe—an astounding amount for Indian country at that time. After another winter had gone by, tribal members contacted me because their elders had not received the pellet stoves promised. I called the pellet stove store referenced by Iron Eyes and was told he had not purchased any from them. I could only confirm three stoves had been installed. One in Iron Eyes' mother's house (the video used in the GoFundMe description was of the installation in her home) and two others in one other person's home. When I asked the Lakota People's Law Project attorney, and later, the 2016 North Dakota congressional candidate, if he could account for the sixty thousand dollars, I received a curt response that they were not legally required to provide that to me. I was familiar with the difficulty of getting a response and the lack of financial transparency in the Wild West of online fundraising.

The article lays out the monumental scope of this issue of accountability, noting there were, at that time, at least ten thousand GoFundMe accounts using the terms "Standing Rock" and "Sacred Stone."

> Over $6 million has been raised through a handful of other private sites, including the Sacred Stone Camp, Sacred Stone Legal Defense Fund, Last Real Indians, Unify, and the Lakota People's Law Project. These private donations are not reflected in, nor will they be included in the Standing Rock Sioux Tribe's budget outlays. The $6 million for private sites in this investigation does not include monies raised on the Internet by thousands of other entities which use the Standing Rock name to raise funds for anything including, but not limited to, cameras, film projects, gasoline, wood, food, legal services, travel expenses, public relations, tiny barns for horses, yurts, tipis and other commodities too numerous to

mention. It is anyone's guess what the total amount is and how to account for it.

The *Teton Times* had sent a set of questions about budgets and charity registrations to Sacred Stone Camp, Freshet (formerly the Sacred Stone Legal Defense Fund), Last Real Indians, Unify, and the Lakota People's Law Project. Only the Sacred Stone Camp, the Lakota People's Law Project, and Freshet replied.

According to LaDonna Allard, the three million dollars she raised via her Sacred Stone Camp GoFundMe was managed by her bank and used to build infrastructure on her "privately owned land." The tribe disagrees with this description asserting, again, Allard's land is primarily on a fractionated allotment of which the Standing Rock Sioux Tribe has a majority interest. The *Teton Times* also found that despite assertions Sacred Stone had an EIN, "when asked for an EIN number, Allard was unable or unwilling to provide it. An Employer Identification Number (EIN) is also known as a Federal Tax Identification Number and is used to identify a business entity. Generally, businesses need an EIN, especially if they have people on a payroll. Allard also made it clear that 'our focus is the people who live in Sacred Stone Camp,' and not the Standing Rock Sioux Tribe."

The Lakota People's Law Project is a program of the Romero Institute, formerly the Christic Institute, which has a fascinating history. After the bombing on May 30, 1984, of a guerrilla outpost in La Penca, Nicaragua, during a press conference conducted by a leader of the Contras, seven people, including three journalists, were killed. Tony Avirgan, an American journalist injured in the bombing, and his wife, Martha Honey, led an investigation in which they concluded that the CIA was responsible. In 1986, the Christic Institute filed a twenty-four-million-dollar lawsuit on their behalf against several associates of Oliver North. The case was thrown out in June 1988, and the Christic Institute was ordered to pay nearly one million dollars in costs to the defendants for filing a frivolous lawsuit.

Following the dismissal, Avirgan complained that Daniel Sheehan, attorney and director of the institute, had mishandled the case by chasing unsubstantiated "wild allegations" and conspiracy theories. The Christic Institute lost its nonprofit status and reformed as the Romero Institute, still lead by Daniel Sheehan. Sheehan, once a highly regarded attorney who pursued notable public interest law cases like the Pentagon Papers and the Silkwood case, also lost credibility due to an obsession with UFOs in the 1980s and 1990s. I spoke to attorneys affiliated with the National Lawyers Guild at the Océti Sakówin camp, who cited Sheehan as a reason they were unwilling to work with the Lakota People's Law Project.

The *Teton Times* found that in December 2015, the Romero Institute had raised more than $1 million with $450,000 spent by the Lakota People's Law Project. An email sent to the institute's executive director and to the Lakota People's Law Project was answered by the press director, who promised an accounting from the organization's treasurer by email that same day, but it never arrived. The paper noted, "The connection between the Lakota People's Law Project, Last Real Indians, and Sacred Stone Camp remains murky."

Freshet was hosted on the crowdfunding site FundRazr, and was heavily promoted by *Vogue* magazine. The fundraiser eventually raised more than three million dollars from more than fifty thousand contributions, which "easily surpasses the IRS's taxation requirements." An email was sent to Honor the Earth's Tara Houska, the fundraiser's administrator along with HTE employee Thane Maxwell, to determine how the money was allocated. Houska responded to the *Teton Times* claiming the "Freshet Collective is a registered 501(c)(4) nonprofit." Freshet never obtained this IRS designation and is registered as a nonprofit solely with the Minnesota Secretary of State. When I reported on the federal defendants' cases in November 2017, I found the families of the defendants composing a letter to Winona LaDuke asking for an accounting of the three million dollars. They had just received letters from Freshet saying they would be cut off from financial support by the end of the year; their cases were going to trial in February and March of 2018. As I covered their cases through 2018, the families raised concerns about how Freshet handled the money raised in their loved ones' names. Concerns continued into 2020 as some were released from prison and had not received payment from Freshet to help them restart their lives.

The *Teton Times* found that Last Real Indians, a news site, was, according to Charity Navigator, "not eligible to be rated by Charity Navigator because it is not required to file the full IRS Form 990." A search on GuideStar yielded an address and the principal officer, Duke Gomez-Schempp, but financials were missing. Two emails were sent to Chase Iron Eyes, the contact person for the website domain (lastrealindians.com)—his address in Fort Yates was also listed—but he did not reply.

The organization Unify was also asked to clarify its connection with UPLIFT (upliftconnect.com), which had a presence at Standing Rock and, at the time the article was written in early 2017, had raised over thirteen thousand dollars through a GoFundMe campaign called "We Are Diné" organized by Lindsay E. Nance. Although Nance was registered as a media organization/journalist at the Morton County courthouse, she was observed praying with protestors outside of the courtroom on December 19. The funding ask said, "We need to be able to pay for lodging to protect our gear and supplies—the warriors depend on us to tell their stories to refute police statements, get the message out, and to raise money so they can stay here for the long term." To longtime journalist Avis Little Eagle, a Native American Journalists Association board member, this description blurred the lines between PR and journalism.

Elliott Rhoades, a regular columnist and a former vice chairman for the tribe, wrote poignantly in the *Teton Times*:

> Those summer and early autumn days of people living together in an organized community with shared traditions and values are gone. The heavy presence of Big Green Environmental groups and opportunistic wolves who prowl cyberspace in search of the gullible and guilty have crushed the

birds sent by the Creator. Creator offered the birds to teach the people how to sing and dance and treat each other with empathy and not indifference.

The sun no longer bathes campsites in warm light while people gather together to pray. Instead, a grandmother is found zip-tied to a chair in a tipi, diaperless, and surrounded by her urine and feces.

Meanwhile, a middle-aged man freezes to death behind a building, and women die for lack of propane, while Indian women in Pendleton jackets party at Hollywood fundraisers and are interviewed on national television.

Jasilyn Charger, interviewed by a local public television program a year after the camps closed, recalls what it was like to be part of the original runs for the water: "We ran because again, no one was paying attention to us. But when we came back, there were like thousands of people here." She says they came because of the sacrifices the youth made running thousands of miles for what they believed in.

But then, Charger says, the youth got swept aside. "All right, you did your part. You're relieved. We got this." But as the weather got colder, people became "more agitated, more impatient." And as they tried to put their bodies on the line for the movement, people got hurt. She was pepper sprayed several times, and her boyfriend was shot.

"It was all horrible," Charger says.

It didn't need to be like that. The youth, the International Indigenous Youth Council, were there at every action to deescalate because we knew, we knew how they felt. We were angry too. At least we can guide them as youth to say, "Hey, if you're fighting for my future, do it this way. Just back off, don't got to say all those things. You don't have to be angry. You don't have to curse at the police. You don't have to throw anything at them"…We came back in prayer, we reminded our people what they were fighting for.

She notes that after Trump approved the pipeline, it was even harder to contain the anger.

The tribal offices of Standing Rock are large and impressive. More so than the small building that serves my dad's Yankton Sioux Tribe. Large even compared to the Navajo Nation president's office and the hogan-shaped Navajo Nation council chambers. But the leader of this tribe, which has about eight thousand living on the reservation, is accessible. Chairman Archambault, nearly a year after the summer the Océti Sakówin camp grew to accommodate thousands, welcomes me into his office. The experience of the NoDAPL fight had at first lifted him up and then knocked him down with the cuttingly effective epithet of "DAPL Dave" taken up by thousands of folks who had never even heard of his reservation until late 2016. We spoke for two hours, and the interview felt like a way for him to come to some resolution. In the fall, he'd lose a reelection bid by thirty-some votes and those who called him names thrilled at his loss.

It's July 2017, and the oil is now running through the pipeline under the Missouri just north of Cannon Ball. And he recalls the beginning. The years of fruitless meetings with the Army Corps of Engineers and Energy Transfer Partners until the youth stepped up and inspired the world to stand with them.

"We go on this route with the buffalo, the buffalo follow the stars," he tells me. "We follow the buffalo. That's our brother. That's our way of life. Every year."

He has asked the USACOE and ETP representatives why they needed this economic development—development that Lakota people would pay for. "You took all of our land," he told them. "You took all of our unceded land, energy, national security. You took our Black Hills for gold and gold is for national security because it backs our currency, this nation's currency that makes this nation strong. We paid for it. We paid for economic development with our land. And we talk about energy independence? And if we look at this river? It used to be a river. They built seven dams, strategically built these damns for not just recreation, but for hydropower. We paid for your energy independence."

Archambault describes the rhythm he had gotten into when times at the camp were at their peak. He would get to the office at six a.m. and head to the camp around noon. There, he would meet people, the tribes coming in, they would sing songs. They had the council lodge set up, and he wouldn't get home until maybe two or three in the morning because people had to talk. Everyone just wanted to talk. When he'd get home at three in the morning, there would be somebody waiting for him. And he would speak with them for a couple of hours. During this routine, young men from different reservations would come up to him, saying, "I want to, I'm ready to die. I'm here. I'm ready to die. Let's go to war." Carrying that, he couldn't sleep, and he sought advice from his elders.

They told him, "We need you to go pray." He went to a sweat lodge, *inipi*, and he prayed, and he was able to let everything go.

"And then, the next time somebody came at me and said, I'm here ready to die. So you need to tell me you're ready to live," the chairman remembers. "I'm tired of people telling me you want to die. You should say, you want to be an uncle. You should say, you're going to be a dad, a good dad. You should say you want to help your families."

The chairman looks at me and says, "Why would you want to create more trauma for your family? We've dealt with enough trauma for the past two hundred years. What's your kids going to do? What's your wife or what's your mom going to do if you die? Shouldn't be saying that you're ready to die. You should say I want to live. So when you ask me what it was like? It was like a nonstop ceremony."

When the attacks and threats became too much, he received help from an unexpected place. A stone was given to him by another tribal leader, Wendsler Nosie, the San Carlo Apache leader who led the fight for Oak Flats, a sacred place to the Apache people. Nosie had been one of the first to come to camp, and he gave him the rock, which was from one of their sacred mountains. It became a touchstone throughout the ceremony against the pipeline. When the attacks were at their peak, Wendsler invited Archambault to the Apache stronghold in Arizona. There they did a ceremony for him and pushed back at what the Apache leader called "the evil." The chairman sweated again, but this time, the heat was nearly unbearable. When the sweat leader offered him a chance to leave, he took it. Outside there was a white man. The man was telling him he had a YouTube channel where he got four million views for his video footage of the awful night at Backwater Bridge at Standing Rock. He could interview Archambault, and he could get those views. The chairman waved him away. Later, Nosie told him the sweat was hard because evil cannot enter there—it was trying to drive the people out. Evil was waiting outside that lodge.

The chairman reminds me how the rock, the Inyan, gave its life for us. It used to be fluid and free, but it gave of itself to give us all life, and it became hard and still. One of our cultural heroes is Stone Boy, Inyan Hoksina. His human mother had swallowed the stone thinking she would die. She had lost her five brothers. Instead, she gave birth to Stone Boy and he grew quickly and went out and rescued his uncles, bringing them back to life by building a sweat lodge for them.

The water, the stones, the land, the buffalo, the People. Dave Archambault had been describing how, in our ceremonial life, we travel across this land that is sacred to us every twenty-eight days. We travel as a People to the Black Hills, Ȟe Sápa. And in this movement, we express our love of life and experience the love our mother has for us. Perhaps that's why even camping together brought back that old excitement. A taste of that old way that is so old it is intrinsic to who we are as Dakota and Lakota, and without it, we are a people lost and sick.

I went back the winter of 2018 to Standing Rock. Visiting the site of the former village, it was hard to believe it was ever there. With the light layer of snow on the ground, I couldn't even make out where flag row had been, where hundreds of flags of tribal nations had once flown and flapped in the dappled Indian summer breeze. It seems like a dream now. The meadow was pristine. The only remaining visible sign was a blue "No Trespassing, United States Property" sign, reattached upside down on the barbed wire fence near the road with the words "Stolen Land" written over it in black marker.

ABOUT THE AUTHOR

JACQUELINE KEELER is a Diné/Ihanktonwan Dakota writer living in Portland, Oregon. She is editor of the anthology *Edge of Morning: Native Voices Speak for the Bears Ears* and has contributed to many publications including *The Nation*, *Yes!* magazine, and *Salon*.

TORREY HOUSE PRESS

Voices for the Land

The economy is a wholly owned subsidiary of the environment, not the other way around.
— Senator Gaylord Nelson, founder of Earth Day

Torrey House Press publishes books at the intersection of the literary arts and environmental advocacy. THP authors explore the diversity of human experiences with the environment and engage community in conversations about landscape, literature, and the future of our ever-changing planet, inspiring action toward a more just world. We believe that lively, contemporary literature is at the cutting edge of social change. We seek to inform, expand, and reshape the dialogue on environmental justice and stewardship for the human and more-than-human world by elevating literary excellence from diverse voices.

Visit www.torreyhouse.org for reading group discussion guides, author interviews, and more.

As a 501(c)(3) nonprofit publisher, our work is made possible by the generous donations from readers like you.

Torrey House Press is supported by Back of Beyond Books, the King's English Bookshop, Jeff Adams and Heather Adams, the Jeffrey S. and Helen H. Cardon Foundation, the Ruth H. Brown Foundation, the Sam and Diane Stewart Family Foundation, the Barker Foundation, Diana Allison, Jerome Cooney and Laura Storjohann, Robert Aagard and Camille Bailey Aagard, Stirling Adams and Kif Augustine Adams, Kirtly Parker Jones, Elaine Deschamps, Patrick de Freitas, Lindsey Leavell, Laurie Hilyer, Susan Cushman and Charlie Quimby, Shelby Tisdale, Stephen Strom, Link Cornell and Lois Cornell, Rose Chilcoat and Mark Franklin, Betsy Folland and David Folland, the Utah Division of Arts & Museums, Utah Humanities, the National Endowment for the Humanities, the National Endowment for the Arts, and Salt Lake County Zoo, Arts & Parks. Our thanks to individual donors, subscribers, and the Torrey House Press board of directors for their valued support.

Join the Torrey House Press family and give today at
www.torreyhouse.org/give.